BIKE BATTLES

BIKE BATTLES

A HISTORY OF SHARING
THE AMERICAN ROAD

JAMES LONGHURST

UNIVERSITY OF WASHINGTON PRESS

Seattle and London

Design by Dustin Kilgore
Composed in ITC Century, designed by Tony Stan.
Display type set in Interstate, designed by Tobias Frere-Jones.

18 17 16 15   5 4 3 2 1

University of Washington Press
www.washington.edu/uwpress

Library of Congress Cataloging-in-Publication Data
Longhurst, James.
    Bike battles : a history of sharing the American road / James Longhurst.
        pages   cm
    Includes bibliographical references and index.
    ISBN 978-0-295-99468-0 (hardcover : alk. paper)
    1. Bicycles—United States—History.   2. Bicycles—United States—Safety
measures.   3. Highway planning—United States.   4. Transportation and
state—United States—History.   5. Cycling—United States—History.
6. Cycling—United States—Safety measures.   I. Title.
    HE5737.L66   2015
    388.3'4720973—dc23   2014035527

The paper used in this publication is acid-free and meets the minimum requirements of American National Standard for Information Sciences—Permanence
of Paper for Printed Library Materials, ANSI Z39.48–1984. ∞

To my parents, Tom and Helen,
who bought me a black Huffy Pro Thunder with
yellow mag wheels from the ALCO drugstore in
Manhattan, Kansas, for Christmas, 1979

CONTENTS

5. 1950s SYNDROME
Excluding Bikes from Suburban Streets,
Interstate Highways, and Adult Lives
152

6. BIKES ARE BEAUTIFUL
The Bike Boom, Bikeways, and the Battle over
Where to Ride in the 1970s
186

CONCLUSION
The Road as a Commons
229

PREFACE

Before we start this ride together, I have to issue some warnings and declarations. Historians prize the noble dream of objectivity, but at the same time we often write about topics we find personally engaging. While environmental and policy historians are slightly more comfortable than others with this type of engaged inquiry, in the interest of full disclosure, I will declare a number of things: I write as a mediocre middle-aged recreational cyclist, regular bike commuter, and enthusiastic cycling advocate. I have a stake in this topic because I wish to avoid being run over.

I'm a newcomer to bicycle history, but my long-standing scholarly interests in political organizing, community formation, and urban environments seem relevant. Like other policy historians, I believe that understanding the decisions of the past can help us to understand the complexities of current predicaments and perhaps make better decisions now and in the future. I particularly believe that public disputes expose unstated assumptions in culture, politics, and philosophy. At second glance, bike battles have deeper, more conflicted meanings than one might think. The episodes of policy debate in this book are offered as evidence that in the United States, the bicycle is an underexamined and meaningful topic in the history of cities, public policy, and the environment.

I hope to bring some of the discoveries of academic historians to a broader audience of decision makers, advocates, and city dwellers, both to better inform current debates and to bring to light many of the useful insights of scholarly research that tend to be buried in specialized publications. This book also reflects my own interest in popular culture to a greater degree than is typical in wonky policy analysis and transportation history. These references to film, television, vaudeville, and comic books are included to make for a more readable book and to give me an excuse to track down forgotten 1950s sitcoms from the more obscure corners of the Internet.

While I'd like to add useful historical insights to current bicycle debates, it is not my purpose to defend the rights of modern cyclists through a selective retelling of history. The record of cycling, like all human stories, is not the spotlessly heroic tale that more nostalgic viewers might wish to see. I wish to complicate the simplistic assumptions often made by all road users, cyclists included.

Fair warning: taking the largely neglected history of bicycle policy seriously means using some unconventional evidence that will surprise a few readers. Some topics—like the sidepaths of the 1890s, the victory bikes of WWII, and the reinvigoration of Japanese bicycle exports during the postwar Allied occupation—can be explored with conventional materials such as primary sources in professionally maintained archives. But examining events during the periods where bicycling was forgotten by the mainstream requires the exploration of less-traditional sources: hokey educational films from the 1950s, cranky letters to the editor in small-town newspapers, slapstick silent films, vaudeville playbills from the 1920s, Boy Scout merit-badge pamphlets, back issues of *Boys' Life*, 1950s television sitcoms, and government-printed comic books.

Many aspects of American bicycle history have been documented elsewhere, including military bicycling, the gender dynamics of bloomers, the occasional popularity of professional competition, and the intricacies of manufacturing and design. European bicycle history is also far more extensive than American research. While much of the historical research in these areas is excellent, these topics are only briefly mentioned here.

In fact, I chose the title *Bike Battles* partly because I liked the alliteration and partly because it conveys the point that I'm not surveying all of the history of the bicycle. These are battles, not the entire war. Instead, this book investigates a few selected episodes of conflict, leaving even more bicycle tales unexamined. These untold cycling stories—suitable for any future dissertation—include early twentieth-century reactions to traffic control, the post office, the Great Depression, the bike-sales booms in the 1930s and after World War II, tariff policy, details of federal bikeway funding, New York City's transit strikes, the late-eighties bike ban in midtown Manhattan, helmet campaigns, and consideration of the bicycle in the context of global history. Amid the bicycle renaissance of the twenty-first century, there is still much left to explore, and more reason than ever to do it.

BIKE BATTLES

INTRODUCTION

A HISTORY OF MY IMPENDING DOOM

I think history is going to get me killed. It all started when I chose to ride my bicycle to work during the gasoline-price spike of 2008. I quickly figured out that my plan had drawbacks: I was entering disputed territory, as other people had conflicting ideas about where—and even whether—my bicycle should be on the road.

At first I thought that motorists were out to get me; many certainly seemed to drive without any concern for whether I lived or died. This suspicion soon yielded to worry that the conflict and confusion were my fault. After all, I had begun bicycling to work out of a desire to burn less gas and more calories, so my shorter life span would be at least partially my own doing. Then, for a while, I thought it was city traffic engineers who were trying to set me up for an accident: surely it was their fault that there wasn't space on the road to ride safely.

But as a historian of urban environmental policy, I eventually began to think about the years of past choices that had created my present danger. The last century and a half of urban development have created a situation in which public roads are the battlegrounds of mismatched competitors: the powerful and numerous internal-combustion automobiles and the vulnerable and far less numerous bicycles. Generally without intention or malice, judges, urban planners, government agencies, trade associations, and interest groups have structured the modern roadway for conflict. Decades of legal, political, and infrastructural decisions have ended up privileging the automobile, and American urban roads quite logically came to be designed for it. But the same decisions failed to erase the fundamental rights of the bicyclists and pedestrians, instead remaining committed in principle to a shared public road that might make sense in an abstract legal sense but in reality has set up an unequal competition of squealing brakes. The conflict is not simply one between the self-interested automobile driver and the equally self-interested cyclist. Instead, prior decisions have set cyclists and drivers on a collision course, and they fight it out on the streets, in the courts, in bitterly contested online forums, and in the editorial pages of small-town newspapers.

For environmental historians, these public fights over responsibilities and rights are examples of the most basic of human disagreements. Bike battles reveal otherwise unstated assumptions about individual rights, the public good, and the proper roles of government. They are instances of sharing a common resource among various parties in a way that is almost never entirely even or fair but can simultaneously never be so unfair as to cause societal upheaval. It is a well-known story of imperfect allocation of scarce resources through group decision making, with the added complication that mistakes might get someone run over, hobble an economy, or ruin the planet. Environmental historians recognize that this debate is as old as human cities and as immediate as our climactically uncertain future.

Thinking of bikes like an environmental historian means considering the bicycle as part of a transportation system that depends on society, culture, politics, geography, natural resources, technology, and the law. It's not about the bike—or not solely. The history of the bicycle has been shaped by a combination of forces far removed from the saddle. The resulting system can appear syncretic, building and running on its own logic, with greater momentum and wider impact than originally conceived. Many scholars describe this sort of phenomenon as a socio-technical system, a technical ecosystem, a landscape, or simply as a component of the modern system of transportation known as automobility.[1]

Considering the technical ecosystem of cyclomobility is useful in understanding not only my own dangerous trip to work but also much larger concerns. Thinking about the interrelationship of many different forces in our cities emphasizes that the environmental predicaments we find ourselves in are very much our doing. It is not in any way preordained that people should spend hours in an automobile on their way to work. It is instead the result of a complex interplay of forces, many of which are within our control. Bike battles—clashes over the use of the public road—bring these hidden issues into the light, excavating layers of unexamined assumptions about politics, society, and our physical landscape.

CONFLICT AT THE STOP SIGN

The modern U.S. city is clearly made for the automobile: it features lanes marked for the width of cars, signals and signage to manage their movement, vast parking areas for their storage, and massive networks of raised or controlled roads to accommodate their speed and weight. All of these are supported by agencies, political constituencies, and funding streams dedicated to automotive needs. Bicycles, on the other hand, move on streets that most often lack designated space for their use. They inhabit an undefined space trapped between the travel lane on one side—filled with fast vehicles whose drivers are impatient with anything impeding their movement—and parked cars on the other, sometimes occupied by oblivious drivers waiting to throw open their doors in the cyclists' path. Few agencies of government take responsibility for managing and encouraging cycling, and those that do typically lack the resources to do it effectively. Signaling technology at intersections, for example, detects autos but often ignores bikes. Major highways or thoroughfares physically block walkers and bikers from crossing, segregating the city and in some places making cars essential

Figure I.1. A typical American city street layout on Milwaukee Avenue, Chicago, in early 2013, with bicycles squeezed between parked cars and moving vehicles. The painted marking on the road is a "sharrow," or share arrow, a recently institutionalized attempt to remind users that the lane is to be shared and to designate a place for bicycles on roads too narrow for bike lanes. Green Lane Project, People for Bikes Foundation.

for traveling anywhere beyond the neighborhood.

The problem that I and other road users confront is symbolized by the stop sign. Cycling on my way to work through the leafy, flat streets of my college town, I regularly pull up to a four-way stop. Coming to rest at the same intersection might be a driver of a large truck or four-wheel-drive vehicle, common here in the upper Midwest. We are equal in some ways: each vehicle is operated by a single city resident and taxpayer, traveling on public roads, using a mechanical conveyance on our separate ways to work. While the law considers us equal users of a shared resource, in other ways we are vastly unequal: the driver is in command of immense energy, measured in hundreds of foot-pounds of torque and horsepower, and cocooned in state-of-the-art safety devices. I am in command of twenty pounds of aluminum, protected by ten ounces of Styrofoam on my head and a blinky light. The driver's knowledge and skill has been at least perfunctorily examined and certified by the state, and the motor vehicle is registered and taxed. I have no license or registration on my person; state law and municipal ordinance allow me to ride on the street, but my riding skill and the mechanical fitness of my vehicle have not been verified, and I have not paid a fee to register my bike with any government agency.

As we eye each other, the driver might be warily thinking: is this one of those crazy bikers who will cut across lanes without signaling, swerve into the road from the sidewalk, roll through the stop sign entirely, ride the wrong way, or even just fall over in the middle of the road? On my part, I worry that the driver might be texting, drinking coffee, fiddling with the radio, or all three. He (or she) might be so insulated from the outside world that he will not see me until after I am wrapped around his rear axle. At some level, we are both wondering who has the right of way here: yes, there's an established law for four-way-stops, but we both know that neither drivers nor cyclists always follow the law. Even *that* law privileges the car: coming to a full stop is safe for the four-wheeled car, but stopping is actually the most dangerous maneuver for the rider of the bike, which depends on forward motion to balance and is at its most wobbly when starting from a full stop. As a bicyclist, I might be confusing to the driver, inhabiting some sort of imaginary lane, to the right of the "real" travel lane for cars but to the left of parked vehicles, and occasionally laying claim to the entire lane through sheer chutzpah. Well-intentioned drivers might wave me through when they have the right of way, implying that my bike is not a vehicle of equal standing with theirs and confusing other vehicle operators who didn't see the interaction. Less well-intentioned drivers might not believe I have any right to travel on the road at all, instead urging me onto the sidewalk with a profanity or a bumper.

If there's an incident, we're both thinking, who will be to blame?

What is the cultural value placed on each of us? Will society, insurance adjusters, police officers, or a jury of our peers side with the cyclist or the car driver? Are cyclists unwanted and dangerous trespassers on the roads, their ranks populated by latte-swilling elites with leisure time? Or are they "invisible bikers," people from poor urban neighborhoods living without cars who should be banished from the paths of more successful and productive members of society? Or are selfish drivers morally culpable before they leave their driveway, threatening the lives, health, and futures of the rest of society with their internal combustion engines and wanton waste of resources? The law recognizes the rights of the bicyclist, but Newtonian physics, America's car culture, and the physical design of the roads clearly favor the automobile driver.

If I make it to work unscathed, I have the privilege of teaching the history of environmental policy to college students. Those who sign up for classes on these topics are often impassioned and sustainability-minded twentysomethings, and they impatiently ask why it is so difficult to take action on pressing environmental issues, especially when the solutions seem obvious and rational to the millennial generation. To an outsider, it might appear that my role in these classes is to crush my students' hopes and dreams, which certainly wasn't my goal when I entered the profession. But whether the students are concerned about pollution, climate, logging, or wildlife, my answers are similar. Legal and political assumptions about property, citizenship, and the proper roles of government predate current environmental concerns, constraining our present-day decisions. In the United States, many of these issues fall into legal space contested by the individual states and the federal government. Wide differences in state laws further complicate consistent, reasoned action. As my favorite textbook points out, environmental policy making combines all of these well-known difficulties and then adds additional complexity: conflicting core values, a tendency to overuse limited resources, predictions clouded by scientific or medical uncertainty, and the possibility of irrevocably damaging the planet.[2]

Like the political struggles over preserving wilderness, conserving resources, responding to pollution, or managing risks to human health, bike battles are negotiations over allotting access to shared property and limited resources. Battles over the public roads resemble Garrett Hardin's famous "tragedy of the commons," where the cumulative effects of unconstrained individual consumption unintentionally destroy shared resources.[3] Commonly held resources are especially difficult to protect from overuse: their varied users do not necessarily share the same interests in maintenance and might not even be aware of each other's existence, making it unlikely that they will cooperate to preserve the delicate balance that makes it a shared resource.

Analysis of the commons has evolved considerably from Hardin's 1968 essay. In his thought experiment, set in an idealized past, no organized force managed access to a pasture that was eventually despoiled through overuse. Scholars subsequently pointed out that almost no commonly held human resource has ever existed without some system of management or apportionment. Economists and anthropologists, in particular, have since become fascinated with the recurring solutions that humans have devised to manage common-pool resources over thousands of years of history. Their concept of the "new commons" examines both the communally held resource and the regime that manages it. This idea is becoming ever more important: As humanity's powers have increased through technology, the mechanisms of the rationalist nation-state, and the myriad interconnections known as globalization, more and more of the planet can be defined as a commons. From forests to fisheries to the radio spectrum to aquifers, all of the physical world is subject to the actions of different groups of humanity. Any one of these groups might encroach on the usage of another, necessitating a regime of management to prevent despoliation for all.[4]

THE ROAD AS A COMMONS

Thinking of the shared road as a commons, rather than a mere location of conflict, lets us rise above the petty squabbles of cyclists versus drivers to see the bigger picture. In fact, treating the road as a commons is a basic precept in Western civilization, dating from the Roman *viae publicae*. The legal code of the Byzantine emperor Justinian, from the sixth century, features a ruler declaring: "I forbid violence to be employed to prevent anyone from freely passing and driving over a public highway, or road."[5] The idea that the passage of individuals and their property on a common viaduct was protected from interference by individual landowners or governments is incorporated into many European civil codes. It also appeared in English common law, through the decisions of courts. Thus a 1599 King's Bench case reportedly declared that "the inheritance of every man in the king's highway is prior to all prescriptions"—a stirring definition of the ancient right to the road.[6] By 1731, this guarantee was written into the name of the road itself: one dictionary explained that "the King's High-way or Common-road" was so named "because it is appointed by him and under his Protection." Fifty years later a judge proclaimed that "from time whereof the memory of man is not to the contrary, there hath been and is a common public king's highway . . . used for all the king's subjects to go, return, pass, and repass, on foot and on horseback, and with their cattle, carts, and carriages, every year, at all times of the year."[7] The road was traditionally a shared property and safeguarded as such.

If—and only if—a road allowed the free passage of all travelers, then it could enjoy an easement of the property rights of the owners of the land over which it passed and be entitled to the legal term *highway*. Courts called this free passage *eundo et redeundo*, or the coming and going of the people. *Thoroughfare* also carries this meaning, referring to both a passage "through" another's property and the right of all to "fare" back and forth along that passage. William Blackstone's widely read eighteenth-century *Commentaries* declared that individuals were entitled to defend that freedom of movement, noting that "if a new gate be erected across the public highway, which is a common nuisance, any of the king's subjects passing that way may cut it down, and destroy it."[8]

Because the courts of colonial America recognized English common law, a right to travel was assumed by judges on this side of the Atlantic and even incorporated into some documents. There were a few differences after the American Revolution: the British concept of the king's highway was expressed in terms of *public* roads. Although the Constitution did not expressly specify a right to travel or freedom of movement, courts subsequently concluded that such rights were implied. By 1849, one Supreme Court justice could declare that "we are all citizens of the United States; and . . . have the right to pass and repass through every part of it without interruption, as freely as in our own States." Decades later, this common-law concept became embedded in the definition of the public roads themselves. A legal scholar pointed out in 1895 that the public right to travel had by then become implicit: "As ordinarily used . . . 'road' means *public* road." Based on centuries-old common law, by the late nineteenth century the word *highway* was likewise defined as a route guaranteeing "the right of all individuals in the community to pass and repass."[9]

This idea of the road as a commonly held resource that could exist only if it served all comers was slightly more complicated in the case of the city street, which served many purposes besides travel. Before the late nineteenth century, a city street was also a marketplace, stockyard, playground, and public gathering place. But as cities became more crowded and horse-drawn vehicles heavier and more numerous, travel became a defining feature of the city streets, overriding previous uses.[10] Still, the city street was a commons, occupied by many diverse means of transporting people and things: gas, water, and sewer lines laid by the city, power and communications lines buried or strung by private companies, trolley lines, public buses, horse-drawn carriages, delivery and construction vehicles, and emergency and private motor vehicles.[11]

The public road is today a common-pool resource: it is a human-made, physically limited, communally funded property that must be shared—however imperfectly—between many different users for divergent purposes that change over time and often necessitate renegotiation. In twentieth-century America, one group of users—drivers of private automobiles—convincingly laid claim to almost the entirety of what had been a successful institution serving disparate and varied users. Recurring disputes over the bicycle's rights to the road are a symptom of the challenges of managing a resource that, according to legal principles, should be accessible to all.

POLITICS, POLICY, AND CULTURE

While much of the philosophy of the public road had evolved before the modern nation-state came into being, examining bike battles means paying attention to communal action as transmitted through the mechanisms of the state. In general, I refer to this communal action as *policy*, by which I mean the deliberations, decisions, and actions of government in pursuit of a shared goal or public good. Politics—or the rhetoric and mechanisms by which groups and individuals come to power—shape the policy decisions that are made, but I distinguish between *politics* and *policy* (what those actors actually do when they get there).

While many forces have shaped bicycle policy, one of the most important has been shifting cultural perspectives over time. The meaning of the bicycle, points out the cultural anthropologist Luis Vivanco, "is closely related to the *when* of a bicycle, that is, its historical period and the diverse social and technical factors that influenced the shape and qualities of the object."[12] Thus, along with all of the other ways to consider a bicycle (as a commodity, as transportation, as a technology, or as a material object), we should think very hard about the various ways that people have considered the physical object. Is it a child's toy or a technological marvel? A nuisance to be discouraged or a solution to crisis? The fad of an elite or a marker of poverty? From the perspective of policy analysis, this cultural background might either be described as *values*—the fundamental, frequently clashing philosophies of different groups that complicate the ability to agree on communal action—or *framing*—the fluctuating rhetoric and assumptions of media that shape specific episodes of policy decision making.

Popular perception should not, of course, be understood as the sole factor determining the success of one type of transportation.

It is sloppy history to claim that Americans travel nearly exclusively by personal automobile simply out of love of metal boxes. Instead, policy and perception should be understood as exerting mutual influences. Many other forces shape how people encounter and experience a transportation technology and whether one system will prevail over another. So, although this book considers popular perceptions of bicycles and their riders, its main focus is on selected public debates over government action that have influenced practical bicycling in American cities. These are what I call bike battles.

THE TWENTY-FIRST CENTURY BIKE BOOM

If the bicycle were truly an out-of-date contrivance destined for the scrapheap—if history were a narrative of precedence in which more advanced inventions always crowd out less-effective solutions—there probably wouldn't have been any bike battles in American cities in the last century. But technology does not seem to work like that: rather, the prevalence of one tool over another is structured by a combination of social acceptance, economic impetus, legal foundations, political will, and random chance. Out of this churn of forces, unexpected results emerge. For example, a century and a half after its introduction and after nearly a century of being overshadowed by the technologically more advanced automobile, the simple bicycle is returning to prominence.

The *Economist* reported in 2012 that total bike trips in America had tripled since 1970 and that the number of cycling commuters had doubled in a single decade. That same year, the U.S. Census recorded a 9 percent increase in bicycle commuting over just the preceding twelve months.[13] The League of American Bicyclists (LAB) has declared that in forty of the fifty states, bike commuting has risen by double-digit percentages when compared to 2005 rates. And in some places, the growth has been even greater: cities across the nation are attempting to emulate Portland, Oregon, where 6.1 percent of all commuters traveled by bicycle in 2012—an increase of 249 percent since 2000 and 430 percent since 1990.[14]

New York City's Transportation Alternatives advocacy group reports that two hundred thousand commuters now cycle to work daily, a significant increase over the last thirty years. The *Washington Post* observes that nationwide, "the number of people commuting by bike is estimated to have increased by 43 percent since 2000," while noting (perhaps hyperbolically) that "the number of bikes in big cities—including Los Angeles, New York, Chicago and the District—has increased exponentially."[15] For its part, the LAB estimated the national increase as 61.6 percent between 2000 and 2012, based on U.S. Census American Community Survey data. This figure represents 865,000 total bicycle commuters in the United States in 2012. Of all these measures, perhaps the most surprising is that teenagers surveyed are less likely than previous generations to look forward to owning an automobile or even getting a driver's license. The bike is back, no matter how you measure.[16]

The increasing number of everyday cyclists is partly a result of attempts to reshape American city streets since the 1970s, but it is also used as an argument for further reforms. From designated on-road bike lanes to bike boxes to separated green lanes to cycle tracks, space for bikes is increasingly becoming a part of the physical roadway. Many of these contemporary efforts in the United States are based on the Complete Streets philosophy, which advocates urban transportation design standards that provide equitably for automotive, pedestrian, and bicycle traffic, as well as public transit, safety, and economic concerns.[17]

A flurry of books by cycling advocates has promoted the bike boom in the United States, with names like *The Cyclist's Manifesto, Pedal Power, Bikenomics,* and *It's All about the Bike*. It feels like a transformative moment: as Jeff Mapes writes in *Pedaling Revolution*, "For the first time since the car became the dominant form of American transportation after World War II, there is now a grassroots movement to seize at least a part of the street back from motorists."[18] Innumerable publications, advocacy projects, and lobbying organizations support that movement, including the magazines *Bicycling, Momentum,* and *Urban Velo;* the LAB's bike-friendly ratings for communities, businesses, and universities;

and national lobbying groups like People for Bikes, the Alliance for Biking and Walking, and the Green Lane Project, as well as countless local advocacy groups.

Scholars and academics are just as interested. In *One Less Car*, Zach Furness provides a cultural analysis of how "support for bicycle transportation is growing in the United States." In *Street Fight*, Jason Henderson examines the tumultuous politics and ideologies of bicycling in San Francisco. The urban planners and scholars brought together by John Pucher and Ralph Buehler in *City Cycling* document "a booming interest in cycling around the world." Together, they have persuasively labeled the boom a North American "bicycling renaissance."[19]

But the boom is not without its problems. As Mapes puts it, "bicycling, once largely seen as a simple pleasure from childhood, has become a political act." For some drivers and pedestrians, bikes have always represented a threat, moving either too slowly or too quickly to be trusted, and the bike boom has resulted in a surprisingly angry response, sometimes termed the "bikelash." On Staten Island, introduction of bike lanes led to a number of road-rage incidents in 2009 and what city council members described as a "wild, wild West atmosphere." In Texas, the death of an off-duty Lubbock police officer on a bike led one letter writer to encourage Americans to "join together and remove these bicycle riders from all roadways and avoid further tragedies." In some cases, these attitudes have led to new legal restrictions on bicycling: bicyclists attempting to pass through Black Hawk, Colorado, were banned from city streets in 2010, and the case went all the way to the state Supreme Court.[20]

Bicycles have also become a topic of congressional debate. After Secretary of Transportation Ray LaHood promoted bicycling in 2010, "Republican House members suggested LaHood was on drugs, dismissed the very idea of bike lanes and derided any change to a car-dependent society," according to press coverage. Rep. Steven LaTourette of Ohio was reported as suggesting that environmental sustainability and bicycle projects had "stolen" $300 million from highway programs, while Rep. Tom Latham of Iowa incorrectly claimed that each new biker was one less person paying into the transportation trust fund and that cycling should therefore be discouraged. Such bikelash triggers further arguments; LaTourette later objected to the media coverage as "scurrilous," saying, "I have to go home over the recess and meet with a lot of people in spandex pants and tell them that I was not serious."[21]

In cities, the addition of bike lanes to existing roads has divided the public. Low points of the debate include accusations that the former New York City transportation commissioner Janette Sadik-Khan was carrying water for "an invasion of socialist-leaning, Eurocentric, limp-wristed Lycra warriors."[22] *New York Post* columnists (when not otherwise engaged in wholesale character assassination of Sadik-Khan) proclaimed a "Bike Lane Bloodbath," claiming that with the institution of a bike-share program, "City Hall is about to flood the streets with 10,000 more weapons of pedestrian destruction." One outspoken opponent of these developments—ironically, a former bike-shop owner—decried plans to increase city cycling, declaring that "the level of emotional and psychological damage wrought by the bicycle . . . is home-grown terrorism. The cumulative effect is equivalent to what happened on 9/11." New York's 2013 mayoral race hinged at least partially on cycling issues, with candidates required to voice their opinion on outgoing mayor Michael Bloomberg's support for bike lanes, the bike-share program, Sadik-Khan, and the closure of parts of Times Square to automobile traffic. "Bill de Blasio Wins the Bike Vote," declared the *New York Daily News*, heralding the arrival of what is now jokingly called the bike lobby—a force not meaningfully felt in American politics for more than a century, and with uncertain power today.[23]

The conflict is not limited to New York City. A Washington, DC, columnist opined that "it's a $500 fine for a motorist to hit a bicyclist in the District, but some behaviors are so egregious that some drivers might think it's worth paying." In Philadelphia, the veteran columnist Stu Bykofsky railed against bicyclists' scofflaw behavior. One 2013 column featured this doggerel, written from the point of view of those he calls "bikeheads":

I think that I shall never like
Anything as much as my bike.
A bike that makes me feel so free,
Because the laws don't apply to me.
I go through lights of red, you've seen,
It doesn't matter 'cause I'm green.

Not all the criticism of bikers came from outside the cycling community. Protesting riders in Chicago streets prompted one experienced but angry cyclist to ask if it was "Revolution? Anarchy? State-sponsored terrorism? No, it's just another Critical Mass in Chicago, allowing anyone with a bicycle to flout the law."[24]

The bike battles of the twenty-first century serve as proxies for other ideological fights. "Particularly in America, the bicycle is emerging as a new conservative front in the culture wars," observed the *Boston Globe* in 2013. The humorist P. J. O'Rourke argues that "bike lanes violate a fundamental principle of democracy." When all are forced to support "a fibrosis of bicycle lanes . . . spreading through the cities of the world . . . so that an affluent elite can feel good about itself" in its "sanctimonious pedal-pushing," O'Rourke sees communist totalitarianism. Similarly, an editor at the conservative *Weekly Standard* warned drivers that "what is going on is the attempt of an organized private interest to claim a public good," stealing from drivers what was intended solely for their use. He argued further that "the bicycle agenda is coming to resemble the feminist agenda from the 1970s, when previously all male Universities went coed. Everything that was ever off limits to the aggrieved minority must be opened up," even while new funds and existing facilities are still reserved for the minority group's sole use. Some ultraconservatives fear that bicycle and pedestrian promotion is the first step in an insidious United Nations plot to undermine American sovereignty and establish a one-world government.[25]

New York City's bike-share program, introduced in the summer of 2013, is an excellent example of how the bike battles are often political debates clad in Lycra. The *Wall Street Journal* raged not only against the bicycles (and the encroachment of bike-share stations on sidewalks) but also against the power of a mayor whom the editorial board had long opposed. In an editorial video, a board member, Dorothy Rabinowitz, worried that cyclists had been "empowered by the city administration with the idea that they are privileged" because of their environmentalist trappings. Rabinowitz chalked up the existence of the bike-share program to Mayor Bloomberg's autocratic overreach, supported by his "ideology-maddened traffic commissioner." Rabinowitz's vehemence attracted widespread attention nationwide as the video went viral. On the *Daily Show*, the humorist Jon Stewart mocked her concern: "They're just [bleep]ing bikes! Slow down, Lady Hunger Games!"[26] As the conflict subsided, the bike-share program was mostly judged a success, and the new mayor, Bill de Blasio, has made an even larger commitment to Vision Zero, an initiative to reduce fatalities and accidents in New York that will likely include further alterations to city streets.

The backlash against bikes and their riders combines legal, political, social, and cultural criticisms—sometimes from cyclists themselves. One writer summarizes: "As bicyclists become an ever more powerful lobby . . . they are discovering—to their sincere surprise—that they are provoking mistrust and even hostility among the public." Another writer notes that "urban bicyclists have an image problem. They've become stereotyped as pretentious, aloof jackasses." Another, in a pro-bike op-ed piece ironically titled "Is It O.K. to Kill Cyclists?," concedes that "every time I drive my car through San Francisco, I see cyclists running stop signs like immortal, entitled fools. So I understand the impulse to see cyclists as recreational risk takers who deserve their fate."[27]

The bike boom and backlash have been even more pronounced in the United Kingdom, Australia, and cash-strapped parts of continental Europe. Italy has reported record-breaking declines in auto sales and concomitant increases in bicycle sales. In London, the increase in cycling might yet lead to dreams of a cycling utopia: "Supporters of 'Peak-Car' theory see a future in which the inner cities are given over to pedestrians, cyclists and public transport, and café culture replaces car culture," wrote a London *Times* journalist in 2012. But according to a 2012 BBC documentary, *The War on Britain's Roads*, that future may be a long way off: it featured terrifying videos taken from cyclists' helmet-mounted cameras showing shouting, finger pointing, hood banging, road rage, and near-death experiences. The show, characterized by the *Guardian* as a "high profile, overly alarmist and somewhat skewed documentary," set off even further debate.[28]

Even stereotypically polite Canadians are engaging in bike battles, which became particularly vitriolic during Toronto's 2011 municipal elections. Then-mayor Rob Ford and his brother, the city councilman Doug Ford, launched a campaign against urban cycling advocates, accusing them of waging a "war on cars," while the Ford brothers waved the populist banner in representation of car-driving suburbanites. The strange contours of this debate have included the prominent Canadian author Margaret Atwood and the flamboyant CBC hockey analyst Don Cherry weighing in on opposite sides, with Cherry characterizing cyclists as "pinkos." Attempts to remove recently installed bike lanes have been blocked by protesters lying down in front of construction vehicles.[29]

These public debates capture the essential difficulty of reintroducing the bicycle to city streets. One view of the problem comes from Toronto's Mayor Ford, who probably expresses the opinion of many twenty-first-century drivers: "Every year we have dozens of people that get hit by cars or trucks. Well, no wonder: roads are built for buses, cars, and trucks, not for people on bikes. . . . [M]y heart bleeds for them when I hear someone gets killed, but it's their own fault at the end of the day." In Ford's view, the history of public roads demonstrates that automobiles were the complete victors in the battle for dominance of the road network, vanquishing all other contenders. But simultaneously, other observers see an end to automotive dominance. In a *New York Times* op-ed, one San Francisco rider declared that "we're at a scary cultural crossroads on the whole car/bike thing," and while bicycles are reappearing, the problem is that "the social and legal culture of the American road, not to mention the road itself, hasn't caught up."[30]

A NEW HOPE

Are today's bike battles something new, with the possibility of resolving the "whole car/bike thing"? Or is this political fight simply a rehash of previous disputes? And why is it so difficult for bikes and cars to coexist on the street in the first place? There are at least two ways in which history helps us answer these questions. First, the debates over bicycles on public streets since at least 1869 fall into identifiable patterns. They can be seen as attempts to support or delegitimize competing interest-group claims to an exhaustible resource. These bike battles have recurred with every significant change in technology or the demographics of road users. Second, these historical debates show how the outcomes of each battle have structured the terms of the next engagement. Each choice, tactic, or failure becomes the basis for the next iteration of disputes over the public resource: for example, traffic signs and painted lanes meant as emergency controls on the automobile in the 1920s and 1930s shaped the experience of cyclists for the coming century. Sometimes, the legacy of a comparatively recent crisis has been mistakenly viewed as an immutable fact of life.

Bike Battles offers a survey of the debate over the public roads in the United States to help us understand our present situation. These battles have been overlooked precisely because historians of the United States, unlike their European counterparts, generally discount the bicycle as a serious topic. Many American cycling enthusiasts and historians of cycling, in turn, do not engage with academic history, archival sources, or policy matters. This book prompts more serious research of bike history to help us understand our cities and their conflicts.

This approach builds on the concept that policy analysts call *path dependency,* or the understanding that our current decisions are constrained by our past decisions and institutions. The bike battles I explore in this book collectively demonstrate the importance of past government actions in privileging or hindering particular modes of transportation. The city in which we live today is path dependent, a legacy of countless past decisions in city halls, courts, and Congress. There is reason for depression here: in the words of the comic strip *Pogo* at the dawn of the modern environmental era, we have met the enemy, and he is us.

But at the same time, there is a new hope for the roads of the future. The legal philosophy that considers the road as a public resource to be shared between diverse users will become ever more important as we add new vehicles powered by hydrogen fuel cells, electric, natural gas, biodiesel, and other still-unknown energy sources. Autonomous or driverless cars will require fundamental transformations to existing law and infrastructure. Ride sharing, enabled by social media, could disturb the taxi industry and reduce private auto ownership. All of these disruptive technologies offer opportunities to transform roads and cities while limiting harm. The double whammy of crumbling infrastructure and declining gasoline-tax revenues to maintain it will require considerable alterations to both roads and political institutions in coming years. All of these trends suggest that the roads of tomorrow will not be what we travel on today.

A century and more of decisions has created the complicated urban landscape of our present-day cities—and the anxieties that I experience when I ride up to a four-way stop. Yet examining the effects of government action also illustrates that collective decisions can improve the situation. Perhaps there is a way out of my impending doom: autocentric America was not created by an uncontrollable love affair with automobiles, by some invisible hand favoring a superior technology, or by the unchangeable dictates of climate and geography. Instead, it came about through the collective actions of the people through the mechanisms of government. If it is true that we got ourselves into the current predicament, then we can get ourselves out of it. The road can be shared. It must be shared, because, like the planet, it is all that we have.

CHAPTER 1

GET OUT OF
THE ROAD!

The Battle over the
Public Roads in America,
1870–1900

There's a lot of history in twenty-four silent seconds. In jerky
black and white, a parade of cyclists rolls slowly down a tree-
lined New York City street in a stately procession, their upright
posture and dazzling bicycle-club uniforms drawing a surging
crowd of onlookers. The mostly male bicyclists are showing off
their status, health, and wealth through public spectacle; their
clothes and demeanor reflect the origin of cycling as high-status
recreation. But more important, the cyclists are riding on a boulevard filled with all kinds of vehicles weaving past each other in
a complex dance. The road is packed with pedestrians, horses,
horse-drawn wagons, and trolley cars on tracks. There are commercial vehicles and private carriages, fire engines and delivery
wagons, public transit vehicles, and private joyriders. But no matter their size, purpose, cost, or capabilities, according to the law
they all had to share the road.

This scene is captured in a film from 1896 titled *View on Boulevard, New York City.* Unseen in America for perhaps a century, the
only known print sits in an archive in the Netherlands. While other

surviving films of this era are treated as treasures, digitized and widely disseminated on the Internet, this one has languished. Its obscurity suggests that among Americans, the road's complex history as a shared resource has likewise been forgotten.[1]

Instead, competing users of different technologies have spent more than a century ordering each other out of the road, starting even before the advent of film. In 1883, one New Jersey bicyclist reported the abuse he received from the drivers of horse-drawn wagons: "Get that thing off the road!" yelled one. Another driver yelled: "Those things are a nuisance, sir! You have no right to the road!" The tables were turned a quarter century later. As the automobile was superseding horse-drawn wagons in 1908, a Long Island driver shouted, "Get out of the road, then!" at a wagon blocking his way, honking his horn at the driver. That particular automobilist only quieted down when the wagon driver produced a shotgun before yelling, "Now stop tooting, dang ye." When bicycles returned to popularity and to city streets in the late twentieth century, automobile drivers again declared that cyclists had no place on the road. A Bangor, Maine, newspaper columnist complained in 1978 that when he went for a bike tour, "drivers tried to rob me of my fair share" of the road, and "when I didn't run my bike into the ditch they roared around me, with a woman in the car shouting 'Get out of the road!'" A driver in Nacogdoches, Texas, made the same point more strongly in 2008, in an all-too-common scene. Two cyclists were riding down the street "when a vehicle passed them and the occupants yelled at them to get out of the road," noted the police blotter. "The riders yelled back and the vehicle stopped and the occupants assaulted them."[2]

These present-day disagreements are just the most recent incarnations of long-running battles between road users with each new incumbent telling the previous generation to get out of the road. But all of these actors make assumptions that belie the fundamental legal principle of the road. How that legal principle has interfaced with physical and political reality is the first of the bike battles.

The story begins long before automobiles existed, as the big-wheeled "ordinary" bicycles of the 1870s and less precarious "safety" bicycles of the 1890s rose to popularity. Their presence on the road frightened horses, sparked fights, and perplexed judges. These conflicts—which originated on street corners but quickly moved to city council meetings, newspapers, and the courts—set important precedents and left important legacies that have complicated the position of the bicycle in city traffic in the present day. In particular, nineteenth-century legal decisions irrevocably mixed somewhat incompatible forms of traffic on the shared space of the public roads.

These developments came in the midst of a revolution in state and local government in the United States. Legislatures and the courts became more willing to strengthen government power, eventually allowing cities to regulate buildings, create public health agencies, tax their residents, and control nuisances. In many ways, today we live in cities that are the physical, legal, and institutional legacies of this progressive era.[3]

The law does not exist in a vacuum: it is, in the words of Justice Oliver Wendell Holmes, a "magic mirror," reflecting politics and society in ways simultaneously illuminating and distorting. *Who* rode *what* mattered to the law. The social groups who dominated cycling in the United States were upwardly mobile middle- and upper-class men, associated with modernity and technological progress. They argued persuasively in courts and legislatures for their rights, but they could also be ridiculed as unrepresentative of the wider public. First the velocipede, then the high-wheeled ordinary, and after that the safety was associated in popular culture with specific groups. These associations occasionally eased and occasionally complicated the groups' claims to the road.[4]

One result of these conflicts was that the law came to understand wagons, bicycles, motorcycles, and even automobiles as legal entities with similar rights to travel on the public road. A bicycle has the same right as an eighteen-wheel semi truck to occupy the same physical space on a city street, though preferably not at the same time. This is the essential paradox of the history of the bicycle, a paradox that is behind both the exasperation of cyclists who insist on their equal rights and the astonishment of drivers who perceive the obvious inequality between multi-ton technological marvels and delicate twenty-pound contraptions. Legal equality won in the courtroom did not eliminate inequality in the physical world, and the right to the road came wrapped in contingencies of social division between groups of riders and drivers.

IS IT A VEHICLE?

A series of nineteenth-century court decisions included bicycles in a long list of legally recognized vehicles, which included cable- or horse-drawn streetcars and all manner of conveyances drawn by horses, oxen, or mules. But these decisions also made it possible for courts to support the regulation of bicycles, to assign bicyclists responsibilities and hold them accountable for negligence, and (eventually) to add automobiles to the same list.

This bike battle rolled through the courts before most legislatures or governments created legislation specific to the bicycle and before ridership increased in the 1890s. Common-law tradition also meant that US legal decisions about bicycle rights and responsibilities were based on earlier British decisions. Under the legal principle of *stare decisis*, these early decisions—whether in the United States or across the Atlantic—set precedents that all later courtroom findings would be required to at least address, if not follow.

The first skirmish concerned long-established definitions of means of transport. Centuries before the invention of self-propelled wheeled contraptions, courts defined what human-powered or animal-drawn constructs—described as *vehicles*—were legally permitted on the road. But before the word *vehicle* became popularly associated with a powered, enclosed contraption for movement, it was used to describe all manner of mechanisms for transport of things and people. Dictionaries from the eighteenth century declared that the word meant anything "which serves to carry or convey a thing; as the *Serum* is a proper Vehicle for the Blood" but also listed as examples the horse-drawn "Cart, Wain, Wagon, or Chariot."[5] The possibility of confusion was obvious: a joke from 1799 told of an old woman advised by a doctor to give her husband some medicine "in a proper vehicle," meaning mixed in liquid. She misunderstood and instead loaded him into a wheelbarrow before administering the drug. By the middle of the nineteenth century, the popular meaning of *vehicle* had been narrowed to refer to a physical means of travel, but it still encompassed a bewildering array of horse-drawn contraptions. Rather than list all surreys, wagons, drays, hackneys, hansoms, caissons, and landaus by name, courts just referred to them all as vehicles.[6] The question was whether bicycles also qualified.

The stakes were high. If bicycles were not legally considered vehicles, then all of the laws allowing vehicles the right to travel on roads and streets would, by definition, disallow bicycles. The default status of bicyclists would be that of interlopers, who could be removed by force: their legal access to the roads would require specific exceptions to the law. On the other hand, if bicycles were judged to be vehicles, all existing laws and legal precedents governing other vehicles would also apply to them.

The King's Highway and the Public Road

Long before the first bicyclist rolled down a street, probably accompanied by shouts of "Get out of the road!," centuries of English common law guaranteed freedom of movement to all on the public road. Unlike the twentieth-century American use of *highway* to describe a controlled-access, high-speed road system, the *high way* in English tradition was a road or path on which travelers were permitted free and unencumbered passage across property that was owned or controlled by others. The rights of travelers *in via regia*, or on the king's highway, were protected in such foundational laws as the Statute of Marlborough, passed in 1267 in the reign of Henry III and still partially in force today.[7] By the eighteenth century, the idea of free passage for travelers was rolled into the definition of the highway itself: one did not exist without another.[8] Since ancient times, other types of roads had also existed, such as turnpikes or toll roads that restricted travel to approved groups and extracted fees; but they were exceptions to the rule, generally requiring the support of the state to enable their operation by private owners or state agencies. By contrast, the label *king's highway* was often paired with the words *public* or *common*, reinforcing the idea that most roads were not privately owned or controlled but were instead communally owned property whose entire purpose was enabling the free passage of travelers. This protected right to travel was assumed in the laws of the early American colonies and incorporated into statutory law after the American Revolution.[9]

Velocipedes

In the earliest decades of the nineteenth century, the first waves of two-wheeled, human-powered contraptions led to some legal bunfights, but these cases did not set significant legal precedents. The first machine to appear was the wooden *draisine*, sometimes known as a hobby horse or dandy horse after the fashionable toffs who straddled the frame and pushed themselves along the ground with their feet. While some European early adopters traveled long distances with these contraptions, poor roads limited their use in the United States to some city streets and to indoor facilities—like skating rinks—for amusement. These uses created little opportunity for legal disagreements that would rise to the level of appellate courts, thereby setting precedent. It was still possible, of course, for their riders to get into trouble: by 1819, a few violators had been dragged before magistrates in Britain for improperly riding on the few paved streets mostly set aside for pedestrians, and a later U.S. Supreme Court case mentioned that New York City had banned velocipedes from city streets in the same year.[10]

The fad died rapidly, only to return half a century later, when the metal-framed velocipedes known as boneshakers appeared. This iteration of the design featured pedals directly connected to the front axle, and, very occasionally, solid rubber tires. But the velocipede, regarded as possessing an "unmanageable nature," was largely confined to indoor rinks in much of the United States: as a mode of transport, it was considered impractical and not seen as warranting the intervention of the courts.[11]

In the few instances when the velocipede came to the attention of the law, it was mostly treated as an anomaly, not as a vehicle that fell under existing rules of the road. In 1869 the borough magistrates of Southampton, England, declared that a turnpike operator was wrong to charge a velocipedist a toll, even if the amount charged was no more than that for a wheelbarrow, because his conveyance was not a vehicle. But in the same year a Hartford, Connecticut, prosecutor made the exact opposite comparison, declaring that a municipal ordinance banning from sidewalks any vehicles powered "by hand" also applied to velocipedes. The ordinance applied to wheelbarrows, went the reasoning: a man using a wheelbarrow used both his hands and his feet to move; and therefore foot-powered velocipedes were covered by the law. Reflecting this confusion, the New York City park commissioners briefly banned the velocipede from park boulevards as a nuisance in the winter of 1868, then reversed their decision the following spring. But all of this may have been moot: as one law journal explained while applauding a court's attempts to ban velocipedes: "We trust this decision may give the *coup de grace* to the velocipede mania, now fast disappearing."[12] While many cities did ban velocipedes in 1869, in the end, there was little need to control or defend the velocipede in law: the fad was self-regulating, with most velocipedists abandoning their machines after only a year or so.[13]

HIGH SOCIETY AND HIGH WHEELS IN THE 1880s

Though the velocipede vanished, its successor was not far behind: the high-wheeler, penny-farthing, or "ordinary" bicycle of the late 1870s and 1880s, with its outsized front wheel, metal spokes, and rubber tires, proved far more popular than any previous design. Because of its expense, precariousness, and association with modernity, the high-wheel bicycle of the 1880s was associated with professional men of the upper middle class. Reflecting this demographic, in 1881 the *Chicago Daily Tribune* determined that bicycling news should be reported under the column headline of "Polite Athletics." The column covered the elaborate uniforms of high-wheeler social clubs, which served to keep out the riffraff and make the new pastime a highly conspicuous form of consumption. "The new uniform of the Ariels includes coat and pants of steel gray corduroy," began one report, "knit Jersey shirt in red and black stripes, polo cap to match, and dark blue stockings." Such an outfit would be sure to attract attention: "It is altogether likely that the Oconomowoc girls will all lose their hearts when the handsome boys in this elegant costume appear at the lake." Besides impressing those choosy Oconomowoc girls, the expense and exclusivity of this outlandish clothing marked inclusion in a fashionable elite: "Plaid stockings of the most fearful and wonderful shades are all the rage just now," noted the paper. "They are imported from England, and everybody is wearing them."[14]

The cost of the high-wheeler was substantial, though prices came down slowly during the 1880s. Late in the high-wheel era, when a high-quality bike cost $125 new and at least $90 second-hand, a used ordinary would still have represented nearly seven months' pay for a farm laborer earning just under $14 a month, or nearly two months' pay for an ironworker making $1.99 a day.[15]

The high price of the ordinary served to exclude the lower classes: "It is for the best that the wheel is something not within the easy reach of all," one rider wrote in *The Wheelman*. With casual prejudice against more recent immigrants, the author argued that high prices ensured "a gentlemanly class of riders that we would not have had were Patsy O'Rafferty and Hans Schneider able to secure mounts without having to make some real effort to that end." High prices, he argued, smoothed the way for those who could afford bikes: "How many road courtesies would be observed if the new vehicle had found its way into the hands of all classes? Very few, I assure you."[16]

"The bicycle is not a toy or a boy's plaything," agreed one bicycling minister in 1882: "A large proportion of its riders are grown men, and many of them heads of families engaged in business and professional life." Speaking as a highly educated and moral leader, he declared of the bicycle: "There is nothing 'common or unclean' about it. Its cost, delicacy, grace and beauty must pre-

Figure 1.1. High-wheel or "ordinary" riders, along with a tricyclist, take a turn around Copley Square in Boston, Massachusetts, about 1880 (with Trinity Church under construction in the background). Their uniform-like clothing signals that cycling is a well-regulated and class-appropriate athletic endeavor. National Archives RG 306 PS D (61–10196).

vent it from ever becoming vulgar. It is a gentleman's fancy." Another author wrote flatteringly of himself and his audience in 1889 that "the average intelligence of the Cycling fraternity can, with justice, be said to be above that of any other association of man and women, devoted to pastime, sport, and exercise, in the world." One advocate declared that 90 percent of high-wheel riders were "'active and pushing' business employees and proprietors, or professional men, such as doctors, lawyers, editors, clergymen, architect and civil engineers."[17]

The association with a male elite was rooted in the extreme nature of the high-wheel: dangerously prone to overturning, with a steep learning curve and little in the way of creature comforts for its rider, the bicycle of the 1870s and 1880s tempted male riders to demonstrate feats of bravery, strength, and pigheadedness. Looking back from the perspective of 1897, one writer observed that "I rather wonder that any one was ever reckless enough or skillful enough to ride it. . . . At best, the big wheels of a few years ago were fit only for athletic young men; they were out of the question for all other persons, and of course for women."[18]

All of these associations were manifested in the activities of the League of American Wheelmen (LAW), a national advocacy, social, and racing organization with local chapters. One historian has described it as promoting "Victorian beliefs in healthy outdoor activities, conducted within the parameters of military pomp, gentlemanly order, and racial exclusiveness." An 1880s handbook called for militaristic uniforms, medals and ribbons of rank, close-order drill, and songs celebrating the riders' masculine courage:

> Now I am a bold Bicycler
> And I ride a great big wheel,
> I'm a member of the brotherhood,
> That binds us firm as steel;
> Whatever way you call it,
> 'Tis band of brothers true,
> It is the league of American Wheelmen
> Or the L.A.W.[19]

Taylor v. Goodwin

It was a good thing that cyclists were becoming more organized in their own defense, because the design innovations of the high-wheeler enabled riders to travel far and fast enough to get into sufficient trouble to involve the courts and thus set lasting precedents.[20] A decade after the velocipede craze had faded, in March 1879, a British court heard an appeal from Charles E. Taylor, who had been charged and convicted of the crime of "driving furiously" on a public road. Perched atop his ordinary, Taylor had pedaled so fast that observers reported to the police that he "had been riding a bicycle on a highway at a furious pace" in contravention of the law. Rather than contest this description of his riding, Taylor's solicitor argued on appeal that the law applied specifically to driving a *carriage* overly fast, and "the fact that a bicycle has wheels does not make it a carriage." The solicitor, a Mr. Rose, argued that it would be ridiculous to declare that "every apparatus by which a man is carried is a 'carriage,'" since such a broad definition would include roller skates and wheelbarrows.[21]

The justices of the Queen's Bench, a division of the High Court of England, were not persuaded. Ruling against Taylor, they declared that a bicycle was a legal vehicle. The statute in question determined that "if any person riding any horse or beast, or driving any sort of carriage, shall ride or drive the same furiously so as to endanger the life or limb of any passenger," then they could be charged. Justice Lush argued that in Taylor's case, "it is quite immaterial what the motive power may be." Whatever Taylor was riding, if he was moving fast enough to worry his fellow travelers, then in the eyes of the court he became both equivalent to them and subject to legal control. Furthermore, according to the justice, the law was future-proofed: "Although bicycles were unknown at the time when the act passed, it is clear that the intention was to use words large enough to comprehend any kind of vehicle which might be propelled at such a speed as to be dangerous."[22]

The *Taylor* decision came at a portentous moment for American cycling. The arrival of the ordinary in 1879 and 1880 prompted a rash of prohibitions, many of which rested on the precedent of the decade-old velocipede bans. Officials in Brooklyn's Prospect Park, Philadelphia's Fairmount Park, and Chicago's Lincoln Park banned cyclists from their grounds. San Francisco had a complete ban on bicyclists in the streets early in the 1880s, and Brooklyn heavily controlled their use. But the most famous of these prohibitions applied to New York's Central Park and Riverside Drive. Bicycles were banned from the park until 1883 and heavily controlled until 1887, long after other such regulations were relaxed. The restrictions resulted in significant political and legal battles throughout the decade, with cycling advocates financed by Colonel Augustus Albert Pope, the nation's most powerful bicycle manufacturer.[23]

Farther south, prospects for cyclists looked even worse in the early 1880s. Kentucky banned high-wheeled bicycles from the public roads entirely. The draconian sweep of this action was tempered only by the fact that there were few bicycles in the state at the time. North Carolina passed a state law in 1885 allowing some turnpike operators to effectively ban bicycles from their privately owned roads, and a similar prohibition was in effect on a turnpike near Hannibal, Missouri. Other cities and towns throughout the United States prohibited cycles from roads in the first part of the decade, including Rome, Georgia; Nashville, Tennessee; Wheeling, West Virginia; Springfield, Illinois; and at least one town in Delaware.[24] It took until 1884 for lobbying efforts, the increasing popularity of cycling, and legal decisions to overturn most of these prohibitions, and it was not until the end of the decade that a New York statute ended the ban on bicycles in Central Park.

This array of local prohibitions was the death by a thousand cuts for prospective cyclists in the 1880s. Only case law that established travel by bicycle as a fundamental right could supersede such a threat. Thus, in losing *Taylor v. Goodwin*, Charles E. Taylor won big for cycling at large, for this decision was one of a handful of legal cases that supported the legal right of cyclists to use the roads.[25] In *The Road Rights and Liabilities of Wheelmen*, the first comprehensive summary of the legal rights of bicycles, Harold Clemenston succinctly summarized the effect of *Taylor:* "The object of the existence of a highway is public travel. All citizens have the right to its use; not alone those using horses as a means of conveyance or traffic, but others as well." Such a precedent had obvious implications for all travelers, he wrote: "Improved methods of locomotion are admissible and cannot be excluded from existing public roads, if not inconsistent with the present methods."[26]

Taylor was immediately seized upon by the lawyers engaged in Colonel Pope's crusade against the New York park-boulevard bicycle ban. The lawyer Charles E. Pratt cited *Taylor* in his presentation against the ban, an argument reprinted by the LAW as a pamphlet and then in the pages of *Bicycling World* in 1881. He argued that *Taylor* definitively declared "that a bicycle is a carriage," and while "the highest courts in this country have not yet passed upon the question . . . it has been raised in one or two of the lower courts, where it has been held a carriage, following the English law."[27]

In his 1892 *Wheels and Wheeling*, Luther Porter called *Taylor* "the first decision on the status of a cycle." This was not necessarily true, but it proves the importance of the case: the Queen's Bench was an exceptionally important court in England, exercising a supervisory role over all inferior courts, and almost all subsequent decisions in United States courts deferred to *Taylor* to determine the common-law rights of vehicles and the road.[28] As local cyclists and the LAW pushed back against local prohibitions in the early 1880s, citing persuasive English precedent was crucial in the absence of guidance from state legislation or American cases. As one American legal treatise later put it, because of the logic of *Taylor*, "the law of the wheel is not *sui generis*"; rather, "it is mainly an application of old and well-settled principles to new conditions."[29] When courts in the United States sought guidance on whether bikes could be banned by cities, *Taylor* provided a solid precedent: the bicycle was a vehicle.

Is It a Carriage?

When riders started using bicycles as transportation more extensively, the courts had to decide whether existing laws for vehicles that carried things and people—that is, "carriages"—included the newcomers. A few existing laws governing tolls and taxation used the word *carriage* as a distinct subcategory of *vehicle*, while others used the words interchangeably. The physical form further confused matters: a single rider sat astride a bicycle much as a rider rode a horse, but a horse wasn't a vehicle, while a bicycle was. Even though the horse and the bike could both carry people and things, a horse was not a carriage, but a bike might be. Idiom made things worse: A horse-drawn carriage was operated by a *driver*, but both horses and bicycles had *riders*, implying that a bicycle wasn't like other carriages. And walking and cycling were both human-powered forms of locomotion, but a cyclist was not a pedestrian. It was enough to drive a jurist round the bend.

When courts could not rely upon legal precedents to guide them, they could fall back on the legal philosophy of *ejusdem generis:* determining if a new thing was like the lists of similar things in statutes. The decision in the British case *Williams v. Ellis* used this approach in considering whether a toll taker was correct in charging a cyclist for riding on the road. An act written before the bicycle's existence had laid out two categories of carriages with two different fares: sixpence for "any coach, sociable, chariot, berlin, landau, vis-à-vis, phaeton, curricle," or similar carriage drawn by animal power, and five shillings for a carriage powered by steam or other mechanical means. The court found that the newcomer bicycle was *sui generis:* it did not fit into either of the existing categories. Therefore, it was not a carriage under this law.[30]

But in most other cases that applied *ejusdem generis* to lists that did not explicitly name the bicycle, the bicycle was judged to be a carriage. "When bicycles appeared as a means of ordinary travel, the same question was argued in America and in England," a 1917 legal monograph reflected. At that time, the courts held that "they were 'carriages' within the common meaning of the expression." The bicycle was a carriage, except when it wasn't: the legal consensus was "not without the reservation that as contrasted with vehicles of an earlier generation they are not *ejusdem generis.*"[31] Although there were complications, most American decisions reaffirmed *Taylor:* "While traveling upon the highways by means of horses has been in vogue much longer, and is more universal at present than by means of bicycles," noted an 1889 Indiana case, "persons traveling by means of horses have no superior rights to those traveling upon the highway by improved methods of travel."[32]

City ordinances and state laws followed these case-law precedents, codifying the bicycle unequivocally as a carriage. The 1887 New York state law that specifically equated bicycles with carriages was widely copied, as in this 1889 Pittsburgh ordinance: "Bicycles, tricycles, and all vehicles propelled by hand or foot . . . upon the public highways of this state, shall be entitled to the same rights and subject to the same restrictions [as] in the cases of persons using carriages drawn by horses."[33]

Nuisance, Negligence, and the Rules of the Road

The fact remained that the high-wheeler was precarious, novel, and comparatively rare. In the 1880s, courts were prepared to define bicycles as vehicles, but only if they did not represent a nuisance to other road users. North Carolina's Supreme Court struck a difficult balance in 1887, deciding that although the bicycle was a vehicle, it was an anomalous and disturbing one. In consequence, it found that the state legislature could make laws restricting the use of bicycles on certain roads. An 1885 state law had forbidden the use of "a bicycle, or tricycle, or other non-horse vehicle" on a specific toll road. When a conviction under this law was appealed in *State v. Yopp*, the court agreed that the bicycle was a vehicle, but it was a strange one, "by reason of its peculiar shape, and the unusual manner of using it as a means of locomotion [which might] prove injurious to others." The court was concerned for "women and children, constantly passing and repassing in great numbers over the particular road mentioned in carriages and other ordinary vehicles drawn by horses." It observed that the strangeness of the bicycle caused obvious damage: "In repeated instances, the horses became frightened at them, and carriages were thrown into the ditches along the side of the road." The judge concluded that the bicycle presented a nuisance to others: "There is no reason why the owner of a particular kind of vehicle, which, because of its peculiar form or appearance, or from the unusual manner of its use, frightens horses, or otherwise imperils passengers over the road, or their property, shall be allowed to use such vehicle on the road."[34]

The *Yopp* decision, which was criticized by cyclists, became largely outdated once the high-wheeler stopped scaring the horses. As judges had found a decade earlier with respect to steam-powered vehicles in *Macomber v. Nichols*, the diminishing likelihood of spooked horses did not alone justify eliminating new uses of the roads.[35] Just two years after *Yopp*, the Indiana Supreme Court case of *Holland v. Bartch* involved a cyclist accused of negligence under rules that governed equally competent vehicles meeting on the road. In August 1885, a woman in a carriage met a young man perched on a bicycle equipped with an unusually large (sixty-inch-diameter) wheel, who was thus able to travel at the extreme speed of fifteen miles an hour. In exact legalese, the plaintiff's attorney declared that the horses "became and were greatly frightened, and became and were wholly unmanageable, and ran away," tipping over the carriage and injuring the occupant. The cyclist was accused of being negligent in his choice of mode of travel, since it "was an unusual vehicle with which to travel upon such highway, and as he well knew was a frightful object for ordinary horses to meet, and was well calculated to and did frighten horses unaccustomed to meeting such vehicles with a rider mounted thereon." But, in contrast to the court in the *Yopp* case, the court rejected this argument. While holding that the cyclist could be held liable for negligent action, it declared that simply riding a contraption that appeared strange to horses could not in itself represent a nuisance to other road users. Of bicycles, the court opined: "To declare their use upon the public highway a nuisance would prohibit their use in the manner in which they are intended."[36]

THE SAFETY BICYCLE AND SOCIETY RIDERS OF THE 1890s

Legal decisions were influenced by characteristics of the bicycle, the number of riders, and their station in society. Just as the courts were coming to a consensus on the rights and responsibilities of the riders in the high-wheeler era, a new bicycle design appeared on the scene, dramatically changing the equation. The innovations of the "safety" bike of the 1890s drove a rapid expansion of cycling. The new design featured pneumatic tires, a chain-driven rear wheel the same size as the front, and frame geometry recognizable to modern eyes. Named for its most obvious advantage over the precarious high-wheeler, the safety opened cycling up to both men and women of a range of ages and abilities.[37] In turn, the proliferation of domestic cycle manufacturers, early developments in mass production, and competition in a mass market made bicycles more affordable.

The result was an all-consuming fad, with cycling featured in magazines, songs, newspapers, social clubs, and parades. While most of this riding was for leisure and recreation, the popularity of the bike boom extended into practical and utilitarian transportation. In a world before cars, the bicycle briefly appeared to be the future of technology, eclipsing horse-drawn trolleys, omnibuses, carriages, wagons and steam trains for personal transport. This boom in bicycling found its way into the courts: there was a consensus that bicycles were here to stay and were not ipso facto nuisances, but also a concern that large numbers of poorly controlled bicycles might constitute nuisances in need of regulation.

Seven years after the *Yopp* decision favoring nervous horses over bicycles, the Minnesota supreme court decision on safety bicycles in *Thompson v. Dodge* stated definitively that "a highway is intended for public use, and a person riding or driving a horse has no rights superior to those of a person riding a bicycle." It continued: "Bicycles are vehicles used now very extensively . . . and the riding of one upon the public highway in the ordinary manner as is now done is neither unlawful nor prohibited, and they cannot be banished because they were not ancient vehicles, and used in the Garden of Eden by Adam and Eve." Contrary to *Yopp*, the Minnesota court found cyclists had no need to show excess deference: "It is not the duty of a party lawfully traveling upon a public highway upon a bicycle, when he sees a horse and carriage approaching, to stop and inquire whether the horse is likely to be frightened."[38]

These decisions continued to refer to the common-law determination that the bicycle was a vehicle, regularly citing *Taylor v. Goodman*. In its *Swift v. Topeka* decision of 1890, the Kansas Supreme Court declared that "each citizen has the absolute right to choose for himself the mode of conveyance he desires, whether it is by carriage, by horse, motor or electric car, or by bicycle, or astride of a horse, subject to the sole condition that he will observe all those requirements that are known as the 'law of the road.'" The court argued that "the right of the people to the use of the public streets of a city is so well established and so universally recognized in this country that it has become a part of the alphabet of fundamental

SOMEBODY BLUNDERED.—Drawn by A. B. Frost.

Figure 1.2. Two "safety" bicycle riders argue
over who is at fault at an intersection on
an unpaved road in "Somebody Blundered,"
Harper's Weekly illustration by A. B. Frost,
1896. National Archives RG 30 (37–787).

rights of the citizen." Four years later, a Pennsylvania county court used the exact same language in finding a wagon driver negligent for running over a bicycle lying on the side of the road. A Pennsylvania Supreme Court's decision in 1898 likewise solidified these rights, observing that bicycles were vehicles but should give way to wagons where appropriate, not because bicycles had inferior rights but because all vehicles had a duty to avoid accident.[39]

Now that they were in the same category as horse-drawn vehicles, bicycles were clearly subject to the basic rules of the road: traveling on the right half of the road when meeting oncoming traffic, overtaking on the left, giving way where appropriate, and exercising due care and vigilance. Following the rules of the road protected cyclists against accusations of negligence, as in the 1892 case concerning Alfred Schimpf of Albany, who, traveling at a tame three miles an hour on the correct side of the road, collided with a faster-moving horse-drawn wagon traveling on the wrong side of the road. The faster speed and greater size of the wagon did not compel the cyclist to give way, said the court, since he had followed the customary rule of the road.[40]

But if the presence of bicycles on the road could not be viewed as a nuisance to the carriage drivers who were already there, neither could the existing street railways be considered a nuisance to the bicyclists, barring some extreme negligence. One cyclist complained in the LAW magazine that "to the wheelman [rail tracks] constitute . . . a constant source of difficulty to himself and damage to his wheel; for he is unable to cross them with safety at anything much less than a right angle," especially after rain. But both the street cars and the bicycle were vehicles, with equal claim to public space: neither could successfully petition to banish the other.[41]

SIDEWALKS

Nineteenth century courts had consistently found bicycles always to be vehicles, sometimes to be carriages, and rarely to be nuisances in and of themselves. But did bicyclists count as pedestrians, with the right to ride on the elevated sidewalk, away from the generally unpaved, often muddy, and occasionally manure-filled street? In May 1884, David Corbin was "standing on a public sidewalk in the town of Rochester," Indiana, when Edwin C. Mercer, on a bicycle, "rode a bicycle against him, threw him down, and severely injured him." The language of the complaint was forceful; Corbin was said to have been "assaulted, beat, and wounded," and later journalistic coverage insinuated that while Corbin was standing on the edge of a fourteen-foot-wide sidewalk, "Mercer stole silently up to him on a rubber wheeled bicycle, ran into him, threw him down and inflicted some painful bruises." When the case reached the Indiana Supreme Court on appeal, fate intervened. After the court had heard the case in November 1888 and subsequently discussed their decision on in February 1889, they retired for dinner. "Three minutes later a reckless bicycle rider ran into Judges Coffey and Burkshire and knocked the former flat upon the stone sidewalk in front of the State House, injuring him so seriously that he has not been able to give attention to judicial duties," according to a Chicago newspaper. "It did not take long for that august body to avenge the insult," commented an Indiana observer. The resulting decision declared forcefully that "sidewalks are intended for the use of pedestrians, and not for use by persons in vehicles." Therefore, "if a bicycle can be deemed a vehicle, then the appellant had no right to ride or drive his bicycle longitudinally along the sidewalk."[42]

Although it was the very definition of irony, the Indiana rundown was not an isolated incident. With the bicycle fad filling city streets with new riders, and journalists excitedly covering the social and cultural effects of this technological marvel, it is no wonder that stories of sidewalk carnage proliferated. Countless legal cases also considered the responsibility of cyclists, pedestrians, drivers, and municipalities. Turn-of-the-century courts agreed upon a general chain of logic: if bicycles were vehicles, they could be banned from places intended for pedestrians, and if cyclists insisted on riding in those places, they could be liable for the resulting damages.

This logic was on display in an 1890 case supporting the ability of cities to ban bicycles from sidewalks. The City of Topeka had previously passed a municipal ordinance prohibiting bicycles on sidewalks and the Kansas Avenue bridge. When W. E. Swift rode his bike over the bridge on a June day in 1889, he was cited and fined a dollar. He appealed all the way to the state supreme court, which responded with a remarkably strong statement protecting the "absolute right" of citizens to choose their mode of travel. But that judgment was followed by an equally strong affirmation of the regulation of that travel: "Sidewalks are intended, constructed, and used solely by pedestrians, and not for the use of vehicles. . . . A bicycle, being a carriage, can properly be excluded."[43]

Other courts agreed that cities could choose to allow or disallow bicycles on some streets or sidewalks, as long as doing so did not completely block the cyclists' right to travel to their destination by other routes. The North Dakota case of *Gagnier v. Fargo* began when the plaintiff rode his bike on the sidewalk on an October day in 1899 but suffered an accident when his wheel fell in a hole. The state supreme court threaded through some complicated logic in its 1902 decision: "Although the sidewalks are primarily constructed and to be used by pedestrians, and the bicycle is a vehicle that under some circumstances more properly belongs to the highway or street," the justices reasoned, "still the [city] council is empowered to regulate the conditions under which the sidewalks may be used by bicycles, or to prohibit the use of sidewalks by them entirely." Since the city council had not explicitly exercised its authority to ban bicycles from the particular section of sidewalk where Gagnier had ridden, he could sue the city for negligence for not maintaining the sidewalk. In a final wrinkle, the court pointed out the result of this logic: the city did not have to look out for cyclists' needs if they were riding somewhere they fundamentally should not. Fargo's "duty is to maintain the walk in suitable condition for pedestrians, and its duty to bicycle riders . . . cannot be predicated upon the mere fact of having granted permission," wrote the justices. The fundamental principle still held sway: since bicycles were vehicles, and sidewalks existed to protect pedestrians *from* vehicles, bicycles could be excluded from the sidewalks, and governments were not responsible for cyclists' safety even if they *were* allowed there. By 1901 it was considered settled law, and an Indiana case could cite numerous precedents in declaring that "a bicycle is a vehicle and has no lawful right to the use of the sidewalk."[44]

LEGISLATING SAFETY IN THE 1890s AND BEYOND

In the decades after the first court cases over the bicycle, new city ordinances and state legislation specifically banning, allowing, or regulating bicycles appeared. Case law alone was simply too piecemeal to deal with the rapid expansion of bicycling. Even while publicizing the *Taylor v. Goodwin* decision that set an 1879 precedent for the legal right to the road, one American law journal wished for the passage of a law that would control furious bicycle driving, "for velocipedes are an annoyance and terror, and are only to be tolerated in the hope that small boys may break their necks."[45] These new laws sparked a further round of court battles, with decisions alternately challenging or affirming their statutory restrictions.

The most famous of these early legislative actions was a reaction to an 1879 prohibition by New York City park commissioners, who had unanimously banned high-wheel bicycles from Central Park. For most of the 1880s, the well-organized and socially well-connected Gotham cyclists challenged this ban in the courts, partially succeeding but leaving significant limitations in place. The fight culminated in an unsuccessful challenge that went all the way to the New York State supreme court, partially financed by the publicity-seeking bicycle manufacturer Colonel A. A. Pope. It was up to the commissioners, said the justices eventually, to decide whether bicycles should be allowed in parks. After that defeat, it was clear that cyclists would find a remedy not in the courts but in a declaration by state legislature affirming the status of bicycles. The Liberty Bill, as supporters called the resulting legislation, declared that park and highway commissioners "shall have no power or authority to pass [regulations] by which any person using a bicycle or tricycle shall be excluded or prohibited from the free use of any of the park highways . . . when the same is open to the free use of persons using other pleasure carriages."[46] A few other states emulated this example, with the League of American Wheelmen lobbying legislatures for support. But even without the specific adoption of statute law, the Liberty Bill's success demonstrated the growing political power of bicycle advocates and made it less likely that individual states would attempt to exclude riders from their roads.[47]

The Police Power and the Scorcher

Outright prohibitions, like those challenged by the Liberty Bill, were less common than laws and ordinances to regulate bicycles—such as those requiring lights and bells or imposing speed limits. In law, the power of the state to regulate or control is known as the police power, easily confused by nonjurists with the individuals organized to enforce those laws, known as the police force. But new laws passed in the 1880s and 1890s regulating the use of private property on the public road were a part of a revolution in state power and legal philosophy in the late nineteenth century. These developments were challenged in court on both practical and philosophical grounds, with some plaintiffs simply objecting to the general expansion of the power of the state. Bicycle regulation was only one facet of a surprisingly powerful nineteenth-century American state, but it was entirely dependent on the affirmation of the police power.[48]

In its 1887 *Yopp* decision, supporting the state legislature's 1885 limit on the use of bicycles on some roads, the North Carolina Supreme Court declared: "The power of government—commonly called the police power—to regulate the conduct of individuals in the exercise of their personal rights, and the use of property . . . to promote the public convenience, safety, and common good, is essential." Although New York's Liberty Bill declared that bicyclists could not be prohibited, it acknowledged the police power: "Nothing in this act shall be so construed as to prevent the passage, enforcement or maintenance of any regulation, ordinance or rule, regulating the use of bicycles or tricycles in public highways, streets, driveways, parkways and public spaces."[49]

Courts believed that city ordinances or state regulations were proper exercises of the police power when they applied to bicycle use that impeded the intended use of the road: the coming and going of all travelers. Any use of a bicycle that interfered with another user's passing became a nuisance, not a protected use. Nuisances included fast riding, greatly feared by bicycle observers in the 1890s. "A bicycle is capable of being propelled at a truly terrific pace, at a rate of speed but little inferior to that of a locomotive," worried one. "Were the choice of the rate of speed to be left entirely to the individual, a nuisance of a dangerous character might spring up, and the proper end and object of the highway's existence be perverted."[50]

This nuisance was related to a moral panic over scorchers, or the fast-pedaling young men showing off in city traffic, although these might have existed more in the fevered minds of observers than in reality. In cities nationwide, newspapers and magazines were filled with stories of speeding youths on bicycles and the damage they did not only to others but also to themselves. An editorial in a paper in Rochester, New York, argued that although such riders made up a small number of the estimated 17,500 riders in that city in 1896, they constituted an outsize threat. "A scorcher is a creature of the human species with imperfectly developed intellect and perfectly developed calves," wrote the editor. He "lowers his handle bars till his back curves like a measuring worm upon a twig, . . . mounts his wheel with the wild glare of demonical glee in his snaky eye; and he runs down a baby carriage at the first opportunity." Behind the wild rider, "like the dead upon the green slope of Cemetery Ridge after Pickett's charge, lie the prostrated victims of the wild, unchained maniac."[51]

The fear of scorchers led to the passage of city ordinances regulating bicycle speed, which the courts generally agreed were acceptable uses of the police power. As a stereotype of dangerous and selfish cyclists, and as a clear abuser of the commons, the scorcher was a useful scapegoat for both critics and cyclists. The LAW threw its weight behind most attempts to limit racing or speeding bikes on city streets, saying that "the scorcher is a nuisance and a detriment to the sport" and promising "special efforts to assist the authorities in bringing him to justice."[52]

Requirements for lights and bells were considered appropriate applications of the police power: they regulated the use of a bicycle but did not prohibit it from the shared road. In 1890, Cicero, Illinois, considered a city ordinance requiring cyclists "to go upon roadways only, to go not more than two abreast, and keeping as close together as possible, and keeping on the right-hand side . . . to announce their presence by ringing a bell, and to always carry a signal light at night." By 1896, a guide to Michigan bicycle routes listed nineteen cities with varying ordinances: some were largely unenforced, but others required lights or bells, banned riding on sidewalks, and limited cyclists' speed to eight miles an hour.[53]

While such regulations passed judicial muster, it wasn't entirely clear how some of them could be enforced. The speed limit was so low that it was generally ignored, contended the *Chicago Daily Tribune:* "With nearly 200,000 wheelmen in Chicago able to easily exceed the speed limits . . . it is not remarkable that frequent and flagrant violations of the rules should happen every hour." The Chicago police would have found it difficult enough to judge the speed of cyclists in daylight; at night, in a city without an extensive network of electric street lights, it was impossible. Mounted and plainclothes policemen scrambled to respond to concerns over uncontrolled masses of cyclists. But when they did so, the class status of the cyclists triggered a backlash in the press: there had been "a number of conspicuous instances where young women and men of perfect character have been treated to rides in a patrol wagon like ordinary criminals," complained the paper. This backlash did not protect all cyclists: "Scorchers, however, will be treated as malefactors." A similar reaction occurred in 1895 in Sacramento, California. After police enforced a largely unpublicized lantern law, "about 300 wheelmen rode through the streets, some carrying big barn lanterns, some ringing cow bells, and others blowing horns." The police were not amused. They arrested a few riders as a public nuisance and (somewhat ironically) cited others as violators of the light ordinance.[54]

Although the courts found these new regulations to be appropriate exercises of the police power, such laws did not necessarily clarify matters. As one observer noted in 1895, although the cyclist "is aware that he has ceased to be considered an outlaw . . . he has no clear idea in regard to that which he may justly claim as his due, nor does he understand the nature or extent of the demands which the public, in the return, may make upon him."[55] That confusion would be a familiar refrain through the next century and beyond.

Paving the Way for Automobiles

By the late 1890s, bicycles were included in the categories of vehicle and carriage in both case law and statutory law. These decisions made it possible for automobiles to receive the same consideration when they came before many of the same judges who had lived through the bicycle boom. The transition in the law was rapid: for centuries, legal references to a *vehicle* or *carriage* had referred to animal-drawn conveyances, but within a decade, the list had been expanded and future-proofed to include conveyances using any possible source of power. For example, the 1891 Highway Code of New York State broke the definition of carriage into two parts. One section defined carriages by their purpose of carrying, and included "stage-coaches, wagons, carts, sleighs, sleds and every other carriage or vehicle," while another listed vehicles that weren't drawn by horses, including "bicycles, tricycles, and all other vehicles propelled by manumotive or pedomotive power." The 1902 Highway Law of New York added "automobiles or motor vehicles" to the first list and vehicles powered "by electricity, steam, gasoline, or other source of energy" to the second. Like bicycles before them, automobiles were now defined as both carriages to move people or goods and vehicles allowed on the public roads, no matter what powered them.[56]

Although horse-drawn vehicles had not been closely controlled by statutory law for centuries, the heavy regulation of bicycle use in the last decades of the nineteenth century opened a philosophical and rhetorical opportunity for the increased management of wagons, carriages, and eventually motor vehicles. As one bicyclist compelled to keep hold of his handlebars complained in 1899, "So this is the latest regulation for the much regulated wheelman.

Everything is done by the city fathers to protect persons from injury by him, but what is done to protect him from injury by teamsters and drivers?" If a wagon driver were making a sudden right turn, risking catching a cyclist in what is today known colloquially as a right hook, "why should he not hold out his whip in that direction as drivers are compelled to do by law in Europe? . . . Is it not time for a letup on legislation for the wheelman and a little attention given to the [disciplining] of drivers?"[57]

The overlap of bicycle and automobile rights carried through decades of legal decisions which established that the road was for many diverse types of users. The 1876 case of *Macomber v. Nichols* laid the foundation for any future users of the road by declaring that "a highway established for the general benefit of passage and traffic must admit of new methods of use whenever it is found that the general benefit requires them." This common-law precept was subsequently cited in court cases that found automobiles to be both vehicles and carriages.[58] An 1897 treatise observed that the best legal minds agreed that "no branch of jurisprudence is more elastic, more needful of adaptation to new inventions, than that pertaining to the highway and its uses."[59] A turn-of-the-century legal reference could thus argue that the bicycle's "position on the public highway is much the same as that of the automobile, and the principles of law applied" to the bicycle should also apply to the newcomers.[60] In 1907, an Iowa court explicitly compared the rights of automobile owners to those of bicyclists and other predecessors: "The owners have the same rights in the roads and streets as the drivers of horses or those riding a bicycle or traveling by some other vehicle."[61] And as one 1921 legal reference work on automobiles later put it, "The position of the automobile and the bicycle, in the view of the law are so nearly alike that it is well to refer briefly to the history of the bicycle" before even discussing the automobile.[62]

Legal precedents involving bicycles were also advantageous to municipalities expanding their power to regulate. Unlike horse-drawn vehicles, which had largely taken to the road without licensing, regulation, or any requirements as to their equip-

ment, bicycles and their operation were subject to numerous laws and statutes. Similar controls were subsequently established for motorcycles and then cars. The only difference was that automobiles, while classified as both vehicles and carriages, were additionally classified into a new category—*motor* vehicles.

Figure 1.3. Carriages and bicycles, both considered legal vehicles long before the automobile, share the road. The well-dressed crowd is heading down Michigan Avenue toward the state capitol in Lansing for a special event; the carriage on the left is riding along trolley tracks, a sign of yet another type of road user. Courtesy Archives of Michigan.

The bicyclists bouncing along that New York City boulevard in the forgotten silent film of 1896 were justly proud of themselves. Their elaborate uniforms, upright posture, and polished bikes were markers of their class and clout, a sign of the social capital that made it possible for them to take to the road with the support of courts and legislatures. The road had long been a commons, legally shared between vehicles with specified rights and responsibilities, and the nineteenth-century legal battle ensured that the newly arrived bicycle would be included in that protected class of users. Many twenty-first-century riders look back at this period with satisfaction, seeing indisputable proof of cyclists' rights to the road. That these rights actually predated those of the automobile and facilitated its introduction to the road seems ironic on today's crowded streets. But in some ways, the legal fight over declaring bicycles to be vehicles was the simplest of the bike battles. The law was not the only force that shaped the history of the bicycle: it was one strand in a complex tangle of forces, including technology, culture, economics, and urban geography. The next battle greatly complicated the status of the bicycle outside the courtroom.

CHAPTER 2

THE RIGHT
SORT OF PEOPLE

The Battle over Taxes,
Sidepaths, and Roads at the
Turn of the Century

Winning the legal battle over the right to use the road did not mean that bicyclists had won the war. An 1891 story in the *Chicago Daily Tribune* describes a grumpy, violent farmer, Absalom Wycoff, with a tendency to whip cyclists who failed to make way for his horse-drawn wagon. "If there was anything Farmer Wycoff hated worse than anything else it was a bicycle," wrote the author, leaving unclear whether this was a factual report or parable. Wycoff was reportedly the author of a proposed municipal ordinance—which nearly passed—holding that any cyclist "should be considered a nuisance and be punished by fine and imprisonment." It didn't matter "that the courts were dead against him on this point, and that the legal status of the bicycle is the same as that of any other vehicle": when he saw a cyclist ahead, he declared, "If that fellow don't get out of my way . . . I'll run right over him, b'gosh!" After horse-whipping several riders, Wycoff picked on the wrong man. "Without a word," the aggrieved rider "laid his machine down, ran alongside the wagon, seized Farmer Wycoff, jerked him out, tore his best coat off him[,] . . . blacked his eyes, threw him down in the road, picked up his whip, and belabored the squirming Absalom till he roared for mercy." The story ends with a handy moral: "And from that day to this he has never claimed proprietorship over more than his share of the public highway."[1]

From the bicycle's earliest adoption, the social markers of bicycling constrained its acceptance and political clout in North America and complicated cyclists' attempts to claim equal access to a commonly held resource. The social division between Farmer Wycoff and urbanites on bicycles was not bridged by appeals court decisions, and that gulf proved fatal for attempts to translate the social capital of cycling clubs into political leverage. In two related political battles—over taxation for roads and a proposed network of separate bicycle paths—social isolation contributed to cyclists' losses.

The social history of bicycling continues to shape popular perception of bicycles and their riders. If the first meaningful legacy of the bike battles was their inclusion in the legal definition of vehicles, the second was the general public's perception of bicyclists as "other." In the United States, the number of people identifying themselves as bicyclists has rarely been large enough to transcend divisions of class, race, and gender. Because of that handicap, and despite the determined efforts of advocates, bicyclists have never been considered fully a part of the larger imagined community of the American public. This imagined community is the way that people in a modern nation state—who would never meet each other personally, and instead learned of new and different groups through the popular press—came to place each other in their personal definitions of "us" and "them." The rules, laws, and accommodations that governments would make for bicyclists depended largely on whether they would be welcomed in the popular conception of the imagined community. In particular, the constantly renegotiated definition of what constituted a public good depended on whether cyclists were considered synonymous with the public, or whether they were instead considered a small subset of elites.

During the golden age of cycling, at least three competing, though interrelated, depictions of bicyclists existed in the minds

Figure 2.1. Representatives from different social groups argue over the right of way on a narrow dirt road in this *Harper's Weekly* illustration by A. B. Frost, 1896. The cyclists may want to overtake on the left, as a vehicle would, or may be ordering the wagon out of their way; the farmer is having none of it. National Archives RG 30 (37–788).

of the public. Positive elitism—mostly within the ranks of cyclists themselves—promoted cycling as a gentlemanly and morally uplifting recreation, and practitioners policed the group's boundaries by excluding immigrants, women, and African Americans. Negative elitism—from farmers and opponents of taxation in support of bicycle infrastructure—portrayed the leisure cyclists of the 1890s as selfish dandies, urban fops, dangerous thrill-seekers, and self-serving, moneyed elites whose amusements got in the way of productive enterprise or local control. Finally, populist views considered cycling a morally uplifting pursuit for the lower classes and for women: these interpretations could be considered an outgrowth of positive elitism. In the end, none of these portrayals is entirely accurate. Each had elements of truth and fiction.

Such stereotypes structured several early political battles over bicycling, including the Good Roads reform campaign and a largely forgotten episode known as the sidepath movement. In both cases, bicyclists were aided by well-developed organizational structures and by their image as progressive, nonpartisan male urbanites. But by the same token, cyclists could be portrayed by political opponents as entitled elites, demanding that the rest of society subsidize their recreational or leisure pursuits.

The Good Roads movement promoted a then-radical proposal to tax the public to pay for state roads, superseding the locally financed and haphazardly engineered dirt roads of the nineteenth century with a road network incorporating technical expertise and bureaucratic control in the first decades of the new century. A great deal of the credit for the success of the Good Roads movement is today rightly attributed to bicyclists: they helped to assemble a vocal and organized political bloc to support road building. But farmers and other foes of general taxation were so effective in their criticism of cycling's urban, elitist image that eventually the League of American Wheelmen chose to separate its cycling promotion from its Good Roads advocacy in order to avoid such criticism.

This perception of elitism spelled doom for another cycling initiative, sometimes known as the sidepath movement, which sought to connect cities and towns by a separate, bicycle-specific network of improved paths, enabled by state law. Sidepath building boomed in upstate New York and briefly flourished in Chicago, Minneapolis, and elsewhere. These successes led excited cyclists to imagine a network of paths allowing them to "go from New York to any point in Maine, Florida or California on smooth roads made especially for them."[2] But because cyclists could not successfully argue that the proposed sidepaths were a public good that would benefit all of society, they could not make a claim on public funding, and the financing was limited to charitable contributions and a user-fee model. By 1905, development of these paths had floundered. After that, bicyclists returned to plans for a single, combined road system, shared by bicycles, wagons, and eventually automobiles.[3]

The fates of these two advocacy movements illustrate the unintended impact of cycling's association with "the right sort of people." As the historians Jesse Gant and Nicholas Hoffman have put it, "Sorting out the sport's proper boundaries would lead to decisions that ultimately undermined cycling's future." The battles over defining the cycling community in the 1890s would have a lasting effect on where anyone could ride for the next century and beyond.[4]

THE SOCIAL BOUNDARIES OF GOLDEN-AGE CYCLING

The last decade of the nineteenth century could be described as the first golden age of American cycling, when the craze for the safety bicycle transformed both recreational and utilitarian cycling. The safety bicycle was named for the innovations that mitigated the considerable dangers of the high-wheel bike. Mostly based on a British model called the Rover, the safety took American cycling by storm. Chain-driven rear wheels allowed the use of gearing, by which a larger front chainring could turn a smaller rear cog. With the need for a massive front wheel thereby eliminated, the rider was closer to the ground, and less likely to go head over heels. Lighter frames made momentum less terrifying, and pneumatic rubber tires made the ride more comfortable.[5] In many ways, the safety resembled a modern bicycle: models built in the 1890s could still be ridden by cyclists today. (Conversely, the brakeless, fixed-gear bikes favored by Brooklyn hipsters in 2015 could easily have been ridden by LAW members in 1892.)

The safety was more accessible not only by design but also financially, thanks to an innovative and expanding American manufacturing industry that pioneered mass production, standardization, and commercial sales. These developments created an interesting social conflict: a machine that had been an expensive, technologically advanced wonder at the beginning of the decade was a common commodity by the end. By the mid-1890s, huge numbers of regional manufacturers were producing as many as three million bikes a year—an incredible number in a nation of sixty-three million people.[6] Prices steadily declined when the nation experienced a serious depression beginning in 1893, and by 1902 department stores were selling bikes directly to children for fifteen dollars or less. But the early association of bicycles with elites and conspicuous consumption persisted.[7]

Hoping to defend the positive aspects of an elitist association, the LAW vigorously opposed opening up the ranks of cyclists. The group "has aspired to be an organization of gentlemen and ladies," wrote one contributor to an 1896 LAW publication. "It doesn't wish 'sporty,' 'freaky,' 'woozy' folks in it. When such persons do get into the League it should be the purpose of the members" to reform them. He continued: "Give them to understand that 'dizzy dazzlers' and 'tiffy-toughs' are quite out of place in this, one of the most respected and respectable organizations in the world." Please, he begged, do no let it be "contaminated by dizzy, whizzy people with whom the good friends of the League do not care to be classed." That August the LAW asked members to vet new applicants in order to keep out the riffraff, with telling emphasis: "We want members, but we *don't want that kind.* The names of all applicants are printed each week in this paper. . . . [I]f you see in the list the name of any one who is not, in your estimation, a suitable person to become a member," readers could object and trigger an administrative review of the application. Bicycling was meant to be a refined exercise for elites, as an LAW editor wrote in 1896: "An overwhelming majority of bicyclists are ladies and gentlemen, and whether on or off the wheel conduct themselves courteously towards others." A Missouri correspondent continued the thought the following week: "A gentleman or a lady can still be gentlemanly and ladylike and present a neat and attractive appearance on their wheels, and there is no reasonable excuse, simply because one rides a wheel, for appearing in public indecently."[8]

Golden Age cycling was not mere transportation; it was a civilized social affair, in which wheelmen "flock together [and] form clubs with full sets of officers, institute races and lend life to asphalt celebrations," according to an 1889 article. Such behavior was unique to cycling, promoters claimed: "Owners of wheelbarrows do not amalgamate on the ground of a common interest in wheelbarrows, nor does property in a hand-cart or a delivery wagon constitute a bond of amity."[9] LAW members found in cycling a number of virtues, including companionship with upwardly mobile men, a desirable association with advanced technology and modernity, and athletic endeavors that were still considered refined and class-appropriate.[10]

Confusingly, a populist argument positioning the bicycle as the salvation of humanity was mixed in with this exclusionary language both in the LAW's publications and in the writing of nonmembers. The suffragist, reformer, and cycling proponent Frances Willard wrote in 1895 that she knew "tens of thousands who could never afford to own, feed, and stable a horse, had by this bright invention enjoyed the swiftness of motion . . . the charm of a wide outlook upon the natural world, and that sense of mastery which is probably the greatest attraction in horseback-riding." The argument was reinforced in an 1897 essay by another writer: "A bicycle is better than a horse to ninety-nine men and women out of a hundred, because it costs almost nothing to keep, and it is never tired."[11]

The most obvious way in which Golden Age cycling was both exclusive and inclusive came with increasing female ridership. The safety design made cycling accessible to women, and cycling in turn became a symbol of changing understandings of femininity

Figure 2.2. Well-dressed women in Rochester, New York, demonstrate the high status of 1890s cycling afforded by the safety bicycle—and the possibilities for personal freedom and recreation, within the constraints of propriety. From the Collection of the Local History and Genealogy Division, Rochester Public Library.

at the turn of the century. The bicycle came to be associated with the "New Woman," an idealization of the educated and independent (yet painstakingly proper) young woman. One proponent of women's cycling declared that "never did an athletic pleasure from which the other half is not debarred come into popularity at a more fitting time than cycling has today."[12]

Yet the exhilarating freedom that the bike afforded women was accompanied by criticism and hostility toward unchaperoned, bloomer-clad women riders. Many women who rode were scrupulous in observing social niceties while cycling, adopting high-status clothing and restricting themselves to structured club activities. The LAW was an organization of men, and although it allowed women in auxiliary divisions and occasionally as members, the language and content of its publications clearly signaled the second-class status of women cyclists. A week after the *LAW Bulletin* published one of its many sexist jokes, a woman writer chastised the editors, asking, "How would you like it if the women were to start a paper and devote it to slurs and jokes about the men?"[13]

The freedom afforded by bicycles made them a common plot device for romantic literature. After all, a couple on a bicycling excursion were traveling without chaperones, and a woman alone on a bike was most likely young, athletic, and adventurous, not to mention revealingly dressed—at least in comparison to constraining Victorian styles. Harry Dacre's 1892 song "Daisy Bell" is the best-remembered expression of this freedom. The chorus became an enduring symbol of the golden age of cycling, frequently referenced in journalistic coverage of bicycling in the coming century: "It won't be a stylish marriage / I can't afford a carriage / But you'll look sweet upon the seat / Of a bicycle built for two." But the words also described the secluded spaces available to a couple: "We will go 'tandem' / As man and wife . . . When the road's dark / We can both despise / P'licemen and 'lamps' as well." A convenient meet-cute between a solitary young man and cycling woman occurs on the first page of the 1901 novel *Rosalynde's Lovers*, as the protagonist, chasing a woman rider, finds "that she was going, indeed, at a racing gait, and against a rising wind, while her fluttering skirts, somehow showing her well-turned ankles and little feet, gave forth a twinkle of yellow and brown."[14] While such displays of properly attired female cyclists were barely acceptable within polite society, more racy exhibitions were taking place under the rubric of vaudeville shows, where trick-riding women wore *tights* before ticket-buying audiences. Immensely popular images of cycling women in skimpy outfits, often captured in postcards and advertisements, made riding a delicate balancing act between socially approved exercise and prurient sexualization.

Although the bicycle promised freedom for women, society still scrambled to set boundaries on that newfound liberty. Cycling women were the targets of jokes about their behaviors and costumes, reflecting nervousness about maintaining traditional gender roles. One newspaper writer observed "a couple dressed exactly alike—caps, coats, trousers, and stockings in a blueish drab material. I couldn't tell which was the man or which was the woman, and went home in despair."[15] Cycling bloomers were the symbol both of the New Woman and a target of sexist mockery. The result was that by mid-decade, according to one woman, "the majority of American women have declared in favor of the skirt in one form or another," whereas bloomers were still for the adventurous.[16]

To modern sensibilities, the most odious form of social exclusion in cycling was racial segregation. In the national meeting of 1894, held in Louisville, Kentucky, the LAW voted to insert the word *white* into the requirements for membership. This change brought very positive feedback from the increasingly segregated South; LAW representative "G. E. Johnson . . . thanked the assembly in the name of the Kentucky division and the South, and promised the league 2,000 new members during the coming year and 5,000 a year following." Black LAW members in Boston and across the nation protested, but to no avail. The vote reflected the fact that segregation was becoming the law of the land: the United States Supreme Court ratified that "separate but equal" society two years later in *Plessy vs. Ferguson.*[17]

The experience of the black professional cyclist Marshall "Major" Taylor powerfully illustrates the effects of the racial segregation of cycling. As a professional cyclist who competed internationally, Taylor was barred from LAW membership, irrespective of his race. But because the LAW sanctioned most races, even his participation was problematic. Although Taylor would go on to win a world championship and set world records, his ability to compete in races with white riders was severely constrained by epic fights within professional cycling unions, and his achievements have been forgotten by many Americans.[18]

The cycling color line was enforced through the popular media. The "darktown" series of lithographs produced by Currier and Ives in the 1890s would today be considered vicious racial stereotypes but were then apparently considered humorous art

THE DARKTOWN BICYCLE CLUB - ON PARADE.

suitable for home decor. The "Darktown Bicycle Club" images in the series mocked the clothing and physical characteristics of black cyclists, effectively indicating that the sport was reserved for a white elite. *The Darktown Bicycle Club Scandal*, a minstrel-show script published in 1897, supposedly portrays a meeting of an African American club. In the mind-bending manner of minstrel shows, the script sets racial boundaries by allowing white clubwomen in blackface to mock black bicyclists' pretensions through role playing, even while imagining the club members as the ones doing the social exclusion by

Figure 2.3. The color line in bicycling was visible in the minstrel shows, exclusionary laws, and racist media depictions that were common across the increasingly segregated United States around 1900. This lithograph, one of a series from the popular printmaker Currier & Ives, mocks the social pretensions of the cyclists: lacking air-filled tires, the central figure has tied pillows onto his wheels to cushion the ride, but the illustrator has him possibly mixing up *pneumatic* for a pidgin form of *rheumatic:* "Hooray for de rumatic! Dont she glide lubly." LC-USZC2–2171, Library of Congress Prints and Photographs Division.

expelling one of their own. The exaggerated dialect of the script derided African American attempts to enter into polite athletics: "Ladies an' fellow-clubbers, I calls you to order to consider de matter ob dispellin' from dis select an' high-toned organization, a lady who has brung disgrace upon it," proclaims one character. The script ends with a particularly egregious song:

> Oh, but de darkey is a scorcher. So
> Look out for club gals, dey're de stuff
> Dey're out in eb'ry shade;
> De Coons take first place,
>   'tain't no bluff,
> When dey turns out on
>   parade.[19]

BUILDING GOOD ROADS AND LEISURE PATHS BEFORE 1898

When cyclists began to organize politically to campaign for improved roads, these opposing currents of elitism and populism became critical. Rural American roads were almost all bad. Unpaved and lacking adequate drainage, most were nearly impassable after rain or snow. In its weekly *Bulletin* and occasionally separate monthly *Good Roads Magazine*, the LAW spent decades pushing for better roads. "The Road is a Creation of Man and a Type of Civilized Society," declared the cover page of many of these publications. In the language of policy analysis, the LAW "captured" the only national-level office responsible for road improvements, the Bureau of Road Inquiry; the LAW lobbied for more money for the bureau, and the bureau in turn sponsored the LAW.[20] But whatever the arrangement, in the decades before the automobile, bicyclists were the driving political force for road improvement.

The state of nineteenth-century roads was a symptom of an essentially local, decentralized system of financing road construction, itself the consequence of weak municipal governments and a distrust of public works. Before the twentieth century, most urban streets were paved only when adjoining property owners— abutters—clubbed together to fund the work. Rural roads were built by the occasional "working out" of road taxes, where nearby property owners were required to provide a week or so of their own labor in a work gang under the supervision of an appointed county "pathmaster." This road gang or "statute labor" system appealed to cash-poor farmers and kept decision making local, but it had obvious limits; one historian has called it "quasi-feudal." Often derided by reformers as a "neighborhood picnic," such gangs lacked engineering or surveying skills, specialized equipment, or incentives to do good work. Most repair work consisted of piling up loose dirt in the center of the road in the hope that it might level itself. The results were predictable: a muddle of randomly built and poorly maintained dirt roads. As usual, Mark Twain summarized the situation best, claiming that if he ever went to hell, then he would want to go by a bad road, so that he would at least be glad when he got to his destination.[21]

Beginning in the 1880s, Good Roads reformers campaigned for improvements. These advocates are early examples of Progressive reformers: they were urban, middle class, efficiency minded, and nationally organized. They favored technocratic solutions over messy and graft-fueled governments, even if their reforms might have unintentionally antipopulist or antidemocratic results. The Good Roads movement began and had its first victories before the internal-combustion automobile even existed: it sought better conditions for the bicycle and horse-drawn vehicle. The great difficulty with such reform, as always, was deciding who would pay. The Good Roads proposal was to fund professional road improvements through state taxes. Farmers, however, feared that they would be forced to pay for nearby improvements to meet the "recreational imperialism" of urban cyclists, following the traditional mode by which abutters funded road construction.[22] "There is altogether too much preaching on the part of the wheelmen," complained one New York farmer in 1893: "It is always easier to advocate the expenditure of other people's money." Along with other problems, these sorts of disputes between rural farmers and urban reformers limited the success of the Good Roads movement before the twentieth century.[23]

Because of these early political divisions, some cyclists in the 1890s created their own alternatives to unimproved dirt roads: separate bicycle paths with packed-gravel or cinder surfaces, financed by voluntary subscription. Cyclists in Chicago proposed a "sort of bridle path, such as is provided for equestrians, except of course with a different surface" in city parks and alongside Douglas Road in 1895. In the next year, Portland, Oregon, riders started with one thousand feet of path along Riverside Road. Cyclists in North Adams, Massachusetts, paid a $1 club membership fee "devoted exclusively to the construction of sidepaths" in 1897. Seattle cyclists enjoyed twenty-five miles of charitably funded trails around the same time and dreamed (unsuccessfully) of building a trail to neighboring Tacoma by selling shares of stock. Denver cyclists funded their own fifty-mile path to Palmer Lake entirely by subscription in 1898.[24]

In Minneapolis, city workers built six miles of paths in 1895, and a path was constructed to connect Minneapolis and St. Paul the following year. The projects were mostly funded through charitable donations, despite the view of some city officials that these should be considered public works. "Several efforts have been made . . . to set aside a special fund," reported the city engineer, "but the public demand for lower taxation has invariably defeated the proposition." He continued to point out the unfairness the following year: "While . . . the custom is to build cycle paths by subscription in different cities, this appears to me a hardship. . . . [T]his should be borne by the people as a whole." Despite the lack of tax funding, nearby St. Paul still built fourteen miles of paths in 1897 by combining private donations with city funds.[25]

These paths had many limitations. Intended for recreational rather than transportation purposes, most of them rambled through parks, forests, or fields, only occasionally linking with roads. And the practice of funding the paths through private donations from users appeared, to some cyclists, "a slow and unsatisfactory method."[26] Beginning in 1896, counties across the Midwest and Northeast began exploring ways to institutionalize and publicly fund not just individual paths but networks of bicycle-specific paths alongside roads, within the existing right-of-way.

The first of these sidepath experiments inspired many subsequent projects. Its originator, Charles T. Raymond, was an avid cyclist and successful businessman in the industrial city of Lockport, New York. In 1890 he had helped to organize the Niagara County Sidepath League, an organization that built short paths funded by club dues that any cyclist could use. This funding mechanism seemed unfair to Raymond, and he "adopted and promulgated the doctrine that 'what all use, all should pay for,'" according to a laudatory article. He drafted an 1896 state law permitting Niagara County supervisors to tax all bicycle owners and build paths with the proceeds; bicycle owners would pay their local treasurer or tax assessor once a year, and those funds would be set aside for path construction.[27] After that law was passed, Raymond drafted a bill that would expand the power to counties statewide.

The LAW, however, was not supportive: it opposed sidepaths as distractions from its own project of building good public roads. According to sidepath proponents, the group's leaders called "upon all wheelmen to strenuously oppose the passage of any such bills." One founding LAW member wrote in an 1896 *Bulletin* that "I fear . . . that the result of obtaining special paths will be a strong feeling by drivers of horses that we don't belong *with them* on the good roads which we have done so much to create." In the same issue, a letter from a New Jersey member condemned "selfish cycle paths" that could only "be of use to but part of the traveling public."[28] With that reasoning, in 1897 members of the New York LAW chapter "went to Albany and spent time and money till the defeat of the Raymond bill was assured." The leadership opposed similar legislation creating separate bicycle-specific paths in 1898, fearing that it would threaten the passage of their preferred Higbie-Armstrong bill. That bill, a major Good Roads achievement, stipulated that the state should contribute 50 percent of the cost of building roads. These types of legislative actions emphasized building improved roads that could be shared by varied users, not separate paths for bicycles alone. Political division among cyclists thus weakened the impetus for sidepath construction, and few counties followed Niagara's lead before 1898.[29]

The next political development was instrumental in both the immediate success and the eventual failure of sidepaths. Not far from Charles Raymond's successful experiment in Niagara County, the city of Rochester (in Monroe County) was embarking on its own initiative. Like Lockport, Rochester was a booming industrial city, and cycling was popular. The Rochester *Union Advertiser* declared in 1895 that the city was "the greatest bicycle town in the country," and that a visitor "would think the whole place moved on wheels."[30] But when an 1896 bill based on the Niagara model proposed to allow Monroe to tax all cyclists one dollar to fund the building of paths, there was a significant backlash, based on the premise that it was unfair to tax all cyclists for a resource that only some would use. The editor of the *Post-Express* claimed that many "regard the tax as an outrage," as it unfairly allowed cycle-path riders "to reap substantial benefits at the expense of others, including women and children." The "vicious principle" of "class taxation" was the central problem, argued the writer: "There is no more reason why the bicyclists should be taxed for cinder paths than that owners of vehicles should be taxed for the construction of better highways." Complaints against the taxation of the many for the benefit of a few—presumably elite male cyclists—was a common refrain: "Twenty thousand wheel owners ought not to be taxed for the benefit of a few hundred," argued the *Post-Express* that May.[31]

The same point was expressed forcefully by a county resident, Franklin Smith, who took the bully pulpit of a national magazine (which eventually became *Popular Science*) to describe the debate in Monroe. He railed against "the most ignorant" minds involved, their "perverted opinions," and "amazing exhibition of selfishness." Smith was not arguing against the sidepaths themselves, which he described as an obvious improvement. Instead, he argued against the political philosophy of taxation for the general welfare. He noted that "[Herbert] Spencer's social philosophy teaches that the improvement shall be undertaken voluntarily by those alone that desire it," he wrote. "What [it] forbids is that they should ever resort to the argument of coercion to secure the aid of others." Smith derided urban leisure cycling, arguing that he was defending "the rights of those bicyclists that might never have time to take an excursion into the country." Hyperbolically, Smith claimed that a privileged group of middle- and upper-class men could unfairly benefit from taxing "the shop girls, the mechanics and laborers, the servant girls and messenger boys, and the impoverished invalids" of the county. There is no evidence that Smith's picture of these social groups reflected reality, but with this sort of opposition, it was no wonder Monroe County's tax proposal failed.[32]

Instead, the county turned to voluntary associations and subscriptions to finance sidepaths.[33] With leadership from the editors of the *Post-Express*, cyclists raised money through donations, subscriptions, an annual trade show, and a "Calithumpian Parade" of bicycle clubs. Smith, for one, found this charitable approach praiseworthy. From its success, he felt justified in generalizing that "no practical problem of social reform has been or can be suggested that can not be solved by voluntary effort." Like many of his contemporaries, Smith felt that government intervention in society for the benefit of any single group was abhorrent.[34]

SIDEPATH SUCCESS AND FAILURE, 1898–1902

While California, Washington, New Jersey, and the Province of Ontario passed state-level sidepath laws before 1899, they were quite limited, allowing sidepaths to exist but not providing funding or directing counties to build them.[35] But the sidepath movement was about to go nationwide and escape the early limits of both the Good Roads movement and leisure-path construction. It began in 1898, by which point six New York counties had passed six different sidepath laws. Hoping to address this confusion, Frank J. Amsden and Charles Raymond collaborated to draft unified statewide legislation after a November 1898 convention of sidepath advocates in Rochester. The resulting legislation sparked enthusiasm and experimenta-

Figure 2.4. Part of a sidepath network stretching hundreds of miles, the Churchville Path in Monroe County, New York, ran alongside the unpaved road through city neighborhoods. According to a 1900 guide, it headed out of Rochester along West Avenue, then ran eleven miles to Churchville and on to Buffalo. From the Collection of the Local History and Genealogy Division, Rochester Public Library.

tion across the nation.[36] New York's General Sidepath Act of 1899 allowed a county judge, "upon the petition of fifty wheelmen of the county," to appoint a commission of five or seven persons, "each of whom shall be a cyclist," to represent the county. These commissioners were "authorized to construct and maintain sidepaths along any public road, or street" with the approval of elected officials. As such, the sidepath commissioners sidestepped the authority of traditional pathmasters, whom Good Roads reformers had dismissed as lazy and corrupt.[37]

Before roads were widened and paved, and before cities required abutters to install (or pay for) concrete sidewalks and curbing, advocates took advantage of the transitional state of the built environment to insert sidepaths into the urban landscape.

The proposed paths "shall not be less than three feet or more than six feet wide . . . and shall be constructed within the outside lines and along and upon either side of such public roads and streets." While they were to be built within the established legal right of way, the sidepaths were separated from both the adjoining road and from existing sidewalks.[38]

The 1899 New York state law, and its 1900 revision, had to avoid portrayals of negative elitism. Although his original Niagara County law was tax-based, the opposition in Monroe County apparently convinced Charles Raymond that "the license system was more equitable and would be more popular." Thus the state law charged only those who chose to ride on the path (in what later policy makers would call a user-fee model).[39] Commissions were to "adopt a form of license, badge, emblem, or device suitable to be affixed to a bicycle." The tag would cost a cyclist at least fifty cents a year, and the proceeds (along with any charitable donations) were to constitute the entire operating budget of the commission. Such funds were to be used to purchase land and materials, to build and maintain sidepaths, and to plant "shade trees along such paths" where appropriate. Because the sidepaths were enshrined in state law, local police could take tagless scofflaws before local courts to extract fines.[40]

The Failure of Bicycle Taxation

The sidepath commission was a compromise between constraining laws and conflicting political philosophies. Its establishment as a commission and not an agency or bureau distanced the sidepath system from coercive government. The state was not directly extracting a tax: instead, like a parks commission, the sidepath commission was a quasi-state entity made up of appointed members of the public commissioned to do the work of government. The fact that it was funded solely by users of the path skirted legal objections against blocking a citizen's right to travel on the public road while also avoiding accusations of elitism or taxation of all for the benefit of some.[41]

There were still a few legal potholes. Courts held, in theory, that bicycles could be taxed as property, but in the decades before the motor vehicle, the practice of levying a special fee as a prerequisite for bicyclists to use a common resource—and banning scofflaws for failing to pay—was problematic. Writing about a proposed special tax on bicycles, one LAW member weighed in, asking "if horse owners are made to pay a special tax to pay for the paths that have been built for their benefit." If not, "it seems a case of prejudice." On the other hand, the legal definition of the bicycle as a vehicle might imply that laws classifying carriages as taxable property would also apply to the bicycle. In Kansas, the *Wichita Daily Eagle* agreed that "as a vehicle it must be taxed. Its value is as great as that of any horse or of any ordinary buggy."[42]

Out of this conflict, courts concluded that taxation was legal only if governments did not block a bicyclist's right to travel on the public roads. Late-nineteenth-century political philosophy held that the police power could be used to regulate, but not impede, a constitutionally protected freedom of movement, and it could not regulate bicycles differently from other vehicles. Along with the philosophical problems, an 1896 Chicago newspaper story argued that it was impractical to even try to exclude bicyclists from the roads: "The trouble . . . lies in the fact that wheelmen will always want to go wherever other vehicles are allowed, and will not be content with separate paths."[43]

Because of these complications, sidepath legislation based on Charles Raymond's original taxation model ran into problems in three states. Oregon's 1899 law, which allowed counties to tax all bikes if they wished, funded nearly fifty-nine miles of six-foot-wide gravel paths in the city of Portland.[44] But the law was challenged by a city cyclist who refused to pay the $1.25 tax and subsequent $1 fine when the Multnomah County Sheriff seized his bike for nonpayment. The state supreme court agreed with the aggrieved cyclist, finding that the bicycle tax violated three sections of the state constitution and, further, that it "constituted double taxation" of personal property.[45] For slightly different reasons, in 1901 the Washington Supreme Court declared its own state law of 1899 unconstitutional. Under that law, Washington cities could require all bicycle owners to pay for a license, create a fund with the proceeds that could be used to build either paths or roads, and fine owners of unlicensed bikes who attempted to take to the city roads.[46] But the justices ruled that the small town of Hoquiam could not charge bicyclists a special fee when horse and carriage riders were not required to pay a similar fee. When two cyclists rode their unlicensed bicycles on the street, the city was wrong to fine them: "A municipality . . . is without power to exact a license fee as a prerequisite to the right to travel on its streets," declared the justices, "and is without power, therefore, to require a license fee as prerequisite to the right to ride a bicycle thereon."[47]

Pennsylvania's tax-based sidepaths also proved controversial. In Bradford County, the sidepath commissioners appointed in April 1899 immediately attempted to collect a dollar tax on all bicycles. The county commissioners objected, noting that by law the sidepath commissioners' tenure did not begin until January of 1900 and that they had no legal power to tax until then. When the sidepath commissioners brought suit, the courts sided with the county: no matter how enthusiastic, a small group of citizens could not forcibly extract money from the entire county without the legal power to do so.[48] This early disagreement led to disaster for the state law, as the same county commissioners successfully brought suit against the sidepath commission's very existence. The county Court of Common Pleas found the entire idea repugnant to the state constitution, which declared that "the General Assembly shall not delegate to any special commission . . . any power . . . to levy taxes or perform any municipal function whatever." As such, in the opinion of the court, "there are no such officers as sidepath commissioners authorized by law and with power to receive funds raised by a tax on bicycles," and all monies previously collected were therefore ruled unconstitutional seizures.[49] When a similar disagreement between county and sidepath commissioners in Erie County reached the Pennsylvania Supreme Court in 1901, the justices declared that special commissions and unelected commissioners were both unconstitutional. Sidepath funding by taxation in the state had two flat tires, and in 1907 the legislature had to arrange to return the proceeds to the general fund.[50]

The Dream of a Sidepath Nation

While sidepath legislation taxing all bicycles was being defeated elsewhere, the user-fee model of New York State was experiencing more success. Following the initial six counties that adopted this model, eight more took steps to create bicycle paths. The scale of these projects varied widely, with those of Niagara and Monroe counties dwarfing all others; Warren County reported collecting only three hundred dollars in 1901, a tenth of Niagara County's budget for the previous year.[51] Monroe County had constructed 150 miles of paths by 1900.[52]

By the dawn of the new century, a nationwide sidepath boom was under way. Avoiding the difficulties of Oregon, Pennsylvania, and Washington, all subsequent state laws were modeled on New York's 1899 act, with legislatures enabling county-level sidepath commissions to raise funds through license sales. Maryland, Ohio, and Rhode Island passed sidepath laws in 1900, and Connecticut, Florida, and Minnesota followed the next year.[53] Massachusetts, New Hampshire, Vermont, and Wisconsin all explored New York-style sidepath bills in 1900 and 1901.[54] Nor was the sidepath boom limited to the United States: the Canadian provinces of Ontario and Manitoba were working on their own cycle-path licensing laws in 1900, with Manitoba's passing in 1901. The sidepath scheme of the city of Winnipeg was eventually hugely successful, with more than eight thousand riders purchasing licenses annually by 1905.[55]

But legislation did not necessarily translate into physical paths. While Florida's law was almost identical to those of other states, there is no evidence that any sidepath commissions were formed. On the other hand, individual cities or counties could establish sidepath schemes without the aid of state legislation. Salt Lake City, Utah; Keene, New Hampshire; Spokane, Washington; and Portage County, Ohio, all created user-fee tag systems or built paths autonomously.[56]

Backed by state laws or not, across the nation, long-standing

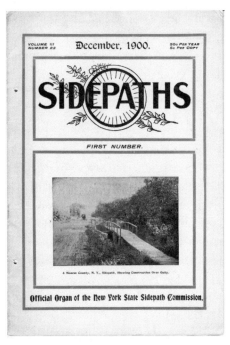

Figure 2.5. A December 1900 cover of the now largely forgotten journal *Sidepaths*, showing a bicycle path and bridge built to the right of an unimproved road in Monroe County. Although the movement originated in upstate New York, the journal covered sidepath politics and engineering across the nation and united a wide audience behind the goal of creating networks of bike-specific paths, financed by user fees and enshrined in state law.

associations of bicycling with elitism continued to make it difficult for advocates to defend paths as a public good. A number of paths had already been built through voluntary contributions in Minneapolis and St. Paul. Despite concerns that the network had too many "free riders," forcing everyone to pay for the resource was seen as unjust. The first city ordinance intended to create "an equitable distribution of the cost of the cycle paths" was quickly vetoed. Approving of the mayor's action, the editors of the *St. Paul Globe* described the ordinance as "radically obnoxious" and objected to the aspects of the plan that smacked of "class legislation": "The public thoroughfares are public property, and their use should be free and unrestricted," wrote the editor. "If it is proposed to tax the owners of bicycles, that is another proposition; but to exclude them from the use of the cycle paths because they have not paid a fee is clearly unjust discrimination and against all true public policy . . . as long as our streets are not private property, we hope never to see" laws prohibiting any group from using public roads.[57]

This debate was conducted in venues both large and small, the heated exchanges highlighting the lack of clear solutions. A journalist at the nearby *Bemidji Pioneer* argued against others' view that "inasmuch as cyclists are the only ones who benefit by paths they should bear the expense." Quite the contrary, he observed: "The bicycle is just as much a means of locomotion as is the carriage, whether the object of its use be business or pleasure. Such being the case, the cycle path should be regarded as part of the highway and maintained as such." Another writer continued to argue for the user-fee model, even while admitting the deficiencies of the voluntary system: "The cycle tag in St. Paul has represented little more than an individual expression of appreciation," he complained in the *Globe*. "The problem is how to make it more than that without invoking compulsory public agencies." Voluntary contributions were not enough to support the goal, and mandatory taxes on all cycle owners were considered unfair. But any requirements to purchase tags were increasingly ridiculed as "class legislation," taxing the lower classes to benefit those above, and the public was not interested in paying for the hobby of a social elite. What could be done?[58]

The New York model was seen as a middle-ground solution, and Minnesota journalists predicted that new legislation could build paths "under the direction of a side path commission similar to the New York commission."[59] The resulting 1901 bill enabled side-path commissions funded by user fees in the largest three counties of the state.[60] The *Globe* felt that the change addressed the "free rider" problem, noting that before the 1901 bill's restrictions, "tags were only bought by the enthusiastic wheelmen, and . . . a great many wheelmen did not think [it] necessary to pay a dollar." By 1902, the private St. Paul Cycle Path Association had declared itself defunct and transferred its funds as well as its officers to the new county sidepath commission. Minneapolis chose not to create a commission and instead stuck with its previous ad hoc alliance of multiple governments, agencies, and the volunteer cycle-path association. But by 1902, both approaches appeared successful: St. Paul boasted 115 miles of paths built for the use of a reported twelve thousand cyclists. Selling tags through the city clerk's office, Minneapolis built a network of more than fifty miles of side-paths by 1902, expanding to seventy-four miles of paths within the city "and perhaps as much more outside the limits" by 1906.[61]

New York's user-fee model looked like a good choice, since commissions designed to avoid taxation appeared to be acceptable to state courts. Helene M. Ryan, the owner of what was then rural property in Suffolk County, New York, brought suit in 1901 to prevent the construction of a path along South Country Road near Bay Shore, on Long Island. But the court found that the path did not "impose an additional burden on the highway" and was thus constitutional.[62]

The first years of the new century were the high point of the sidepath movement, fostering dreams of a two-wheeled future. Newspapers imagined a network of bicycle-only paths stretching uninterrupted "from New York to Buffalo and between Detroit, Chicago, Milwaukee and Minneapolis," thus creating a "transcontinental highway" of sidepaths, putting Europe to shame and making the United States "pre-eminently the country for tourists." Some of this actually got built: Monroe County had expanded its network of bicycle-specific paths to cover two hundred miles by 1901, and a few other counties across the nation were experiencing more limited success. The sidepath commissioner in Oneida County, New York, was prepared to claim victory, claiming at the 1900 sidepath convention in Utica that "the building of side paths, which was started as a matter of sentiment by public spirited citizens through voluntary subscriptions, has passed the experimental stage, and is now a matter of business."[63]

By the end of the century, even the LAW seemed to have overcome its previous objections. The group had still been hedging its bets in 1898, when the LAW president grudgingly committed to "the construction of cycle-paths in those parts of the country where good roads are not found and cannot reasonably be looked for in the near future." But for several years after 1900, sidepath and Good Roads advocacy existed side by side in LAW publications; one article proclaimed that "within five years this country will possess a system of sidepaths that will extend almost everywhere."[64]

The Sidepath Not Taken

But the dream of a national network of sidepaths was already fading, hamstrung by the insularity of cyclists. Like a receding tide revealing rotten piers, by 1905 the decline of the exuberant bike fad left the sidepath movement exposed and unable to support itself. The decline in public interest exposed the inherent weakness in the movement's structure: a small, insular group proved unable to create lasting infrastructure without broader support.

The mismatch was obvious in Genesee County, New York, from the start. When the sidepath commissioners organized a public auction for sidepath licenses in 1899, "the auction wasn't the complete success that was hoped for." Just eighteen tags out of the planned one hundred were purchased. At the next year's auction, Commissioner James A. Le Seur tried his best: "You people don't act as though you wanted these tags very badly," he hectored the crowd. "You want sidepaths, but you must know that they can't be built without money."[65]

Le Seur's words were not enough: the sidepath commission ran out of funds at the very beginning of the summer construction season, bringing work to a halt on June 14. The *Genesee Daily News* tried to put a good face on it: "As soon as the Commissioners secure additional funds the path from Le Roy east to the county line . . . will be completed." But at the start of 1901, the commissioners had a grand total of $1.78 in the bank. They scaled back both fund-raising and operations, canceling the public auction "as so little interest was manifested." They also declared that "no new paths should be undertaken at the outset, or at any time during the season, unless the sales of tags warranted." By May, there were not enough cyclists purchasing tags to even cover repair or maintenance. "The wheelmen seem to take little interest," mourned the *Daily News*. "Without funds the Sidepath Commission can do no work on the paths, and there is no way to get money except from the sale of tags. The paths . . . are not in firstclass condition and cannot be improved until coin is obtained. . . . It rests with wheelmen to decide whether the necessary improvements shall be made."[66] The decision was in the negative: after 1901, the *Daily*

News carried no stories about either the sidepath commissioners or their creations. In Genesee and elsewhere, the much-ballyhooed sidepath network was falling apart.

The last gasp of the sidepath movement was an attempt to reintroduce the idea of taxation. While some counties were still successful with funding paths through user fees, Fulton County's *Gloversville Daily Leader* lamented that "in many the receipts are largely expended in repairs, and few extensions are being made, and in some counties the commissioners have given up and resigned in despair." At a state convention of sidepath commissioners, Charles Raymond argued that "the time has arrived, when a part of the construction should be borne by the entire community and not thrown upon the shoulders of a few wheelmen." Road building offered a handy comparison: "No one would think of attempting to build all the roads in the state from the proceeds of a license on vehicles using them," argued the *Gloversville Daily Leader*. "The slogan of Mr. Raymond would be 'What is of benefit to all, all should pay for.'" With that change, opined the newspaper, the state could still be "gridironed with a perfect system of sidepaths."[67] But Raymond's new proposal never made it to the state legislature.

As the commissions weakened, their sidepaths eventually disappeared under newly paved and widened roads. The *Brooklyn Daily Eagle*, after describing the exhaustion of the long-suffering and often-sued Suffolk County sidepath commissioners in 1907, worried that "it is possible that when the state engineer comes along" to survey for newly-funded state roads, "he will demand that the entire width of the roadways where sidepaths now are, be graded, which would cut out the sidepaths." With prescience, the newspaper opined that "it is to the interest of everybody, school children especially, that the sidepaths be allowed to stand, as it is too dangerous in these days of automobiling for a bicyclist to be compelled to ride in the road."[68] But that appears to be exactly what happened: comparing maps from different decades indicates that sidepaths simply disappeared under widened roadbeds. At the time, many cyclists were delighted by the newly paved roads; few realized then that automobiles would eventually threaten their travel. This outcome would have been inconceivable to the *Daily News* journalist who confidently predicted in 1900 that the paths would never disappear, since legal sources assured him that "a strip of land 'once a sidepath, would always be a sidepath.'"[69]

THE PROBLEM WITH ELITES

The funding mechanisms for sidepaths were determined by arguments over whether the paths served a public good. The LAW employed language that claimed the benefit of roads for all, arguing that the prior "work gang" system of rural road building was an "injustice" to the general populace. "Equality of taxation is a familiar principle," argued one Good Roads advocate, "yet nothing would be more unequal than to tax farm property alone for the construction of roads which ultimately benefit the entire community." While such arguments had already been applied with success in securing funding for public schools, they failed in the case of sidepaths. It was just too difficult to argue that "cyclists" and "the public" were one and the same. As such, the failure of the sidepath movement was primarily one of social class and social capital. The movement had begun with urban and elite cyclists who were fed up with rural opposition to road improvement. As one cyclist complained 1896: "Why should the bicyclist carry the farmer like a millstone around his neck? What has the farmer, the man most interested, done for good roads when left to himself?" But such distinctions doomed later appeals for public support, and the rhetoric soured attempts to claim that bicycle paths could be counted as a public good. In Monroe County, attempts to tax all cyclists to build sidepaths proved disastrous, susceptible to arguments that an elite group of middle and upper-class men were unfairly benefiting from the taxation of all. For similar reasons, all subsequent sidepath projects were limited to essentially voluntary funding. The sidepath movement was just too early for its own good, emerging before the growing acceptance of twentieth-century funding mechanisms that overcame objections of taxing all for the benefit of some (as in the cases of public schools and urban infrastructure). These developments might have made path building possible.[70]

If cyclists lost the sidepath battle partly because of the rhetoric of exclusivity, they simultaneously won and lost the Good Roads battle for the same reason. The LAW fought against accusations of elitism for more than a decade, claiming that the interests of urban and rural, rich and poor, were served by good roads. But according to one historian, the association of the bicycle with the urban upper class "threatened to scuttle the campaign for better roads," leading the group to "downplay their cycling interests when they discussed highway politics" after 1900.[71] Success eventually came through alliances with farmers, which required the Good Roads reformers to obscure their associations with cycling. But hiding bicyclists' political investment in the new commons, even when the Good Roads movement succeeded, meant that the bicyclists lost. Without broad public support, cyclists were limited to essentially charitable projects, dooming cycling infrastructure.

Farmer Absalom Wyckoff's habit of horse-whipping cyclists looks a bit different from this perspective. The newspaper related his story as an allegorical tale of overcoming an outdated objection to competing use of the roads, with Wyckoff being taught a hard lesson by a cyclist. But from a modern-day perspective, the crux of the story is the social division between the farmer and the cyclist. This division has persisted in one form or another to the present day. Bicycles were originally identified with dandies in Europe and then with urban elite males in the United States. In the early twentieth century they were associated with childhood; since then they have been variously linked to urban poverty, jobless hipsters, effete environmentalists, and immigrant groups. Whatever the association, bicyclists commingling with motor vehicle traffic are still considered oddities: not fully American; not equally deserving of protection or public expenditure; parasites on the gasoline taxes paid by automobile drivers; and symbols of white, middle-class, urban, environmentalist elitism. Bicyclists remain "them," not "us."

CHAPTER 3

THE RULES OF THE ROAD

Bicycling in the
Automotive Age,
1900–1930

In the first three decades of the twentieth century the still-new medium of film silently captured the rapid transformation of city streets and rural highways. A 1900 Edison film of an automobile parade hints at an increasingly complex road: led by wobbly bicycle cops, a handful of bouncy, open-top autos make a turn in front of a stationary camera. The road has no lane markings. Pedestrians, bicyclists, and carriages intermix freely, and a horse pulling a two-wheeled hansom expresses its displeasure when the faster automobiles cut it off. By 1906, some remarkable footage showed even more intermixture of vehicles in the increasing masses of automobile traffic along San Francisco's Market Street. Fast-moving automobiles, slowly trotting horse-drawn carriages and omnibuses, electric trolleys on tracks, daring pedestrians, and bouncing bicycles weave around each other. Without signals or lane markings, the traffic is fluidly chaotic. Everyone crosses intersections at their own discretion.

More than twenty years later, the 1928 Harold Lloyd feature *Speedy* showed the terror that automobile traffic had become on unmarked, uncontrolled city streets. While the mayhem is exaggerated for comic effect, the film shows wide New York city streets completely without defined parking areas, traffic lanes, or center lines; intersections without controlling signage of any sort; and wildly mixing pedestrian, horse, auto, and trolley traffic, all hemmed in by masses of parked and double-parked cars. The occasional traffic towers and white-gloved cornermen are small signs of a coming attempt to impose order.[1]

In response to the chaos surrounding the rise of the automobile in the first decades of the twentieth century, a new system of road engineering, traffic rules, and signs would be created explicitly for the use and control of cars. Engineers paved roads with a center ridge and sloping sides, cambered curves, and uniform widths. Standardized national signage and road numbering systems were created. A nationwide Uniform Vehicle Code set out the rules of the road. Speed limits, painted lanes, stop signs, and intersections were designed such that "roads and cars operated almost seamlessly as two complementary parts of a vast, unified technological system," according to one historian.[2]

Although bicycles did not entirely disappear, and indeed thrived in a few niche areas, there was no significant attempt to safeguard their riders or cater to their needs in this new order. Instead, as historians like Clay McShane, Peter Norton, and Christopher Wells have pointed out, all eyes were on the automobile. Public debates addressed road construction, public financing, and the control of traffic, but bicycles and their riders were absent from this policy battlefield. Although bicycles, pedestrians and horse-drawn vehicles retained a theoretical right to the road, by the middle of the century the road itself had changed beneath them.

THE DECLINE OF SOCIETY CYCLING

It is a phenomenal irony that just as the streets of America came to be more regulated in the first decades of the twentieth century, bicycles became much less common on the road, their demise hastened by the end of the upper-class interest in recreational cycling.

The census charted the collapse in numbers, seeing a boom and bust cycle that estimated 1905 sales at one-sixth and the number of shops at one-third of their 1900 figures. According to one observer, in "the prosperous days of 1894 to 1896 . . . people went cycle mad; the bicycle industry appeared to be an Eldorado, and there was a rush to engage in it." But "then followed the decline in popularity, with the resultant dull times and failures among the manufacturers." By 1905 the bike boom was increasingly dismissed as a temporary fashion; observers of the rapid rise of the automobile argued that the auto's "remarkable growth is not, like that of the bicycle, based on a fad, and so liable to as sudden a decline."[3]

Bicycling did not vanish entirely: as a spectator sport, cycling remained popular, as in the multiday velodrome competitions in Madison Square Garden, and trick riding still found a place on stage. "Our antique friend, the bicycle, came back at the Orpheum yesterday," reported *Variety* in 1915, describing a titillating vaudeville act: "Despite the antiquity—now—of the wheel, put a pretty girl atop of it, in few enough clothes, and it still makes a stunning turn."[4] But the social clubs and recreational cycling of the 1890s declined precipitously. Upper-class cyclists migrated to other elite pastimes that could not be soiled by the common people: "Golf, of course, has been responsible for a great deal of the falling off of the popularity of the bicycle among society people," wrote a Chicago reporter in 1899, "but the cheapening of cycles has also been a cause."[5]

Commentators still did not miss the opportunity to belittle women's cycling: "I think that the most noticeable decrease of the public interest has been among the women," opined one male cyclist. "With the women wheeling was almost entirely a fad, few women taking long rides because they really cared to do so." Criticizing female commitment might have provided an easy excuse, but such potshots didn't explain the overall decline. *Scientific American* thought that the mechanisms of conspicuous consumption as a signal of class status were more probable culprits, noticing in 1905 that one "cause of the decline was the introduction of cheap bicycles, and the placing of the wheel within reach of everybody who could find the necessary forty or fifty dollars." With that, "bicycling became unfashionable."[6] In the view of a *Motor Age* writer in 1914, the cycling fad of the 1890s was one "in which the safety bicycle was taken up by the wealthy classes, made a sport of, and finally reduced in price so that cycling became a universal pastime with all classes." Then came "the period of decay as a sport, when the exclusive element abandoned long-distance riding, and, finally, cycling altogether, because of the elimination of the bicycle as a luxury, followed by the gradual falling off of popularity in the middle classes, and finally by the working classes."[7]

With the sudden decline of cycling came a similarly precipitous decline in the political power of the LAW, which had reported "over one hundred thousand paying members" in 1898 but after 1900 "collapsed." Ignominiously, by 1920 the former LAW president Sterling Elliott had reportedly joined the American Automobile Association (AAA) to maintain a role in road advocacy.[8] In 1936, the once-powerful national organization acknowledged its decades of decline in an internal history: "With a diminishing activity the interest in the affairs dwindled, [the league's] records were not maintained, and the membership rolls neglected."[9]

Without the LAW to represent cyclists, the bicycle industry was left to fill the void. By 1920 a national consortium of bicycle dealers, first known as the United Cycle Trade Directorate but later renamed the Cycle Trades of America (CTA), was attempting to revive the upper-class associations of the bicycle through "a comprehensive plan for molding and shaping all avenues of public opinion that can be reached," including ads and photographs. In reports to the manufacturers and shop owners who funded the group, the directors worried that "one of the great obstacles the bicycle industry has to overcome is the feeling in the minds of the layman that to be seen on a bicycle puts him in the 'soft shirt' class rather than in the 'White collar brigade'" ("soft shirt" here meaning working class or blue-collar). Replaced as a symbol of conspicuous consumption by luxury automobiles, and displaced at the other end of the spectrum as the workhorse of the poor by the mass-produced Model T, the bicycle was stuck in the middle.

The CTA campaign worked at both ends of this image problem with advertising that tried to sell the bike to everyone under a slogan targeting the upper class. One 1919 ad declared, slightly insistently, that "cycling is fashionable!" Under a picture of an impeccably dressed pair of young riders, the copy declares that "society started it in the Southern winter resorts and now they have it back to the North. Cycling is popular at Vassar, Smith and other women's colleges." Indeed, the bicycle was said to be back "among people of taste, and *Vogue* has decreed in our spring styles in sport clothes that they be suitable for bicycle riding."[10] The group continued to work behind the scenes, donating a bicycle to the White House, subsidizing cycling events in the new phenomenon of the Olympic Games, and distributing "photographs of prominent society people" riding bikes in Florida to newspapers. The promoters were justly proud of an editorial in the *New-York Tribune* in 1920, which hoped for a return of the "Aristocratic Bicycle" for fashionable, upper-class adults. But the ad men were trying to hold back the tide: such propaganda was needed precisely because the adults of America were uninterested in cycling.[11]

Bicycles themselves were also becoming scarce. By 1926, bicycle production had been drastically curtailed, falling by nearly one-third in a single year. A folksy local historian wrote of the disappearance of bikes in Quincy, Illinois: "Do you remember when people started talking about the last days of the bicycle? Well about 1925, 6 or 7 or along there, everybody thought the bicycle was out." By the mid-1920s, in downtown Quincy, "one could see one or two, whereas several years before that there were hundreds."[12]

FROM BLANK SLATE TO AUTOCENTRIC ROADS

As bicycles faded from the public's attention, motor vehicles took their place as both possessions and problems. Like Golden Age bicycles, cars began as high-class recreational status symbols but then captured the imagination of the young, the upwardly mobile, and the technology obsessed.[13] Most importantly, as automobiles proliferated, discussions about controlling their existence and movement replaced bike battles on the public agenda. Whereas the American road had been managed for bikes and farmers' wagons at the turn of the century, in the twentieth century the systematic regulation and control of roads focused on automobile traffic.

It may be hard to imagine now, but the nineteenth-century road was largely a blank slate, both legally and literally. It lacked traffic laws, signs, lanes, or signals. In the mid-nineteenth century, there was only a single rule of the road: stay on your own side. Thus in 1881 Supreme Court Justice Oliver Wendell Holmes could refer in the singular to "the rule of the road," which allowed courts to narrow the question of liability from "the vague one, Was the party negligent? To the precise one, Was he on the right or left of the road?" An 1876 treatise comparing road laws in England and America concluded that the law was simple: "In the old country the three laws are: First, on meeting, each party shall bear to the left; second, in passing, the passer shall do so on the right hand; and, third, in crossing, the driver shall bear to the left and pass behind the other carriage." In America the directions were simply reversed: drivers kept to the right. Governments rarely set speed limits, did not license or inspect horse-drawn vehicles, and imposed few requirements on the equipment or design of vehicles. Carriage and wagon drivers had no legal obligation to indicate their turns or stops and lacked standard hand signals even if they wanted to.[14]

"Prior to 1903 in American cities there were no rules for driving known to drivers or police," wrote one observer in 1922. "Vehicles made their way as best they could through the inextricable mass of other vehicles headed in every possible direction." The unmarked roads outside cities, usually just a single vehicle's width across, meant that road users had to decide for themselves how to pass or when to pull over to yield to oncoming traffic. The lack of regulation led one unnamed bicyclist to suggest in the LAW *Bulletin* that everyone use the system of bells used by overtaking steamships on rivers.[15]

Before automobiles allowed speedy long-distance travel, navigational signs were unnecessary, since travelers rarely ventured beyond places they already knew. Not until 1901 did a meeting of New York automobile enthusiasts, LAW representatives, and horse-carriage pleasure drivers decide that one of their first orders of business should be "signs at the corner of every street, giving its name." These signs were merely descriptive, not regulatory, but they were the first marks on the blank slate.[16]

Transforming the Law

As the historian Peter Norton has wryly pointed out, "Cities treated the arrival of the automobile as they might any other emergency." Automobiles presented a crisis mostly because they were per-ceived as the cause of an unprecedented bloodbath, with crashes in 1915 knocking off more than twice as many New Yorkers as were murdered that year.[17] It was this life-threatening chaos that was portrayed in the 1928 silent film *Speedy*. The experience of tearing through New York streets terrifies even the paragon of masculinity Babe Ruth (playing himself), who declares to his taxi driver, via title card, "If I ever want to commit suicide I'll call you."

Clearly, the growing mass of automobiles required completely new regulatory regimes and physical controls.[18] A 1911 treatise on automobile law included the observation that "to persons riding along our public roads . . . the rapidly moving automobile is a constant source of danger." In the words of one judge, "Their great weight, speed[,] power, and resulting momentum render the con-sequences of a collision with them much more serious than with ordinary carriages moving at even a higher rate of speed," and their path was much less predictable than street railways. As such, while automobiles (like bicycles before them) were classified as vehicles, and "drivers of automobiles and bicyclists have an equal right to use of the street," a consensus was building that automobil-ists should be "held to a stricter obedience . . . than drivers of lighter and slower moving vehicles."[19]

With the increased crowding of cities and the rising number of motor vehicles in their streets, urban police forces were given the task of bringing order to the chaos. This additional realm of police responsibility was to be called "traffic" control, a new word for a new problem. With the support of the traffic-control hobbyist and "eccentric gadfly" William P. Eno, New York City's police department produced the first "traffic code" in 1903, an example that many other cities emulated.[20]

State after state created entirely new bureaucracies to respond to the needs of the automobile. The public and the courts found it sufficiently different from previous vehicles that it needed a new legal category, that of *motor* vehicle. Whether powered by the rare steam boiler, the surprisingly common electric motor, or the eventually dominant internal combustion engine, motor vehicles were distinct from all previous types of vehicles. Eventually their sheer numbers merited the creation of that pinnacle of civilization, the Department of Motor Vehicles.

Treating motor vehicles as a distinct category allowed a previously unthinkable level of regulation: licensing first the vehicles themselves, and then drivers. No private horse-drawn vehicle or operator had ever previously needed a state-issued license to take to the road, though teamsters and other commercial vehicles had been regulated in various ways. But a 1901 New York law proposed at first to require automobile owners to paint their initials, and later a license number obtained from a government office, on the side of their vehicles. The California Code of 1905 followed suit in an entirely new section of laws applying only to motor vehicles, which included the requirement to register them with the state.[21]

By the 1930s, the Chamber of Commerce's National Conference on Street and Highway Safety was proposing a further step: managing the automobile menace by issuing driver's licenses *only* to qualified applicants. "The continually increasing volume of motor traffic accidents, within a million injuries and deaths a year, is one of the most serious questions facing the 48 states at this time" wrote the director, A. B. Barber. "The answer . . . is clear and unequivocal. It is restriction of the driving privilege to competent and capable drivers. This means the licensing of drivers," with the legal ability to *revoke* a license for violation—something previously considered an unconstitutional restriction of freedom of movement.[22] The needs created by the motor vehicle were transforming the fundamental relationship between citizen and state, as legislatures and newly empowered municipalities began imposing unprecedented controls on behavior.[23] Over time, the license certifying the knowledge and skill of the motorist would unintentionally become a de facto government identification card in the United States, serving as a proof of age, name, and place of residence.

Rebuilding the Road

Requiring driver's licenses was a surprising development, but it was only one component of the way the physical and regulatory environment was being refashioned to meet the demands of the automobile. These innovations included one-way streets, traffic-control signs, electrically lighted signals, painted lanes, raised sidewalks, and the entirely novel concept of "parking."

Then as now, urban intersections were the most complicated and dangerous locations on the road. Before signs that indicated that traffic should come to a halt and laws specifying precedence—or lights that allowed some vehicles to move while others were stopped—intersections were either uncontrolled or required a uniformed human presence. These "cornermen," equipped only with a whistle, white gloves, and nerves of steel, were a new addition to the police force, itself newly professionalized in the late nineteenth century. Even as they increased in number, they were still no match for the growing host of automobiles, and city authorities soon sought to solve the matter with technology.

Before the stop sign or the traffic light, the "silent policeman" was the first piece of physical infrastructure designed to control vehicle movement. It was a post planted at the center of a road intersection, forcing left-turning drivers to take a wide path around it rather than cut across lanes. First proposed in New York City in 1904, the post replaced an actual policeman who would have stood in the same spot, and the name conferred the authority of the human onto the proxy. Many observers doubted, however, that motorists would defer to nonhuman authority. Indeed, after drivers started running over and destroying the vertical posts, the more sturdy "Milwaukee mushroom" became popular—a cast-iron bump in the center of the intersection, which could survive the impact of a vehicle while still forcing drivers to make a wide left turn.[24]

In response to the automobile menace, authorities also began to divide up the road to control the flow of automobile traffic. Marking center lines and lanes, a practice that began in 1915, regulated traffic flow and enabled police to cite drivers of vehicles that improperly left their lanes. These markings promised a much more ordered system than the terrifying interweaving of trolley car, horse-drawn omnibus, motor vehicle, and bicycle traffic on display in the 1906 San Francisco film. It was slow to catch on, however, in part because road paint was not yet all that durable. Painted lanes still had to be explained to the readers of *Good Roads* in 1922: "Paint is now being extensively used to direct traffic . . . in the division of roadways into lanes, thus separating the traffic." While the author believed paint was "here to stay," he cautioned that "care must be used to educate the public as to the meaning of the painted strips or confusion may result."[25]

Protecting pedestrians from auto traffic meant separating their space on sidewalks from that dedicated to motor vehicles with something a bit more substantial than painted lanes: concrete curbing. For pedestrian crossings, additional measures were warranted. "Where it is necessary for pedestrians to cross streets filled with swiftly moving automobiles and other vehicles," noted a 1922 report in *American City*, "it has been found expedient to establish *islands of safety* in the center of the roadway," offering foot traffic "a safe and secure stopping-place." These structures can be seen in the 1906 San Francisco film, with scurrying pedestrians rushing to perch on the raised curbs in the center of the road, peering out skeptically at passing traffic.[26]

Automobiles created new problems and demands even when they were not moving. For most of the history of the road, it was not acceptable for people to leave horse-drawn vehicles unattended in the public street. "Private premises must be procured . . . to stop in during the interval between the end of one journey and the commencement of another," thundered the Lord Chief Justice of England in 1812. "No one can make a stable-yard of the King's highway." Nineteenth-century American courts cited these precedents, arguing in 1889 that "the highway may be a convenient place for the owner of carriages to keep them in, but the law . . . prohibits any such use of the public streets." This decision echoed the long-standing philosophy of the road by stating that "the primary use of the highway is . . . the passing and repassing of the public, and it is entitled to unobstructed and unoccupied use of the entire width of the highway for that purpose." Indeed, early traffic code in New York completely banned leaving personal property in the public road.[27]

With the increasing popularity of automobiles, that philosophy was soon overtaken by events. Drivers began to leave their rigs alongside the travel lane, perched on the strips of grass that bordered some roads. Because these types of roads were known as "parkways," leaving one's automobile on the public road became known colloquially as "parking" it. By 1936, one observer in H. L. Mencken's irreverent *American Mercury* magazine was declaring that the twenty-three million "car owners of the Republic have taken over its streets and highways as a permanent possession." The essayist Fletcher Pratt complained that "twenty-four hours a day [they] pre-empt space along what are euphemistically known as *public* highways—parking, parking, parking, for one hour, two hours, all night, a week, a month, as long as it suits them." If anyone told a driver "that the streets are intended for traffic rather than storage, he becomes more indignant, pointing out that he helps pay for those streets . . . and therefore they belong to him." But "is his right to occupy a portion of the highway any more legal than his right to move in on Dr. Roosevelt . . . because his taxes help pay for the upkeep of the White House?"[28] Eventually authorities bowed to necessity and began marking strips of urban streets as areas for parking motor vehicles.

However, marking the road with paint offered visible proof of the marginalization of the bicycle. While painted lines marked parking areas and travel lanes for automobiles, no space on the road was marked for the use of the increasingly rare bicyclist, and the lanes designated for moving vehicles were not sized with bicy-

clists in mind. By basing lane width on the dimensions of the automobile, traffic engineers made bicycles an oddity on the road,
adrift in a wide lane not matched to their size and surrounded on
all sides by parked or moving motor vehicles. By 1936, the much-
reduced LAW counted the development of on-street auto parking
as a significant blow to cycling, mourning that bicyclists "were
finally deprived of the use of the roads they helped to build by the
speeding motor car, plus the fact that our streets have been permitted to become public parking places."[29]

Detroit—the Motor City—was a very early experimenter in the
1920s with both painted lanes and a traffic-light system, controlled
by a nearby policeman. For traffic management professionals, it
was clear that the automobile brought the need for signals: "It is
impossible to go back to the days of the horse and buggy when
there was plenty of room on the street," wrote *Good Roads* magazine. But "it is just as impossible to widen" the roads already in
existence. Painted lanes and controlled intersections offered a
specific response to the traffic menace that avoided re-engineering
the road, which was fairly unlikely anyway.[30]

Human-operated traffic lights were placed at busy downtown
intersections already staffed by cornermen, but beginning in 1914
in Detroit, a new, octagonal sign was posted on less-important
roads to stop traffic before it crossed main boulevards. Originally
called a "boulevard sign" and only later a "stop sign," it was not
meant to slow down the mass of dangerous vehicles but instead to
speed the way of priority traffic. Local neighborhoods opposed the
signs in what Clay McShane has called a "battle of the streets." For
a short time in Illinois, courts ruled stop signs illegal because they
encouraged speeding for prioritized traffic and infringed on pedestrian freedom of movement.[31] But the neighborhoods lost out to the
automobilists and the authorities who were attempting to accommodate them, and stop signs proliferated.

When unmanned stop signs were installed at all four corners of
an intersection, it wasn't clear who got to go first. One early practice was to give the right of way to north-south traffic—an idea
developed in New York City, where most major thoroughfares had

that orientation. But outside Gotham, it became necessary by 1918 to propose that vehicles pulling up simultaneously to a four-way stop sign should give the right of way to the vehicle on the right. This practice was not universally accepted: it wasn't until 1929 that Wisconsin codified the four-way stop rule.[32]

Taming the unruly intersection also required another entirely new behavior of vehicle operators: signaling their intentions. Signals were necessary because twentieth-century auto design was tending toward enclosing drivers, thus hiding their body language. Cars were also moving so quickly that travelers needed to anticipate where other vehicles were going, not just observe where they were. But signals took a while to catch on, and even when required by law, they weren't standardized: "There are at least two systems of hand signals in fairly general use" on the opposite ends of the continent, noted the Boy Scouts in 1930. The electric-lighted turn signal wasn't common in automobiles until the 1940s.[33]

One technological solution for the automobile menace was the proposal to limit speed with mechanical governors. In the early 1920s, Cincinnati considered a city ordinance requiring a control device that would shut off the engine if a car exceeded twenty miles an hour. Automobile interests instantly mobilized against such threats, becoming very well organized in the process. The foolproof speed governor was supplanted by voluntary speed limits, occasionally observed by fallible drivers and irregularly enforced by imperfect human police.[34]

The fight over controlling automobiles in American cities ironically ended up controlling pedestrians by forcing them to leave the street. The nineteenth-century road had been a place for many types of movement and interaction by pedestrians, street vendors, animals and humans; but the twentieth-century street was entirely usurped by motor vehicles. Big-city automobile clubs invented the term *jaywalking* to shame walkers who stepped into the street at any place except intersections and at any angle save the perpendicular, and they embarked on campaigns to "educate" walkers for the benefit of drivers.[35]

The auto was now becoming philosophically dominant. "On the

most fundamental legal level, English common law had held that all street users were equal," one historian has noted. "At the urging of traffic engineers, however, city councils replaced this ancient rule with new ordinances that gave cars the right of way, except at intersections." In 1916 the AAA supported this approach, arguing that pedestrians should be protected at corners but that "drivers of vehicles should have precedence between crossings. They should have a right to expect that they will only have to look out for other vehicles." The road was now for cars, a logic visible in a 1923 Colorado Springs proposal to fine pedestrians who had the temerity to get hit by an automobile while crossing anywhere but at an intersection.[36]

In the end, none of the innovations of the early-twentieth-century, traffic-regulated street were designed with cyclists in mind. Bicycles traveling in the newly-marked road lanes were perceived by drivers as unfairly taking up more space than they needed and impeding faster traffic. The new practice of allowing vehicles to be left standing on the side of the road blocked cyclists' passage and forced them to thread between opening doors on the right and moving cars on the left. Stop signs designed to halt and establish an order of precedence among intersecting automobiles also compelled bicycles—which are balanced only when they are rolling forward—to come to a complete halt and awkwardly restart (something that would have been impossible in the high-wheel era). Traffic-light sequences and speed limits were tuned to the speeds of automobiles, not bicycles. Copying automobilists' hand signals forced cyclists to take their hands off the handlebars and brakes. No standardized road signs referred to bicycles in any way. Most tellingly, there was, literally, no design standard for a sign telling users to "share the road." It was all for the auto.[37]

Writing a Uniform Vehicle Code

Between the two world wars, American roads were rebuilt—and in the absence of a powerful cycling lobby, both the roads and the rules that governed them were designed for cars. These changes made it possible to reimagine the shared resource of the road as solely the province of private automobiles, and planners began to consider what historians now call "completely car-centered landscapes."[38]

Perhaps the most important physical changes happened after the Federal Road Act of 1916 and the Highway Act of 1921 matched state funding with federal money, fulfilling the long-standing dream of the Good Roads movement. In order to receive matching federal funds, states had to create their own highway departments, staffed by professionals and adhering to standards laid down by the federal Bureau of Public Roads (BPR).[39] By 1917, according to BPR engineers, "standards governing the . . . plans, specifications, and estimates for Federal-aid projects were adopted and issued, and all States have since been working in absolute conformity to these standards." Planners even began to apply federal standards to projects that were not receiving federal money, leading to "standardization of the details of specifications and methods used in the construction of the various types of road the country over." A century of spending began with an explosion of road building in the 1920s and 1930s, when, in the words of the historian Christopher Wells, road construction became "the second largest object of government spending behind education."[40]

The physical standards for these interurban highways were tailored to the automobile, not the now-eclipsed bicycle or rapidly disappearing horse-drawn vehicle. Standards governing the width of lanes, cambering, bridge engineering, and sign size and legibility were optimized for the needs of the faster, heavier, and more numerous cars. The Committee on Standards of the American Association of State Highway Officials specified road-building guidelines that were promulgated nationwide after 1928, with ten-foot-wide lanes, concrete pavement, and a center "crown" to encourage water runoff.[41]

Most importantly, surfacing materials for intercity highways that had been acceptable for other users were replaced in response to the needs of the automobile. While macadam (precisely engineered and close-packed gravel) was fine for bicyclists and farmers of the early Good Roads movement, it produced too much dust and provided too little support for heavier automobiles. Further innovations were necessary. Tar sprayed over previously laid macadam led to the product named tarmac, otherwise known as bituminized macadam. Concrete was used for highway construction, but it was impractical for frequently excavated city streets and expensive in general. Another option was artificial asphalt, created by premixing tar-like bitumen with aggregate and sand into a malleable, yet durable surface. While naturally occurring bitumen deposits had been imported or exploited since the late nineteenth century for city streets, it wasn't until World War I that the volume of petroleum distillation created enough inexpensive byproducts to make practical the extensive use of an engineered asphalt surface. Carefully engineered asphalt, with Portland cement as a binder, was by far the most popular paving choice by the 1930s. Under federal direction, these engineering choices became standardized across the nation.[42]

This new technology of paving and road engineering was embraced by urban and transportation planners who were responding to increasing traffic congestion with grand blueprints for the future. The French modernist and architect known as Le Corbusier offered plans through the 1920s and 1930s that reimagined the city on a massive scale, with broad highways cutting neatly past rows of identical apartment buildings, each the size of a city block. His sketches of ten- and twelve-lane thoroughfares were scrubbed clean of pedestrians, delivery zones, parking, intersections, and bicyclists. While few of Le Corbusier's plans were built, his rationalist vision of a streamlined, concrete future captured the imagination of American urban planners. In New York, Robert Moses was only the most visible of an entire generation of public officials who began to reconstruct the city around the automobile. Supported by the engineers of the federal BPR, they built huge highways that traveled directly through downtown areas, enormous elevated structures that cut across neighborhoods, and parkways with wide shoulders that encouraged high vehicle speeds and required the demolition of vast swaths of urban property.[43]

While cycling was being erased from the nation's new roads, the most obvious mark of bicyclists' reduced legal status came with the development of the Uniform Vehicle Code (UVC). Beginning in 1920, the proliferation of divergent state motor-vehicle laws prompted the creation of a set of national driving standards. A National Conference on Street and Highway Safety, staffed mostly by lawyers, combined the power of the private chamber of commerce and automobile interests with that of the federal Commerce Department to embark on this project of bureaucratic rationalization. The resulting UVC was a set of guidelines for legislation, not a law itself. Repeatedly updated, it summarized legal and business opinions about traffic management and influenced subsequent state legislation. The UVC gave priority to the automobile and weakened the status of the bicycle that had been established in nineteenth-century courts.[44]

While the UVC was aimed at rationalizing the jungle of state legislation, it opened the door for a subsequent project to reform city ordinances. The lukewarm reception among motorists for the first UVC sample laws prompted President Herbert Hoover's administration to stack the deck in favor of automobile interests for this second project. The resulting Model Municipal Traffic Ordinance (MTO) was created not by a committee of lawyers but instead by a group of automobile enthusiasts, manufacturers, and dealers. The chair was the director of the Detroit Automobile Club, an executive with the AAA, and the owner of a Cadillac dealership. Representatives of street railway companies were outnumbered by more than two to one on the committee, and there was never any mention of including representatives of the weakened LAW or any other pedestrian or bicycling group. The resulting MTO, produced in 1928, reflected the makeup of the group; according to the historian Peter Norton, it "codified pedestrians' confinement to sidewalks and crosswalks" and limited any rules that threatened the freedom of automobiles.[45]

In law, definitions matter. The details of the first version of the UVC, presented to the public in 1926, defined a vehicle as any thing in which people or property could traverse a highway, "excepting devices moved by human power." A legislative fiat added to the final draft stipulated "that for the purposes of . . . this act, a bicycle or a ridden animal shall be deemed a vehicle." After that grudging admission, the 1926 UVC proceeded to ignore bicycles except for a requirement that they be equipped with lights or reflectors. The idea was that, with the special exemption in the definition, the rules of the road for motor vehicles in the UVC implicitly also covered bicycles.[46]

A 1930 revision of the UVC continued to treat bicycles as a special case but now explicitly stated that the rules of the road applied to them: "Every person riding a bicycle . . . shall be subject to the provisions of this act applicable to the driver of a vehicle."[47] It was a kind of shadow existence for the bicycle: the law considered it a vehicle, but with reservations.

The language of the MTO went further in negating 1890s case law by allowing bicyclists to ride on sidewalks under certain conditions. Summarizing decades of decisions, a 1922 legal guide noted that "the running of a cycle along a sidewalk is frequently prohibited . . . sometimes absolutely. But even in the absence of a statutory regulation, it is presumptively improper to use a sidewalk for this purpose," since a bicycle was a vehicle and vehicles were not allowed on sidewalks. But to get bicycles out of the road, the MTO allowed them on sidewalks as long as they were not running over pedestrians, ridden in downtown business districts, or otherwise banned. One alternative form of the MTO sample legislation allowed any cyclist younger than fifteen to ride a bicycle on sidewalks without restriction. This exception fudged the definition of bicycles: whether a bicycle was a vehicle now depended upon the age of the operator.[48]

This put the bicycle where it previously had been forbidden, and the Boy Scouts of America noted the change in its bicycling guide in 1930: "A generation ago, when there were few automobiles and many bicycles ridden by men and women as well as young people, riding on sidewalks was strictly forbidden." Although city laws from the previous era banned sidewalk riding, the guide continued, "these are generally not enforced on residence streets," and the situation was increasingly misleading: "In fact many children, especially beginners, are told that they must ride on the sidewalk and not in the street because of the danger from automobiles."[49]

Court decisions of the era similarly tended to erode the status of the bicycle as a vehicle with equal rights to the road. A 1912 Indiana case argued that although automobiles and bicycles were legally charged with the same responsibility, "it is obvious that more is required from the former, to fully discharge the duty, than from the latter. The great weight of the automobile, the high speed at which it may be driven, and the ease with which the great power of its motor engine may be applied, distinguish it, in the matter of danger to others, from the light foot-power bicycle." A 1919 Iowa decision in a fatal accident declared that bicycles now had to coexist in the automobiles' world: "The overwhelming majority of vehicles . . . at the present time are motor vehicles . . . [A]ny other vehicle using the highway concurrently with such motor vehicles should adopt itself to the general rules of the road which are imposed by statute or ordinance upon the great body of vehicles moving thereon."[50]

Motor vehicle laws that implied bicycles weren't vehicles were being laid on top of common-law precedents that had previously determined that they were. This is exactly the sort of confusion that law should clear up, not create. This fact was not lost on the Oregon Supreme Court, which in a 1931 case "was confronted with the duty of determining the status of a bicycle rider upon a public highway," something that had been decided through litigation decades before. But the court found that the existing Oregon law, based on the UVC, "excludes bicycles from the statutory provisions of the Motor Vehicle Act in so far as such provisions apply only to vehicles." The court reasoned that the motor-vehicle law did not apply to the case, since "the only reference to bicycles appearing in the Motor Vehicle Act is the provision that they shall be equipped with a front lamp and a red light." But with no governing legislation to guide it, the court was left to its own reasoning. The justices deplored "the necessity of applying rules of the common law to bicyclists while the operators of nearly all other vehicles are governed by the Motor Vehicle Act; but it is the duty of the court merely to declare the law, not to amend it." There was a solution, urged the justices: "If, in its wisdom, it is so minded, the legislature could . . . include bicycles within the meaning of the term 'vehicle.'"[51]

A court in New Jersey had a similar problem reconciling the state's new motor vehicle act with reality in 1933. Was a bicycle a vehicle or merely a device? "It is true that the definition of a 'vehicle'" in the state law excluded "devices moved by human power," reasoned the court. "A bicycle is of course moved by human power. Whether the legislature regarded it as a 'device' is not so clear." Based on that confusion, and on observable reality, the court thought the legislation's language had to be set aside: "Whether a bicycle be a vehicle within the definition, it is clear that it is entitled to use public highways like other 'devices' which are 'vehicles,' and it would be idle, we think, to say that a bicycle is not controlled by the general regulations concerning vehicles."[52]

Relegated to second-class status, bicycles were increasingly controlled by a new breed of traffic laws having to do with "impeding" the forward progress of other road users. The 1930 UVC declared flatly that "it shall be unlawful for any person unnecessarily to drive at such a slow speed as to impede or block the normal and reasonable movement of traffic," with minor exceptions.[53] The word *unnecessarily* here was open to interpretation, leading some to argue that if wagons and bicycles were going as fast as they could, their operators were not impeding others. But others thought that any obstruction that slowed the auto was unnecessary. A 1934 revision specified that this edict applied to motor vehicles impeding other motor vehicles, but the original language had already appeared in many state codes and lent support to the movement to push bicycles out of automobile travel lanes and cap their numbers to limit the chance that they could block faster traffic. The 1938 revision of the UVC specified that bicycles did not have full access to the entirety of the road: "Persons riding bicycles upon a roadway shall not ride more than two abreast," and that furthermore, they "shall not impede the normal and reasonable movement of traffic and, on a laned roadway, shall ride within a single lane." In some interpretations, bicycles were thus not traffic but an impediment to it. The newly created lanes were not even meant for them: by 1944, a new addition to the UVC declared that bicyclists "shall ride as near to the right side of the roadway as practicable, exercising due care when passing a standing vehicle or one proceeding in the same direction."[54] While lawyers would log many billable hours in the coming decades debating the terms *practicable* and *due care*, the import of the UVC and subsequent state laws was clear: bicycles were not equal inhabitants of the roadway, and they were to be shunted toward the side, out of the way of more worthy road users.

Despite the MTO's desire to push them there, bicycles were not welcome on the sidewalks. The BSA noted the strangeness of this marginal state: "The careful cyclist yields to pedestrians on the sidewalk as a matter of courtesy and law observance. He yields to motor vehicles on the highway as a matter of self-protection. This may sound like the cyclist got the worst of it both ways—but it is the only safe thing to do." Pedestrians and bicyclists now cowered together, pushed out of the path of heavier and faster travelers. Both were discounted as valid users of the road; just as the campaign against "jaywalking" had diminished the rights of walkers to the public street, declaring bicycles as risky threatened to erase their presence as well. In passing, a 1919 sociology textbook could simply declare that "the bicycle is a dangerous conveyance in large city traffic."[55]

Bicyclists lost this battle because they were outgunned by a power bloc of traffic engineers, increasingly powerful municipalities, and automobile trade groups—"a large, self-reinforcing, international, professional community." In drafting the MTO, government and business worked to advance one vision of transportation's future. Policy analysts describe this sort of alliance as an "iron triangle" consisting of interest groups, regulatory agencies, and elected representatives locked into a shared worldview. Their vision of the future was of personal automobiles for transport, bicycles for recreation, and limited public transit only where absolutely necessary.[56]

BICYCLING AFTER THE BOOM

Some Americans continued to ride bicycles even after the 1890s fad had dissipated. But their presence has been easy for historians to overlook for two reasons. First, practical cycling in the United States was minimal in comparison to Europe, where urban transportation on two wheels remained important. Second, practical cycling in the early twentieth century is difficult to document in the United States: the conspicuous consumption and enthusiasm of the 1890s recreational boom generated copious published accounts from excited upper-class participants, but very few accounts of workaday bicycle commuting in the early twentieth century were recorded by journalists, novelists, politicians, or the riders themselves. Yet even if they were beneath comment, the riders were still there. As one observer put it in 1919, "Today bicycling has its place. The young, the strong, those too poor to own motor cars, ride bicycles." Telling the story of these diverse groups requires the methods of social and cultural historians: finding scattered evidence in demography, film, photographs, and ephemeral sources that document the experiences of those who are not privileged to write their own histories.[57]

Adult Bicycle Commuting

A remarkable film from 1899 captures the continuation of bicycle commuting. It shows nearly a hundred employees of the Detroit drug firm Parke-Davis leaving work—on bicycles. Upright women in dresses and high-collared white shirts make up a surprising number of the bicycle commuters, mixed in among men in suits, ties, and hats. A few scorchers whiz through the crowd, their handlebars turned downward for optimal aerodynamics. There are no cars or horse-drawn vehicles for the commuting employees; only pedestrians and cyclists pass the camera.[58]

As recreational biking faded at the turn of the century, cycle commuters like those in Detroit continued to ride. "Cycling has become a utility and not a pleasure," wrote a Chicago newspaper in 1899, with one commentator echoing the sentiment: "Bicycles are now a convenience, not a machine for racing, as they were originally." One observer noted a decade and a half later that bikes were increasingly regarded "as a commercial vehicle and as a utility rather than a luxury," and "the bicycle has disappeared altogether as a sporting vehicle." A sociology textbook agreed, declaring that "by 1915, the bicycle was only a business conveyance for men and a sport for boys."[59]

Various attempts were made to count bicycle commuters. To settle a bet, several Chicagoans set out in 1896 to count the number of cyclists heading to work in the morning. The group found that more than four thousand Chicagoans were commuting on bicycles, and another count in 1898 yielded more than ten thousand. "No better evidence of the utilitarian purposes to which the bicycles today applied is perhaps possible than the ocular proof offered every morning on the boulevards of Chicago," declared the *Chicago Daily Tribune*. If the Chicago sample was representative of the rest of the nation, "then from out the breadth and length of the land . . . a vast army, 150,000 strong, is daily urging, between the hours of 6 and 9 every morning, its [bicycles] citywards."[60]

In 1910, the Minneapolis city engineer, conducting his own head count, found that 1,258 cyclists passed a single busy downtown intersection on one pleasant day in July, and he counted an average of 669 cyclists per day during twelve months of observations. Although this figure was a fraction of the nearly three thousand horse-drawn wagons that passed the same point, it was only two hundred less than the average number of automobiles.[61] Visual evidence also captures otherwise undocumented commuting: at the National Cash Register factory in Dayton, Ohio, the company built a shed just inside its gates to accommodate bicycle commuters, and hat- and suit-wearing employees were photographed in 1902, presumably mounting their rides for home.

Columbia, a manufacturer of top-of-the-line bicycles in the golden age of recreational cycling, tried to change with the times. The company's 1910 catalog noted the shift, introducing "a bicycle specifically designed throughout for everyday hard, practical service," in response to "an extensive demand during the past three

years for a bicycle possessing greater strength and durability than the ordinary pleasure machine." The 1911 catalog echoed the theme: "As a vehicle of daily use, and as a saver of time and carfares for those who would otherwise ride in the street car, there is nothing that gives so much return for a moderate investment as the bicycle." It was an early business case for cycling: "Many are the occupations in which it can be put to practical everyday use. A great army of men and women daily ride to and from the store, factory and office; by its means policemen cover long beats and are employed in a variety of service; the letter car-

Figure 3.1. Bicycle commuters in 1902. Homeward-bound employees, dressed for white-collar work and sporting pants clips, mount up outside company-provided bicycle parking at National Cash Register in Dayton, Ohio. In the bike barn behind them, notices declare that the lower rack is reserved for female employees. Detail of LC-DIG-det-4a20572, Library of Congress Prints and Photographs Division.

TI 48-41

Figure 3.2. In the 1919 silent comedy *Bill Henry*, the actor Charles Ray portrays Bill Henry Jenkins, who depends on his bicycle for his work as a rural door-to-door salesman. Although less prominent than the recreational cycling of the 1890s, adult cycling continued into the new century for commerce and transportation as well as recreation and was occasionally portrayed in vaudeville and film for comic effect. WHS-90296, Wisconsin Center for Film and Theater Research.

rier finds his long route a comparatively easy matter to cover; telephone and telegraph lineman quickly and more easily reach the scene of their work; and thousands of boys on bicycles give to merchants the most economical of any quick delivery service." To serve that metaphorical army, Columbia offered the "Pope Daily Service" and the "Pope Messenger Special," both named after the company's founder. The trade publication *Motorcycling and Bicycling* documented these practical uses, as in the 1915 photograph of four heavy-duty tricycles sold to the Chicago Telephone Company in Joliet for the use of linesmen.[62]

On Time

A million workers make the trip to and from work a pleasure and recreation by Riding a Bicycle.
Do you?

She live in the clean, quiet suburbs where living costs are less, and let their wheels save their car fare. They arrive *On Time.*

Do you?

They earn more money because the healthful exercise of riding enables them to do better work and more of it.

Do you?

RIDE A BICYCLE

Figure 3.3. As a part of its "Ride a Bicycle" campaign, the United Cycle Trade Directorate produced this 1919 advertisement directed at upwardly mobile bicycle commuters and reproduced it in the organization's third annual report. Other ads in the series targeted delivery boys, fashionable college students, and respectable middle-class homemakers, attempting to distinguish new uses of the bike from those of the 1890s golden age with the line "This time it is not a fad, it is a utility."

Scattered advertising and films demonstrate that some Americans continued to commute by bicycle for the rest of the decade. The 1919 silent film *Bill Henry* featured a character with a practical use for the bike: a small-town innocent selling electric vibrators (a modern technology ostensibly intended to "relieve sore muscles") door to door. His entrepreneurial spirit is temporarily crushed when the bicycle is destroyed, but the bootstrap theme eventually wins out in that film and elsewhere. "RIDE a bicycle to and from work and you not only are assured that you can save money but all the while you are building up health," enthused a 1919 Connecticut newspaper advertisement targeting the working class. Differentiating these practical applications of cycling from the recreational boom of the 1890s was a major advertising goal: "This time it is not a fad; it is a utility," declared an ad from the United Cycle Trade Directorate. Another advertisement in the same series directly targeted commuters. The illustration shows a smiling and nattily dressed young man with neatly knotted tie, three-piece suit, and soft cap, wheeling his bike into work to clock in. Through an open door, the boss cocks an ear to his punctual bicycling employees. Perhaps the ads worked; the U.S. Tariff Commission observed in 1921 that "there has remained a steady demand for the bicycle as a utility, widely used as a means of cheap transportation by laboring people and by boys."[63]

Bikes in Battles

Bicycles also found practical uses in the armed forces. Military planners repeatedly experimented with the bike as a replacement for the cavalry horse, at least for scouting functions. A signals officer in the Connecticut National Guard reported in 1896 that "the bicycles have been taken by the corps over hills and mountains, through woods, thicket, sand, newly cleared tracts, and the troops have with them forded rivers, crossed marshes, ridden in cart paths and pastures, on shell beach and on railroad tracks."[64] Later that year one expedition experimented with "Kola-nut" caffeine pills to help them ride 1,142 miles from Omaha to Chicago and back. "I feel confident that an average of fifty (50) miles per day; for an indefinite number of days, can be counted on, and twice that for a forced march," reported the optimistic and probably over-caffeinated lieutenant leading the three-man team.[65] But that adventure was insignificant when compared to the epic two-thousand-mile overland trip from Montana to Missouri undertaken by twenty African American soldiers in 1897. The infantrymen who did the actual pedaling were marginalized within the military: no account of the trip in their words exists, and the soldiers were driven to the edge of endurance in a way that would never have been attempted with white soldiers. Their expedition was a grueling and lonely trip, captured in their white officer's words: "In mud

and rain, we were plodding along one after another, rolling our wheels up hills and with much care riding down slippery hills. Every once in a while we would strike an Indian cabin and the dogs' barking would announce our approach, while the occupants would run to the door and gaze at us. Our shoes were filled with mud and it was very difficult to keep our feet on the muddy pedals."[66]

Despite this proof of concept, the bicycle did take not take the military by storm. This did not stop dozens of civilians from promoting the idea of bicycles in war to the adjutant general of the army in the coming decades. At the outset of the Spanish American War, at the height

Figure 3.4. Soldiers of the Twenty-Fifth Infantry Division pose with their fully loaded bikes on an eight-hundred-mile trip to Yellowstone Park in 1896, which they followed the next year with a two-thousand-mile trek from Montana to Missouri. Countless advocates experimented with the bicycle in military applications, and bicycles were in fact used by many armies in World War I, but the bicyclist and the soldier were never really connected in the American popular consciousness. National Archives RG 111 SC (88516).

of the bicycle craze, one Minnesota man volunteered to form an entire company of bicyclists; three days later a Pennsylvanian did the same. In 1917, an officer serving in World War I wrote to the adjutant general's office recommending that engineers deployed "for service in France for whom horses are not provided, be equipped with [bicycles] of general design used in French Army."[67] Despite these entreaties, and despite the fact that many armies employed bicycles in the early twentieth century, the occasional image of bicycling soldiers did not influence Americans to associate the bicycle with adult masculinity or practical weapons of war.

AMERICAN EXCEPTIONALISM

While commuters and utility riding persisted in the United States, the technology of bicycling diverged from European design. In the late nineteenth, cycling technology had been similar on both sides of the Atlantic, featuring pneumatic tires on chain-driven safety bicycles with a single fixed gear. Lightweight frames were valued by recreational cyclists. But in the new century, European innovations meant that the technology diverged: by 1921, the federal government could observe that "the British bicycle is usually a higher developed machine than the American; it often has or two or three speed transmission, two hand brakes, chains and gears protected by guards, and is of the highest quality of workmanship." American boys and adult laborers weren't interested in these refinements, according to the U.S. Tariff Commission: "These machines, of considerably higher price, do not find a market here, where such refinements would be looked upon rather unfavorably by the class which uses bicycles." Protected from imports by a steep tariff, American manufacturers increasingly produced comparatively heavy bikes, usually equipped with just a single speed and some version of a coaster brake (applied by turning the pedals backward).[68]

These simple, durable, heavy bikes eventually came to mimic motor vehicles. By 1934, Columbia was advertising "just the slickest thing you ever saw on two wheels," a bike that sounded more like a motorcycle or a car. Its "balloon tires, electric lights and horn, large stream lined tank and luggage carrier" pointlessly mimicked cars and motorcycles: obviously no bicycle actually needs gas tanks, streamlined or otherwise. They were instead signifiers of desirable automobility.[69]

With adults embracing the personal automobile, bicycling in America became increasingly associated with childhood. Children were the sole reliable market, as *Motorcycling and Bicycling* pointed out in 1915: "EVERY boy and girl of ten years and upwards is a bicycle prospect. It is the natural vehicle for the adolescent period between ten and sixteen." The bicycle industry was conflicted on this point: although it relied on a booming youth market and produced bicycles and advertising that featured kids on bikes, it still embarked on various sales campaigns to recapture adults. *Motorcycling and Bicycling* opined that although many young bikers would be lost to "the universal spirit of the age which demands motor vehicles" after they reached the age of sixteen, there was still hope. Somewhat plaintively, the magazine insisted that "myriads of grown-up people find health and recreation in the use of the bicycle and others find it indispensable in going to and from their daily business."[70] It is clear that whereas society found it normal for a child to be on a bike, seeing "grown-up people" on two wheels required explanation.

The bicycle industry had mixed opinions about this association. In 1920, the CTA tried to sell bicycles to both boys and adults at the same time; spring ads were placed in *Collier's, American Magazine* (whose readers the CTA identified as "good upstanding citizens who help mold public opinion"), *Christian Herald* ("great small town circulation"), *Popular Mechanics* ("mostly young men of a mechanical bent"), *Popular Science,* and *Sunset* ("folks on the Pacific Coast"). But in the run-up to Christmas, executives added the *Saturday Evening Post, The American Boy,* and *Boys' Life* to the list at the last minute. The association seemed to consider that it had captured the "boy market" and was reaching for more: "The Committee felt that this message should be directed straight from the shoulder to adults. Not overlooking the boy market so rich in possibilities . . . the message went straight to grown-ups." In an ad that the CTA described to its industry sponsors as "Helping the Boy Market by Talking to Parents," the group proclaimed, "Not only boys and girls, but men and women get both pleasure and profit out of bicycling. . . . Give them the opportunity to grow up healthy, rosy women and robust, four-square men." The Goodyear Tire Company of Akron, Ohio, figured out the benefits of advertising to children in 1917: "The bicycle riding boy of today is the automobile owner of tomorrow," theorized their ad. "We have got to make you a good bicycle tire now if we expect to sell you an automobile tire in the future."[71]

Boys on Bikes

Print advertising and press coverage of bicycling increasingly focused on boys, whether as telegraph messengers, scouts, or schoolboys. "Boys and bicycles were made for each other—the chummiest of chums," read an ad in 1925. Advertising copy and boys' adventure stories emphasized the bicycle as a masculine technology, promising mastery, strength, and freedom. By 1932, the industry group was causally linking these themes in a publicity campaign: "The BICYCLE is your best PAL!" declared an ad from the Cycle Trades of America. "Like every American boy you deserve and should have a bicycle. . . . The bike is your birthright." Another ad in the series declared that boys and bikes were as "inseparable as ham and eggs. . . . [A]s soon as they step out of the crib they reach for the handlebars . . . and all through boyhood two-wheelers are their constant and happy companions."[72] A 1930 pamphlet announced that "you will be surprised how much a bicycle will help a fellow make something of himself when he grows up. . . . [M]ost athletes, aviators, racing drivers, track stars, boxers and all others whose success depends upon rugged health and strength, use the bike now as a big part of their training." By 1935, the ads were becoming even more explicit in selling male traits: "You'll find that bicycle riding builds muscles . . . and makes for increased ruggedness." According to advertisers of bicycles, at least, "all boys should have bicycles."[73]

Businesses employing bike messengers reinforced the associa-

Cycle-logical Ways
to
Happier Days

Figure 3.5. Although American bicycle retailers periodically attempted to entice adults back to riding, for most of the twentieth century their core market was children. This 1930 Cycle Trades of America brochure demonstrates how bicycle riding came to be increasingly associated with childhood, and how advertisers sold bicycles as promoting a path to manhood. Here the spirit of Hermes, the Greek god of speed, athleticism, vitality, and messenger services everywhere, accompanies two boys. Courtesy of the Strong, Rochester, New York, July 2014.

tion with boyhood. The historian Gregory Downey has pointed out that while adult recreational bicycling faded after the 1890s, boys on bikes were paid to deliver telegrams, newspapers, groceries, and packages for the next fifty years. One such young rider was captured in a silent film in 1903, executing the type of flying dismount made possible only by youthful tendons and disregard of mortality while rushing to drop off a letter in Washington, DC. *Motorcycling and Bicycling* magazine covered what it called "commercial" bicycles through the teens, highlighting photos of "rival delivery boys in San Jose," California; a "delivery boy for the Chinese store"; and the "corner grocery special" in 1913. By 1930 the Boy Scouts of America were suggesting that scouts seek employment making special deliveries for the Post Office, delivering goods for small merchants or printers, taking over newspaper routes, or "canvassing for magazine subscriptions in rural districts." According to the BSA, "a hustling boy on his bike could easily visit a big territory" and create employment for himself. The CTA, somewhat self-servingly, suggested that bike deliveries could fund the purchase of a bicycle: "Any wideawake boy with red blood in his veins and a fair share of spunk can get a bicycle" by running errands and earning enough to buy his own.[74]

Telegraph companies powerfully increased the association of bicycles with youth. "There goes a Western Union Messenger," read an ad in *Boys' Life*. Subsidized by the company, "his speedster bicycle cost him far less than what less fortunate boys have to pay. . . . It's great work for a wide-awake boy!" But in reality, messenger work was dangerous, as a 1904 appeals case in Louisville, Kentucky, documents: "Albert Jahn, a messenger boy for the Western Union Telegraph Company, 15 years old, while riding his bicycle on Main street . . . was struck and instantly killed by a delivery wagon drawn by a runaway horse."[75]

Indeed, courts were filled with liability and tort cases concerning telegraph messenger boys and their bicycles, both running over pedestrians and being struck by horses and cars themselves. By 1916 the stereotype of speeding messenger boys was so commonplace that an Atlanta, Georgia, plaintiff tried to bring suit against the Western Union company based on only a brief glimpse of the culprit: "He did not know how he was hurt, and his witness testified that . . . [the plaintiff] was struck by 'a boy on a wheel.' . . . He 'did not know whether it was the Western Union Company's wheel or not, but the rider had a uniform on.'"[76] A 1916 messenger boy in Birmingham, Alabama, cheekily refused to give his name when he collided with "the plaintiff while she was waiting at a proper and customary place on a street crossing for the purpose of boarding a street car." The company was easy to identify, however, as lawyers demonstrated that "the boy in question, at the time of running against the plaintiff with his bicycle, had on a cap bearing the inscription, 'Postal Telegraph-Cable Company.'"[77]

Many of the legal battles over telegraph boys concerned whether their employer could be held legally liable for their actions. If they were employees, then the court considered them "servants" of their employers, making the company liable, but if they were independent contractors, then the boys themselves were on the hook. Therefore company lawyers often argued for the independence and temporary status of the bicycle messengers to avoid liability. Testimony established that one boy in Kentucky in 1918 was paid "at the rate of two cents for each telegram," or in other words, as piecework and not an hourly wage. The lawyer also emphasized that the messenger "paid for his own uniform and furnished his own bicycle which he used in the said employment, and paid for the upkeep and repairs thereon, and also paid for his daily lunch."[78] Lawyers also portrayed delivery as a boy's after-school work, not a man's career. In Tennessee, when a fifteen-year-old bicycle messenger was killed by an automobile in 1924, investigation revealed that both the cyclist and his employer were skirting truancy and child-labor laws. Lawyers representing the boy's mother pointed out that "at the time of his employment the defendant . . . did not have on file" paperwork excusing him from school. Furthermore, "the mother was ignorant of the boy's employment." Although child-labor laws prohibited employment after 7 P.M., the fatal accident occurred twenty minutes after the deadline. The court found Western Union provably negligent, requiring the payment of $13,500 to the boy's mother.[79]

Whatever the employment status of messenger boys, the association of bicycling with boys reinforced the conception of bicycles as children's vehicles in the public consciousness. "Western Union Messenger Service is the BOYS' BUSINESS with a *future*," declared one 1926 ad. The telegraph companies might have benefited from emphasizing this idea in order to keep wages down: work done by children certainly didn't merit a man's wage.[80]

This was one reason that American bicycle culture was diverging from that of other nations: design and advertising were shaped to appeal almost solely to boys' aspirations to manhood. One bike was "Just Like a Motorcycle!" according to a 1916 ad in *Boys' Life:*

Figure 3.6. The muckraking photo-journalist Lewis Hine captured bicycle messengers across the United States as part of a report on child labor, documenting children working late, during school hours, or in morally dangerous circumstances. The National Child Labor Committee labeled this image "A typical Birmingham messenger," but they and Hine may have been attempting to emphasize youth and vulnerability in their choice of subject and presentation. It shows an Alabama messenger in uniform with his fixed-gear bike, October 1914. LC-DIG-nclc-03935, Library of Congress.

"You have the style lines, the electric light, the whole snappy motor-cycle appearance when you own an Indian Motobike," which, despite the name, had no motor. "The electric Model has an Indian Gasoline tank style of battery container, an electric light with reflector, double forks, long braced handlebars—the real motor-cycle effect," the copy continued, intentionally blurring the bound-aries between the child's bicycle and the adult's motorcycle by offering two very similar product names. Any boy riding the Indian Motobike could be "just as proud as the big fellows who ride the Indian Motocycle," which, unlike the Motobike, actually *was* a motorcycle. Like its competitor Harley-Davidson, the Indian brand exploited the fact that it made both motorcycles and bicycles: a 1917 ad promoted "not just an ordinary bicycle, but one that has all the streamline effect and snap of a big motorcycle, so dear to the heart of every red-blooded youngster." Columbia's ads likewise appealed to boys dreaming of manhood: "It looks just like a motor-cycle, with its roomy spring saddle, long handlebars, storage tank, lighting outfit, [and] rear stand."[81]

The Boy Scouts of America, working in lockstep with the bicy-cle industry, contributed to the ongoing association of boys and bikes. The "Cyclist" badge was one of the original fourteen "badges of merit" that could be earned by scouts in 1910. Incorporating Lord Robert Baden-Powell's original British spelling, the 1910 American scouting handbook required that the "Cycle Scout" would own "a bicycle in good working order, which he is willing to use for service of the Government in case of emergency, such as national defence, carrying despatches, etc."[82] The badge was unusual because most of the merit badges were awarded for out-door skills and fieldcraft: marksman, master-at-arms, horseman, pioneer, stalker. Nevertheless, it was obviously popular: the cyclist badge continued to appear in subsequent editions of the guide, becoming the "cycling" merit badge in 1911. The requirements were fairly simple: riding fifty miles in ten hours, completing basic repairs, scouting ahead, and reading a map.[83] By 1919, a separate BSA merit-badge pamphlet was orchestrated by C. F. Olin of the industry group eventually known as the CTA:

[Olin] planted the thought with the advertising manager of *Boys' Life*, the official organ of the Boy Scouts, to include cycling as one of the regular recognized activities. . . . [T]his headquarters took up the idea, and followed it up with Boy Scout Headquarters persistently. It was two years ago that finally they consented to take up cycling in the thorough going fashion that they follow other pursuits, such as scouting and woodcraft. It was then that they asked us to furnish copy for this pamphlet which is issued to Scouts and Scoutmasters. . . . [T]he major portion of the booklet is written by Mr. W. T. Farwell of our staff.[84]

In other words, the Boy Scout merit badge pamphlet on cycling was largely written by bicycle industry lobbyists. Farwell was an advertising copywriter, and Olin was an organizer of the Million Bicycles Campaign, an industry campaign to promote bicycling. The text in the merit badge pamphlet bears a remarkable similarity to subsequent CTA advertising, such as the 1930 brochure "Cycle-Logical Ways to Happier Days" (fig. 3.5).[85] The association's text remained in the scouting merit-badge pamphlet until its 1949 revision, demonstrating the success of the bicycle industry in capturing the Boy Scout market.

Badge requirements were overtly masculine and militaristic, reflecting scouting's original interest in training young boys along military lines. According to the 1930 version of the scouting pamphlet, the bicycle gave the scout "the advantage of speed which makes it easier for him to move silently and unseen. His knowledge of the country surrounding his home town is greater. . . . He can study the roads and map them so every soft spot, bridge, hill, curve, etc., can be mapped and any information of value noted." The scout could then make all this valuable intelligence "available to his Local Red Cross, his home government and the National government in times of disaster and crisis like that caused by the World War." Scouts were encouraged to play "stalking and patrolling games" while cycling, learning where to avoid an ambush and taking care to "studiously conceal" their dispatches, even using fake messages to distract potential captors. After all, noted the pamphlet ominously, "emergencies will arise." Thankfully, there

were no directions on how messengers should withstand torture.[86]

From its inception in 1911, when it described troops organized along military lines taking to the road, the scouting magazine *Boys' Life* was filled with bicycles—in stories, in advertising, and as contest prizes. The bicycle manufacturer Iver Johnson advertised its own "Boy Scout" model in 1915, the "snappiest, easiest riding, fastest boy's bicycle we know how to make." A 1923

Figure 3.7. The Boy Scouts of America endorsed bicycling as a healthy boyhood activity from its inception, furthering the association of cycling with childhood in the popular consciousness. Detail of panoramic photo from "Annual Boy Scout field meet," McNulty Park, Tulsa, Oklahoma, May 1926. Collection # 1000.017, Special Collections and University Archives, McFarlin Library, University of Tulsa, Tulsa, Oklahoma.

column declared, with the perennial hope of the bicycle advocate, that "the popularity of the bicycle is on the increase. . . . [M]ore boys and girls are buying bicycles now than several years ago. . . . A bicycle does not cost much nowadays, and bicycling is healthful exercise." *Boys' Life* also included coverage of professional bike racing, describing Olympic athletes and the six-day professional bicycle race fad that surged in the 1920s and 1930s.[87]

These semiromanticized representations of daring military scouts and Olympic athletes in Boy Scout publications depicted cycling as a suitable preparation for manhood. The prospects of improved physical fitness, independent travel, mechanical skills for future car drivers, and soldiering would continue to appeal to boys even as adult interest in bicycles faded. But this tactic had a drawback: associating bikes with scouts decreased their appeal to the general population. "Many automobile drivers despise the man on a bicycle," warned the scouting pamphlet, surely a poor sign of things to come.[88]

A BATTLE WITHOUT BICYCLES

The battles over traffic in police departments and city governments in the years before World War II were not specifically intended to exclude bicycles from using the public roads. Professional traffic engineers, city politicians, and automobile advocacy groups were responding with every tool at their disposal to a surprising expansion in a new class of road users. They were attempting to provide access and manage risk for the vast majority of travelers—those in cars. But whatever the intent, the road was transformed into a self-sustaining system of "automobility" combining infrastructure, law, and politics in a way that promoted and privileged automobiles over other road users.[89]

Bicycles—dwindling in numbers, no longer the object of desire of a politically organized elite, overtaken as a symbol of modernity by the internal combustion engine—were no longer significant either politically or legally. The biggest challenges for planners were rationalizing, regulating, and optimizing the flow of automobile traffic. That meant discouraging any uses of the road that presented complications for automobile users. Groups who might speak for other modes of transport were overruled or ignored. Cyclists were largely voiceless in this period because they were few in number, politically disorganized, and perceived as children. Scofflaw messenger boys, scouts, and kids on their way to school lacked the social capital to influence decision making.

Amid the new traffic signs, painted lanes, police enforcement, and physical engineering of the road to accommodate the automobile in the first decades of the twentieth century, almost no space remained on the road for other users. No marked lanes or signage were provided for cyclists, and their legal status was ambiguous. There were also fewer riders on the road. It is this history that has made it possible for casual observers in the present day to believe that the road was originally meant for the automobile alone, and to assume that nothing changed after the advent of the car to challenge that dominion. But they would be wrong: for a brief period, Americans were about to become far more interested in the bicycle.

CHAPTER 4

VICTORY BIKE BATTLES

The Debate over Emergency
Transport in World War II

THE LEGEND OF THE VICTORY BIKE

It is a funny image, good for both newspaper circulation and morale: a big man in a three-piece suit is riding a bicycle with a young woman stuffed into the front basket. Ready for her wartime secretarial job, she is wearing lipstick, slacks, saddle shoes, and an expression combining equal parts of fear and a desire to go along with the joke. Young and adventurous, she looks ready to ride. He, by contrast, is an unlikely cyclist, dressed in a pinstriped suit and chomping on an unlit cigar. A headwind is pushing back the brim of his fedora, making it look like an unfashionable homburg, or perhaps the rolled-brim work hat later worn by Ed Norton on *The Honeymooners*. Although he looks silly, he sports a playful grin, as if this is the most fun he has had all day. Maybe it was.

The photo, from 1942, is of Leon Henderson, director of wartime consumer rationing in the fledgling Office of Price Administration (OPA), and he is riding a prototype bicycle intended to conserve gas and other resources to aid America's war effort.[1] Nicknamed a Victory Bike, the prototype was lighter than typical bicycles of the

day, made without frills to reduce material consumption, and sized
for practical adult transportation rather than child's play. While
wartime planners were halting the production of nonessential consumer goods at the beginning of 1942, they were also deciding
whether bicycles counted as essential. Should the federal government allow the manufacture and controlled sale of a limited number
of bicycles to replace the completely frozen production of new automobiles? Or, given the military demand for steel and rubber, and
with natural rubber supplies cut off by Japan and little synthetic
rubber yet available, should the production of new bikes and bike
tires be curtailed entirely for the duration of the war?

Henderson's ride was staged on the gravel paths of the Mall in
Washington, DC, for the benefit of newsreel cameramen and newspaper photographers, and the image proved useful to the narrative
of wartime sacrifice. Reproduced in *Life* and countless newspapers,
the image of the cigar-smoking Henderson seemed to express a
good-humored commitment to do whatever was necessary to support the war effort. Months later, cartoonists could reference the
image in their work, depicting cheerful bankers wheeling their ste-
nographers about while dictating letters. Journalistic coverage of
the photo opportunity tended to end with a punch line: one reporter
claimed that the pictures revealed Henderson's "executive ability,"
since "he was able to manage the bicycle, a wide-brimmed hat, a big
cigar and a stenographer on the handle bars simultaneously."[2]

Some news coverage adopted a flirtatious tone. Henderson's
ride reminded the *New York Times* of the unchaperoned "New
Women" and "bicycles built for two" of the 1890s: "The photographs
of this occasion are not only a delight for the eye; they have a value
for morale. . . . Some of us, in riding bicycles again, will be turning
back the clock and in some degree recapturing our youth. We have
a notion, after looking at Mr. Henderson, that it may be fun."[3] Much
of this coverage emphasized the "pretty Betty Barrett" and Henderson's teasing attempts to dump her out of the front basket, as
if the two were out on a date.[4] The journalists were straining to
make their point: the bicycle had been associated with childhood
in the minds of the American public for nearly four decades. It took

Figure 4.1. In one of a series of widely publicized photos, Leon Henderson, head of the wartime Office of Price Administration, rides a Victory Bike prototype on the National Mall in Washington, DC, with his secretary, Betty Barrett, in the front basket, January 1942. This particular model was never approved for production, and the federal government had an internal debate over whether or not it should allow the manufacturing of any new bicycles or tires during the war. United Press International.

a world war—or a pretty girl—to make it seem appropriate for a well-to-do adult male to bike around Capitol Hill in 1942.

Even after the war, the image of Henderson on the Victory Bike continued to resonate as an image of a can-do spirit and home-front willingness. The Victory Bikes—along with Victory Gardens, rubber recycling drives, and bond rallies—were potent symbols of cheerful unity in the face of rationing and enforced frugality. In popular memory, the Victory Bike was more of a commemoration of patriotic will than it was an accomplishment of American bicycle culture: it was in this spirit in 2006 that the Smithsonian Institution acquired for its collection a Victory Bike, originally manufactured by the Huffman Corporation.[5]

The legend of the Victory Bike has, however, missed a lot that is hidden beneath the surface of Henderson's photo opportunity. Federal plans were not limited to producing new-model "Victory Bicycles." Strategists wanted to set national production targets for iron, steel, and rubber, with the materials apportioned among the army, navy, and civilian production; establish production quotas of new bicycles to meet military and civilian needs; limit production of bicycles to a handful of companies with government contracts to keep industry focused on strategic goals; ban production of anything but the new, lightweight adult bikes; reserve most of those for military use; regulate the prices of used bicycles nationwide; limit civilian purchase of new bicycles to those with government permission and demonstrable wartime need; and, finally, reserve the right to prosecute any producers, wholesalers, or retailers who did not follow regulations.[6]

The dual status of the wartime bicycle, as both childhood toy and strategic imperative, resulted in some strange juxtapositions. For example, in May 1942, one OPA director had to respond to a child who had written to the president to ask why she couldn't buy a bicycle. "President Roosevelt has asked me to answer your letter," Robert Sessions opened, like an elf filling in for Santa Claus.

> He is a very busy man, you know. It would be splendid if you, Betty, and every youngster like you who wants one might have a bicycle.

Perhaps if we weren't in the war, that might be possible. You have your brother, Joe, in the Army. Joe must have a gun to fight. Guns and bicycles are both made of the same metal. There just isn't enough metal to manufacture all the guns we need, and all the bicycles we want. You can see that guns are more important than bicycles. . . . I'm sure, Betty, that you will be willing to be a good soldier for your country, just as your brother is. You can do this by waiting until the end of the war for your bicycle.[7]

As Sessions's letter shows, the Victory Bike program was more than just a bit of patriotic fun. Government agencies were engaged in an undertaking rare in American history: a centralized program of resource conservation, consumer rationing, industrial policy, economic regulation, and transportation management. The goal of the Victory Bike project was to find the most efficient way of moving war workers and citizens between home and office, school, or factory. But when federal regulators attempted to manage the supply of bicycles, they faced a string of challenges. Despite media coverage suggesting cheerful unity, behind the scenes the OPA dealt with considerable opposition to rationing in general, the incredible difficulty of enforcing price controls on the used-bike market, nagging complaints and requests for exceptions, and internal debates over the wisdom of committing resources to manufacturing and maintaining bicycles in the first place.

It is this last aspect that holds the most relevance for the present day. Long before the environmental movement, before the discovery of urban smog and certainly before concerns over peak oil, engineers and economists employed by federal agencies vigorously debated which was more efficient, the bicycle or the automobile. In the panicky first year of the war, many were convinced that such comparisons could mean the difference. Complex calculations were made in attempts to assess the costs of all phases of the two competing systems, and passionate arguments resulted. The Victory Bike battle on the home front marked the first policy attempt to privilege one mode of transport over another on the basis of sustainability and efficiency.

HOLLYWOOD AND AMERICAN BICYCLING IN THE 1930s

Even in the years immediately before the outbreak of the war, the landscape of American bicycling was complicated. Bicycling had been the object of a brief surge of interest in the middle of a decade of bad news. Summarizing the sorry state of the bicycle industry in 1934, in the midst of New Deal attempts to respond to the Great Depression, the National Recovery Administration observed that "because of the advent of other forms of transportation the popularity of the bicycle has suffered a great decline." Agency bureaucrats wrote that "in order to maintain some semblance of popularity," the bicycle industry was forced to slash prices, cutting into profit margins, and "the demand for the bicycle as a means of transportation became secondary to its demand as a plaything for children." As a result, in the two decades after 1914, the peak annual production had been less than half a million bicycles, and from 1923 to 1932, a New Deal government report noted, "the decline in production, except for 1929, has been consistent."[8]

Although it was minuscule compared to the 1890s bike boom, the 1930s did witness a minor increase in cycling popularity. Partially sparked by an industry campaign to make America "bicycle conscious," the 1930s fad emphasized recreational riding for health. Hopeful bicycle advocates overreported any increase in cycling. "The bicycle of today has staged an amazing come-back in the past two years," wrote *Popular Mechanics* in 1935. Much of the magazine's reporting on the subject is more wishful thinking than reality, consisting of rewritten ad copy from brake and bike companies: "With 3,000,000 cyclists already riding . . . the springing up of bicycle clubs all over the country and the revival of the famous American Wheelmen of America [*sic*], . . . plans are being made for the building of bicycle paths along the highways," bragged the magazine prematurely.[9]

Throughout the 1930s, stories about bike-riding movie starlets appeared in the Hollywood press, where the boom seemed to originate. According to an apocryphal story in the magazine *Movie*

Classic, it all began when one Hollywood star borrowed his gardener's bike in 1933, and soon there wasn't "a gardener anywhere around that could find his 'bike' when he wanted it." The miniboom "received social approval when taken up by Mary Pickford, Joan Crawford, and Janet Gaynor," resulting in much light-hearted coverage in movie magazines: "Almost any bright, sunny day [in] Beverly Hills . . . you're likely to see a bicycling party out for whoopee and slim waistlines. In Palm Springs it isn't safe to risk yourself on the streets. You're liable to come to with Janet Gaynor, and her bicycle, in your lap." In what was almost certainly a ghost-written press release, "Goldwyn Girl" Vivian Keefer was quoted in a 1933 wire service story as declaring that the bike was her beauty secret: "I ride a bicycle to and from work because I like the exercise. Besides, with the bicycle on the lot, it's easy at odd moments to pedal about—and that's more exercise, as well as fun!"[10]

Onlookers were cynical about the promotion. One fan magazine, *Photoplay*, was certain that this was all an organized publicity stunt for the benefit of the cycling industry, reporting that "a bicycle magnate is giving a couple of luscious little blondes ten dollars apiece every Sunday, bicycle ensembles and bicycles, just to spend the day on the highways and byways of the countryside."[11] The *Rotarian* reflected in 1938: "Somewhere about the year 2 of the great depression, Hollywood press agents were running short of ideas for keeping the names and figures of their beautiful employers before the movie-going public. . . . A publicity man one day put his luminary on a bike, called a photographer, " and soon everyone was doing it. After a while, "people began to notice that there was also a bicycle in the picture."[12]

The themes of the starlet campaign included recreation, health, and an appeal to women cyclists. In this last respect, it succeeded: as the *Rotarian* reported, "Forty percent of the bicycles manufactured are now women's models; formerly the figure was only 8 percent." In 1939, *Life* magazine weighed in: "According to over-enthusiastic commentators on the U.S. scene, the sport of bicycling has just started to show an amazing return to popular favor. This is nonsense. The truth is that bicycling has never been out of

Figure 4.2. Even while cycling was generally on the decline among American adults, Hollywood actresses and hopefuls regularly appeared on bicycles in the popular press in the 1930s, reflecting both the continuing popularity of cycling in sunny California and the studio system's desire to publicize starlets in skimpy clothing. Here Rita Hayworth poses at the Beverly Hills Hotel on a heavyweight American fat-tire bike, in clothing appropriate for the pool but impractical for the bike. #3209347, Hulton Archive/Getty Images.

popular favor. Over a million bicycles have been sold in the U.S. every year since 1936. . . . It is true, however, that socialites have lately discovered that nothing is more fun than bicycling." By socialites, *Life* meant young women of the upper classes who photographed well: the story was accompanied by a racy photo spread featuring society women changing into their bathing suits during a vacation ride in the Maine woods.[13]

While this kind of promotion contributed to a discernible increase in adult bicycle purchases in the late 1930s, it did not present cycling as a serious pursuit: instead it established a new connection to leisured California elites while perpetuating an association with recreation and fitness. According to figures from the Bicycle Manufacturers Association, the boom was temporary, too: from 643,000 in 1935, bicycle manufacturing in 1936 spiked to 1.2 million before falling back to 870,000 two years later. American adults still did not cycle in large numbers. The Rotary Club summarized the differences across the Atlantic: "In Europe, pappa, mamma, and the children never forsook the bike. While in American only telegraph messengers and here and there a fun-loving youngster pushed a few isolated pedals in the stream of millions of gas accelerators, in Europe the cross-country bike race and the bicycle tour remained in vogue."[14]

Along with the numbers of adult cyclists, the technology of cycling in the United States had fallen behind that of Britain and Europe. While lightweight, three-speed adult bikes became popular in the United Kingdom after 1900, and advanced multigear derailleur technology developed in France became standard by the 1930s, "American cyclists fell down a hole in the road and continued to ride single-speed coaster-brake bicycles for the next 60 years," according to Frank Berto, a historian of bicycle technology. At the end of the 1930s, lightweight, multispeed adult bicycles were rare in the United States, and the most common design was a heavy frame encumbered by metal fenders and decorative features, including dummy gas tanks. "Most U.S. bicycles have too many gadgets," complained an article in *Life* in 1939, accompanied by a photo whose caption repeated: "Bicycles are too gadgety."[15] The

American company Schwinn pioneered much of this design, including the fat tires that supported all the weight and distinguished American-style heavyweight bikes from the rest of the world.[16] The Boy Scouts warned merit-badge seekers against buying these heavier bikes; they recommended that scouts who were already saddled with such a clunker should prepare it for useful riding "by taking off all large or heavy and useless gadgets."[17]

The design of American bicycles diverged from that of the rest of the world partly because both European and Japanese manufacturers were kept out of the market by a high import tariff. One Japanese manufacturer, Mitsubishi Shoji Kaisha, tried unsuccessfully to break into the American market throughout the 1930s. The staff of the company's Seattle office wrote back to their Osaka bosses that a touring executive had concluded it was too difficult: "There is very little demand here for bicycles at best, but what demand there is would be chiefly for American style, type and size. . . . Therefore, as to your question of selling chains here of British size, we would say that this would be quite out of the question." By 1935, fluctuations in the import duty had further cramped Japanese imports; the tariff was at least 30 percent of the value of the imported product and could fluctuate up to 40 or even 50 percent, making American buyers antsy: "They are not so anxious to develop a market for Japanese bicycles and parts if they are to assume any risk on the import duty," wrote the San Francisco office to Osaka, especially since "there is so much agitation being carried on in the newspapers" concerning the threat of Japanese imports in a depressed domestic economy.[18] Thus American markets were largely limited to heavyweight kids' bikes through the 1930s, a weakness that likely contributed to a stagnant ridership once the 1934 boom ended.

American roads were, in any case, unprepared for anything more than a token resurgence, as the *Rotarian* noted in 1938: "In Europe, where bicycles are economically important as means of transportation, special cycle lanes have long been in use." By contrast, "America's billion-dollar highways, many of them barely wide enough to accommodate two lanes of two-ton machines hurtling at 40 or 60 miles an hour in either direction, are death traps to the cyclists. Pedestrians don't want bicycles on sidewalks; they are barred from many parks." That left very few options: "Where, then, ask 4 or 5 million young Americans, can we ride?" The solution, suggested the *Rotarian*, was to "build cycle paths of gravel or rolled grass on shoulders of highways, say the growing number of adult cyclists." In other words, observers were calling for something like the 1890s sidepaths, though without the name, fees, tags, and commissions. Three years later, another safety-conscious bicycle advocate in the *Rotarian* suggested "the proper conditioning of the shoulders along State highways so that automobile and bicycle traffic can be physically separated."[19] But this call was in vain, at least in the 1930s.

The 1940 census provides evidence of the decline of cycling in the previous decade. Although bicycle manufacturing and sales increased in the early 1930s, the increase was in comparison to the census data from 1929—evidence of overall recovery from the Great Depression, not a return to a golden age of cycling. In fact, when figures are adjusted for inflation, sales of bicycles and motorcycles in 1939 were only $534 million, a fraction of the $701 million worth of bikes alone sold at the height of the previous boom in 1900.[20] By 1941, at least two cars were made for every bike. And because cars were so much more expensive than bikes, the economics of transportation were almost all wrapped up in the automobile.[21] As World War II began, the automobile was clearly the dominant transportation mode in America.

WORLD WAR II AND BICYCLE RATIONING

The demands of wartime were about to disturb that dominance, at least temporarily. Even before direct American involvement in World War II following the attack on Pearl Harbor on December 7, 1941, the federal government was already moving to manage strategic resources and to specify production goals for arms and munitions provided to Allied nations under the Lend-Lease policy. Wary residents of the eastern seaboard had been purchasing bicycles at a higher rate than normal throughout 1941. Justifying their fears, just ten days after Pearl Harbor, the government announced that bicycle production would be controlled during the war.[22]

While the bicycle initiative was just one of ten major consumer-rationing programs on the home front, it was as complicated as any of the rest.[23] Like other attempts to control inflation and distribute scarce resources, bicycle rationing was marked by continuous changes as federal agencies moved to close loopholes, respond to retailer and consumer concerns, and manage the changing realities of production. The program lasted for only two and a half years, from April 1942 until September 1944. In that short span of time, federal agencies confronted a host of new problems and concerns.

Bicycle rationing was piecemeal, with dramatic stops and starts. It began rather innocuously, when, in the months after the Pearl Harbor attack, various federal agencies announced the end of production of children's bikes and set targets for bicycles produced for military use. In April 1942, the War Production Board (WPB) temporarily froze all bicycle production and sales for civilians. Although broad hints of this measure had been made since at least the previous December, the civilian rationing order was still the most draconian action of the entire wartime bicycle-rationing program. "The order was a panicky reaction to perceptions of hoarding in the months following the declaration of war," notes one historian. The announcement declared that "no bicycle may leave a factory, a jobber, a wholesaler, or a retailer's place of business after 11:59 tonight."[24] Eventually the freeze was to be replaced by some sort of rationing system.

There was a delay while various agencies figured out what an alternative system would look like and navigated bureaucratic obstacles. After weeks of bureaucratic run-around, OPA administrators thought that the WPB was the holdup, with one WPB lawyer concluding that the paperwork putting the rationing system together "couldn't be signed before because the last man who was available to sign it has gone fishing." But by May 13, the WPB had issued the "supplementary directive" to the April freeze, declaring that new bicycles could be purchased by the army, navy, and other arms of the federal government and delegating the OPA to control sales of bicycles to civilians under Rationing Order No. 7 of May 15. The "full-fledged" rationing program was outlined in a July order. Government restriction of bicycle sales would be significant: whereas all of the combined bicycle industry had built 1.8 million bikes in 1941, many for children, the plans of early 1942 called for only 750,000 new bikes per year to be built by a limited number of makers. The only bikes that were approved for manufacture were stripped-down, lightweight adult models; although Leon Henderson had ridden a prototype cargo bike with a small front wheel, large basket, and heavy-duty kickstand in January, such refinements were deemed unaffordable luxuries when the final decisions were made five months later.[25] And there was still some question as to whether new bikes should be built at all.

BICYCLE VERSUS AUTOMOBILE

During the spring and summer of 1942, at the same time that bicycle rationing was being institutionalized under the OPA, various federal agencies debated the wisdom of committing any strategic resources to bicycles for civilian transportation. Today, this obscure internal debate can be traced only through records kept by the OPA, now in the National Archives. Not publicly discussed at the time, it was eclipsed after the war by the positive narrative of voluntary Victory Bike riding promoted in the popular media.

The debate involved a bewildering variety of offices and agencies of the executive branch. Ironically, those charged with controlling automobiles—the Automobile Rationing Branch of the OPA—ended up strongly advocating bicycle transportation, while a group charged with managing consumer purchasing—the Civilian Supply group of the WPB—opposed the continued sale of bicycles to civilians.[26]

The confusion was real and the situation dire. Amid all the difficult strategic decisions required by the shift to wartime production in early 1942, it might be surprising that parts of the federal government were arguing about whether it was more efficient to ride a bicycle or drive a car to work. But multiple outcomes were possible in this crucial debate: the government could choose to promote civilian travel by automobile, railroad, bus, or bicycle; attempt to equitably support all modes of transport; or enact a strict austerity program that minimized civilian transport and produced only military goods. Given that oil, rubber, nickel and steel were now both scarce and deemed essential for strategic needs, which mode of transport promised the best return on the use of these materials? This debate was never allowed to leak to the public, who were instead assured from the earliest stages of the war that commuting by bicycle was a desirable and patriotic sacrifice for the war effort.

While the Victory Bike battle was one of innumerable debates taking place in Washington at that time, it involved a limited set of actors. Although it took place within the federal government rather than within industry, it was, like debates within metal recycling and materials companies, kept from the public. Nor did it include representatives from the auto industry. Detroit had its hands full in 1942, as a complete conversion to military demands taxed the productive capability of existing industry and eliminated nearly all sales of new automobiles to civilians. Producing new cars for nonmilitary use was not an option.[27]

The choice between maintaining existing automobiles and building new bicycles was surprisingly difficult and continuously revisited. Federal agencies could easily have decided to favor automobiles or public transit over the bicycle or eliminated the manufacture of new bicycles altogether. Instead, the bicycle rationing program was constantly modified in response to shifts in consumer behavior and availability of resources. For example, the OPA tinkered with the quotas of available bicycles on a state-by-state basis for the next two years and even increased the quota of bicycles for the East Coast after a regional reduction in gasoline availability.[28] Similarly, when jittery consumers made a run on bicycles before rationing began, the WPB stepped in with its draconian freeze order.

In the spring of 1942, federal agencies seemed poised to encourage bicycle usage, a logical choice given the conclusions of their own internal reports and the influence of bicycle industry lobbyists. One April 1942 report from the Bicycle Manufacturers Association of America (BMA) concluded that bicycles represented a more efficient use of resources than automobiles did. Furthermore, according to the slightly self-interested BMA, the war was "forcing the bicycle forward to a position of importance more commensurate with its current development in other countries." The bicycle manufacturers' calculations of efficiency clearly favored bicycles, with reports comparing the three thousand pounds of metal in a contemporary car with the forty-pound weight of the typical 1940s American bicycle. Even allowing for six riders in every car, five hundred pounds of metal and rubber were required to move a single worker by automobile. Encouraging bicycle commuting "would permit a saving in essential materials of 960,000 pounds or 480 tons per 1,000 workers" across the nation, according to the BMA.[29] It wasn't much of a debate: the bicycle was clearly a better use of a small amount of metal and a better conserver of gasoline.

But rubber for use in tires was rapidly becoming a scarce resource, and the proper use of rubber presented a much more complex and dire problem. Before the war, crude rubber was mostly sourced from rubber plantations in Asia. By 1942, nearly 97 percent of the crude rubber used in the United States came from areas under the control of imperial Japan. Rubber was thus the first consumer commodity to be rationed by the OPA in January 1942. Since a bicycle was so light, it wore down its rubber tires at a much slower rate than cars did, and encouraging bicycling could therefore be viewed as an important strategy for conserving rubber.

These claims were supported by an analysis circulated by the OPA in the early summer of 1942. The assistant branch chief, R. E. Stone, submitted an engineering report declaring that "the question is whether a bicycle weighing 31 pounds plus the weight of a passenger, and going at not over ten miles an hour on the average, is easier on rubber than the private passenger automobile weighing 3000 pounds and running at 30 to 45 miles an hour." Stone's initial analysis strongly favored the bicycle—by a factor as high as ten—

but with an engineer's comprehensiveness, he proceeded to ana-
lyze various permutations. He eventually concluded that "the same
amount of crude [rubber used to make tires] in a bicycle goes only
8.75 times as far per passenger mile as the same amount of crude
in an automobile."[30] A separate OPA report on rubber usage showed
bicycles to be far more efficient, with a pound of crude rubber supporting eleven thousand miles of bicycle transport per person compared to only three miles of auto transport per person (with the
optimistic assumption of five occupants in a car at all times).[31]

Based on these calculations, on June 4 the OPA made an early
exception to its April freeze on bicycle production. In a press
release, the office noted that "heaviest demand has come from
California aircraft plants where transportation problems have
been intensified" as war work put pressure on both public buses
and private cars. The ten thousand bicycles released were divided
among the war manufacturers Douglas, Lockheed, Grumman, and
Raytheon for distribution to employees. Thus, as of early June, the
OPA considered the bicycle a solution to a wartime need.[32]

No New Bicycles

Stone might have thought that his detailed report about resource
use had settled the matter of bicycle production, but instead the
debate was just getting under way. He had written that "if any new
rubber is to be allocated for transportation purposes, it ought to
go for bicycles" instead of automobiles. In an exhaustive document
circulated on June 22, A. G. Richtmeyer of the Office of Civilian
Supply of the WPB challenged the prior assumptions of the OPA,
arguing instead that no new rubber should be allocated for any
transportation purposes during the war, whether for bicycles, cars
or buses. Instead, the huge surplus of automobile tires should be
exhausted before new rubber bicycle tires were provided for civilian use. "In terms of passenger miles per pound of new crude rubber, it is more economical to continue the use of existing passenger
cars than to produce new bicycles," he wrote. Completely ceasing
tire production would result in great savings in "the most critical
years" of what was thought would be a long war, argued Richt-

meyer, at least "until synthetic rubber shall become available in volume." He figured that existing stocks of auto tires, used carefully, could yield 2 trillion passenger travel miles.[33]

Richtmeyer's calculations were based on very different assumptions from Stone's. He tried to take into account not only the initial production of tires but also a comprehensive inventory and lifespan estimate of new tires, those currently in service, and tires in warehouses. He also assumed the ability to reclaim or repair tires to extend their usable life. Richtmeyer's report estimated 11,765 passenger miles per pound of crude rubber for automobiles versus 10,101 miles for bicycles.[34]

Richtmeyer's report created a stir, eliciting immediate and detailed responses from multiple offices and an all-hands, multi-agency meeting on June 24. John Fennelly of the End Products Committee of the WPB hurriedly produced a rebuttal. He estimated that "it ought to be possible to get nearly 9,000 miles out of a set of bicycle tires," contradicting Richtmeyer's estimate of three thousand. But even using the most pessimistic estimates of bicycle tire wear, Fennelly still asserted that "an automobile will consume more rubber than a bicycle by a slight margin."[35]

The reports not only compared autos to bikes but also contrasted predictions of their consumption of something new: reclaimed rubber. The "crude" rubber or latex described in these documents would today be described as natural or gum rubber, almost all of it produced in Asia. Decades-old schemes to cultivate rubber in Central America and domestically had never yielded fruit, so to speak, and there was little hope for a last-minute save now. Synthetic rubber was envisioned as a technical possibility, but development of the technology would certainly not be cost-effective without massive government investment.[36] The only other option for easing the shortage seemed to be massive recycling: either resurfacing existing tires (also known as retreading or recapping) or melting down old tires and using the rubber to make "reclaimed" tires. Richtmeyer believed that recycling could supply enough materials to eliminate the use of new rubber, but Fennelly was cautious "in view of the low results of the President's drive for scrap rubber." Considering the likely availability of both new and recycled rubber, argued Fennelly, "it would seem a shame to stop the production of bicycle factories and compel people to rely solely upon automobiles for all forms of local transportation."[37]

After running the numbers with the Office of Civilian Supply's pro-automobile assumptions, Fennelly did the same thing with his own preferred data. He came to a devastating conclusion: "The use of our automobiles is a raid on our greatest stockpile of crude at a rate . . . 50.9 times as wasteful of crude as a bicycle." He summed the matter up definitively: "There is no set of uses or combination of uses of reclaim or of crude rubber in which the automobile tire is not found more extravagant of rubber per mile than bicycle tire."[38]

More information about how wartime rubber compounds would wear was called for—and, indeed, Fennelly reported that a different agency was "now having boys out pedaling bicycles and men driving automobiles in order to get a real standard of comparison." The matter led to a direct confrontation between the WPB and OPA offices, with Fennelly directing the two sides to organize a high-level meeting to square the discrepancies. But by Saturday, following their attempts to find agreement on facts, the OPA was instead reporting that there was a fundamental difference in philosophy between the two offices. The OPA representatives had persuaded the Civilian Supply division chief, Donald Longman, to concede that "more additional miles per passenger per pound of crude rubber expended may be obtained by its use in a bicycle as against its use in an automobile." That admission, however, seemed to now be beside the point: Civilian Supply was advocating extreme steps of austerity for *all* modes of transportation, over and above the bicycle debate, based on strategic pessimism. As the OPA summarized the issue, the Civilian Supply division was arguing for austerity across the board: entirely halting the manufacture of bicycles, freezing resources for railroad passenger cars "due to necessity of pulling freight," cutting auto trips to 60 percent of prewar distances by rationing gasoline, and providing "no rubber for new busses." In the critical words of the OPA, "at a time when more transportation facilities are needed," Civilian Supply was proposing to "cut down still more on transportation facilities" while "eliminating the form which is most economical." The OPA attacked this approach as one that would hamstring civilian transportation at a time when it was urgently needed; it also criticized the WPB as making bad decisions based on limited information, arguing that "Civilian Supply recommends that we immediately stop production of bicycles . . . before it can be determined statistically by the Office of Price Administration under its rationing plan what are definitely the uses and needs for bicycles." Even while arguing against the WPB's dramatic plan, the OPA was still cautious about its own commitment to bicycle manufacture, preferring only that it "should be continued at least for a few months" until more data was compiled through the summer.[39]

Harry DeSilva, head of the Research and Quotas Section of the Automobile Rationing Branch, went far beyond his boss's moderate arguments in favor of bicycles. He wrote more argumentative and passionate policy memos than his fellow bureaucrats, including an eight-page report titled "We Need Plenty of Bicycles during the War." In plain language, he reasoned that since

> there is a growing demand for home-to-work transportation far beyond that of peace time, . . . [therefore] in view of the adequacy of the bicycle for short trips, for persons who work at irregular hours and live in out-of-the-way places, and who on account of the financial burdens of the war are unable to afford automotive transportation, and in view of the fact that the bicycle can carry light pay loads, is easily reparable, requires no gasoline, is extraordinarily economical in its consumption of rubber and is little used by adults for pleasure purposes, it would seem highly desirable for us to provide an adequate supply of bicycles for adults.

DeSilva's background as a social psychologist shaped this approach. After completing a PhD at Harvard in 1927, he found his professional opportunities constrained by the Great Depression and embarked on a peripatetic career in public policy. He appeared to go wherever funding existed for research on the psychology of automobile driving, including the famous Bureau for Street Traffic Research, housed first at Harvard and then at Yale. Under the New Deal, DeSilva oversaw Federal Emergency Relief Administration and Works Progress Administration projects on traffic design. The most prominent of the resulting publications was a 1942 book about psychological factors in automobile accidents, setting DeSilva up for his wartime position in the Automobile Rationing Branch of the OPA.[40]

With the onset of war, DeSilva's expertise enabled him to craft more persuasive and humanistic appeals for the bicycle than those of his technically minded colleagues. In a section of his memo titled "Psychological Warfare," DeSilva noted that "It has often been said that wars are fought on the psychological front as well as on the battlefront. . . . What will happen to the morale of the people of this country if the government at Washington attempts to immobilize them?" He argued the calculus of efficiency should allow some leeway to enable the populace to use their cars and bikes for nonproductive purposes. Unlike public transport, these modes of transport gave individuals the ability to travel when and how they liked. In some ways, it was a very American argument: in criticizing the communal drudgery of public transit, DeSilva was emphasizing the individual freedom afforded by both autos and bikes as an American birthright.[41]

While DeSilva examined the psychological and cultural aspects of transportation options, the efficiency argument continued, and like-minded analysts kept DeSilva supplied with evidence favoring the bicycle. A lengthy July 9 memo from Fred Myers, for example, was particularly strong, criticizing "certain assumptions made by Mr. Richtmeyer that are in error, confusing, and possibly included in his study to force a ratio" in favor of the auto. Myers definitively concluded that "the use of new bicycles to provide worker transportation will deplete the stockpile *less* than one-half as fast as the automobile."[42] By August 1942, DeSilva could declare that "the results favoring the bicycle are at wide variance from those originally presented by the Office of Civilian Supply" of the WPB.[43]

DeSilva's triumph was short-lived, however. At the end of August, the WPB, with renewed concerns about strategic resource consumption, overrode OPA's implementation of the rationing program. The WPB cut the total number of approved bicycle manufacturers

Figure 4.3. Harry R. DeSilva researching driver-reaction time for the Bureau for Street Traffic Research at Harvard University, September 1936. Despite his background in automobile research, DeSilva became a proponent of the bicycle in wartime, arguing that individual bike ownership would give Americans a sense of freedom and health that would compensate for the rationing of cars and gasoline. SF 12169, ACME Newspictures/Corbis.

from twelve to two, cut production quotas, and allowed consumers to purchase new bikes only after military needs were filled. Though the production freeze was brief, the quota of available bicycles for consumer purchase fluctuated throughout the next year. The restrictions were informed by remnants of Richtmeyer's argument about using up the existing stock of tires: until January 1943, those who already owned automobiles could not purchase new bicycles.[44]

New bicycle production for civilians was never eliminated entirely during the war. Equipped with DeSilva's reasoning and rhetoric about the efficiency and psychological benefits of bicycle use, the OPA not only argued for the continuation of new bicycle production but actually called for the End Products Committee of the WPB to increase the quota for new bicycles.[45] Although that did not happen immediately—the bicycle quota was instead constantly adjusted throughout the next two years—the OPA's view prevailed, and the federal government encouraged and supported the use of bicycle transportation as a strategic imperative for the duration. The Victory Bike had won.

CYCLING AS A PATRIOTIC ACT

The OPA's carefully investigated statistics on rubber use were perhaps not the deciding factor in the wartime bike battle; Leon Henderson's widely disseminated photo might have been more influential. In some ways, the OPA won the debate not through reasoned internal argument but by default: widespread promotion of personal bicycle transportation and its association with patriotism had already won over the public. Because cycling had declined before the war, any adult seen traveling to work by bicycle in 1942 was assumed to be acting out of patriotism. Riding a bicycle to work fit the narrative of voluntary sacrifice in support of the war.

The patriotic theme was strong in media coverage of cycling. One journalist observed that "voluntary use of the bicycle whenever possible as a personal contribution to the war effort can save considerable quantities of gasoline." The headline declared that "both for business and pleasure the bike is replacing the vanishing motor car." A story in the *New York Times* in January 1942, featuring a photo of a well-dressed female cyclist, reported that women were taking up bicycling as a patriotic act, clad in appropriate attire: "A hood, . . . fleece lined mittens and sturdy shoes complete a well-planned cycling costume for current months." The ultimate career woman was already an example: "Mrs. Franklin D. Roosevelt is among those who have acquired bicycles in the last few months." By March, the *Times* was suggesting that some streets in Rockford, Illinois, should "be reserved for bicycle traffic during specified hours every day" and that the "'bicycle streets' would be cleared of motor traffic during hours when children and laborers were pedaling to and from school and work." The national press pitched in, reporting that bicycle use had quadrupled in Chicago in the first months of 1942.[46]

Because of this coverage, the bicycle was undergoing a significant transition in cultural meaning. "Previously accepted as a child's plaything or an exercise device for fresh air enthusiasts," said the *Chicago Daily Tribune*, "the bicycle is expected to come into its own as a result of conversion of the auto industry to war production and the severe rationing of tires."[47]

For the rest of the year, cycling was vigorously promoted as a patriotic exercise: *American Bicyclist* reported that by June 1942, bicycle transportation among workers at Lockheed had "rapidly increased," partly due to a program by which the aircraft manufacturer subsidized the provision of thousands of bicycles to workers. In July, the magazine ran an article observing that "thousands of workers are now depending on bicycles to get them to their jobs" across many industries. "The bicycle is assuming a position of prime importance in the transportation field, and is certainly doing its part to win this war." By the end of the year, this patriotic language was well established in the popular imagination: "Just now it seems a matter of patriotic wisdom to start using bicycles wherever possible by employees to and from war production plants as well as in commercial establishments."[48]

The link between wartime bicycling and patriotism was supported even in the absence of actual bicycles: Cleveland Welding, the maker of the Roadmaster bike, ran a fascinating ad in *Life* in 1943. Under an illustration of a playing toddler, the copy directed: "Buy him War Bonds today—and when he's older he can buy his own bicycle." The problem for the ad men was that the company was temporarily out of bicycles to sell: "Today, Roadmasters are not being made, that's because the manufacturer of these popular bicycles is doing 100% war production work." But there was a solution: "Buy that youngster of yours war bonds today, earmark them for a Roadmaster Bicycle and put them away."[49]

The increase in bicycling necessitated increased regulation of bicycle traffic. "Adults who have not ridden for years are riding to

Figure 4.4. Girls riding their bikes to school in Pocatello, Idaho, July 1942, several months after bicycle rationing began. The Office of Price Administration halted the manufacture of all new children's bikes, but used bikes, a limited number of new adult bikes, existing stock, and new bicycle tires were still available for approved buyers, and bicycle travel was encouraged by rationing gas and automobile tires and halting all new automobile sales. LC-DIG-fsa-8c32556, FSA/Office of War Information, Library of Congress Prints and Photographs Division.

work," worried one 1943 report from the AAA. "With increased bicycle use, accidents are likely to increase unless effective measures for their protection are taken." That report, and another completed later in the same year, both recommended increased efforts to register bicycle as vehicles with local police and proposed the extension of municipal traffic ordinances governing bicycling.[50]

Even before the fall of 1942, when OPA determined that the math favored the bicycle, the narrative had already been set in the public mind. It would have been difficult for the OPA to reverse course at that point. Indeed, the debate over bicycling within federal agencies took place within broader framing that cast much recycling—both within industry and by consumers—as a necessary and patriotic act to reach strategic goals. While the idea might seem entirely logical, it is not clear that the act of recycling on the consumer side—outside the industries themselves—had anything more than a symbolic effect on strategic resource needs. Wartime rubber recycling drives were an important marker of communal effort but not a practical solution to the problem of scarce resources.[51] Wartime rationing was a difficult pill for the public to swallow: it had to come coated with patriotic fervor. Rationing on this scale was not only unprecedented in the United States, but it was also culturally unsettling: no other wartime measure "conflicted more sharply with traditional American values," according to the historian Richard Polenberg. For "a society that cherished the ideal of material abundance," he reasons, "the resort to rationing seemed almost a confession of inadequacy." In the end, the cultural and emotional impact of rationing might have been greater than its strategic effectiveness. It had the power to promote a controversial and surprising attitude: for a brief period, Americans considered automobile travel as a wasteful practice that needed to be severely limited for the greater good.[52]

LIFE DURING WARTIME

One result of restricting bicycle production while encouraging bicycle use, unsurprisingly, was an unmet demand for bicycles. To address the problem, the federal government ran a complicated bicycle rationing program for the duration of the war. This included managing used bikes, distributing new stock, month-by-month planning, and enforcement aimed at controlling the inevitable black market.

As bicycle rationing was implemented, hundreds of letters poured into the OPA from dealers, manufacturers, defense plants, and consumers. Most expressed deep confusion about the program; many asked for exceptions; all represented the varied purposes of the bicycle on the home front. Joseph Geiger of Denver, Colorado, wrote that "I am seventy-one year [*sic*] of age & have a farm and do the work myself but do not live there"; he asked for permission to buy a new bike to commute the fourteen miles to the farm. Brother George of the Franciscan Monastery in Paterson, New Jersey, wrote in May 1942 that "I would use a bicycle to carry out my duties and thus save on the use of gasoline for a car. The prices asked for second hand machines are a bit too high for me to consider due to the fact that the new article was fairly reasonable in price before they were froze." One young correspondent wrote plaintively in July 1942: "Dear Mr. Roosevelt: I have always wanted a Bicycles [*sic*]. And now you can not get one with out an order. Please send me an order." A representative of the General Electric River Works in West Lynn, Massachusetts, wrote in May 1942 that "there are approximately one hundred employees coming to work on bicycles. This number has increased from ten in the last six weeks," and it would increase further if more employees could get bicycles. In the view of plant management, "the more employees that will purchase bicycles the better, because it will aid the traffic and parking congestion."[53]

Some correspondents were angry. Evan and Janet Gawne, bike shop owners in Arcadia, California, were upset that aircraft manufacturers were allowed to provide bikes for employees at or even below cost during the sales freeze. They asked Leon Henderson to consider the "legitimate bicycle dealer": "Aircraft employees are well paid and do not need this reduction, so this seems an unnecessary blow." The Gawnes' complaint was slightly passive-aggressive: they argued that impoverished local bike dealers "will themselves

Figure 4.5. In Burbank, California, Lockheed Vega Aircraft Corporation swing-shift workers mount up at 12:30 A.M. Some of these bikes were provided by a company-run lease program; employees could sell them back when they were no longer needed. In the wartime rationing of new bicycles, military needs were met first, but employers were offered new bikes at controlled prices to provide to employees before they were made available to consumers. LC-USE6-D-004523, FSA/Office of War Information, Library of Congress Prints and Photographs Division.

become a burden, and will indirectly, if thoughtlessly, aid the Axis through their bitterness and loss of faith in their government. . . . All necessary sacrifices will be made cheerfully, but none of us will sit patiently by while the results of our hard work are handed over to people in much better circumstances . . . who have not earned, in any way, such benefits."[54]

The OPA had to develop form letters to respond to most of these requests. Gone were the days of Robert Sessions's personalized May 1942 attempt to fill in for FDR in responding to young Betty; by January 1943, a form letter declared robotically that "your letter to the President has been referred to me for reply. Under Amendment No. 7 to Revised Ration Order No. 7, school children who meet certain needs requirements become eligible to obtain new adult bicycles. . . . You may file an application with the local War Price and Rationing Board serving the area in which you live."[55]

Despite the Gawnes' anger, the OPA worked hard and exercised close oversight to make sure that industry was getting all the assistance it needed in providing bicycles for employees. Meeting the needs of the armed forces was a different challenge. Faced with the problem of regulating how bikes were sold or leased at post exchanges on overseas bases, the OPA decided that "due to the need for military secrecy . . . we are unable to make the usual investigation as to need" and let them manage themselves.[56]

The OPA also organized meetings with bicycle manufacturers and dealers—under the auspices of the Bicycle Institute of America— to manage existing dealer stock and to redistribute it from regions where few civilians were qualified to make purchases. At one December 1942 meeting, industry types gathered at the BIA headquarters provided "many suggestions for liberalizing our regulations" governing civilian purchases of new bikes. "Some proposed school children to obtain bicycles. Others advised using bicycling as supplemental transportation in the Eastern area. Another suggestion was that housewives be permitted to acquire bicycles and still another was that anyone gainfully employed be made eligible."[57]

Although eligibility rules for bicycle purchases were significantly relaxed in 1943, the overall numbers of bicycles sold to civilians were smaller than projected. Early newspaper stories had anticipated 750,000 new Victory Bikes per year. In 1943, however, the total number of new Victory Bike models manufactured by the two approved manufacturers, Huffman and Westfield, was 154,586, with 95,913 intended for civilian use. Only 72,798 new bikes were actually released for sale to civilians during the year.[58] These were apportioned to the states through a quota system. In March 1943, the entire state of Alabama was allotted a total of 1,919 new adult bicycles to sell to approved civilians, up from 1,886 the previous month; the 72,798 newly manufactured bikes added to existing stock held by retailers and manufacturers meant that just 88,000 new bikes were available nationwide.[59]

By the middle of 1944—still almost a year before victory in Europe—government officials were arguing about the efficacy of rationing an increasingly small number of bicycles. The War Production Board pointed out in February that manufacturing quotas were yielding fewer and fewer bikes to be rationed: "Consequently, there will be no production of civilian bicycles as such, and the only ones that will be available for distribution will be those remaining after military needs are satisfied." According to the WPB, the time seemed "opportune to discontinue the present rationing program" for civilians. Reports from the field were marshaled to support this point. Rationing officials from Vermont reported that "we should discontinue rationing this commodity as the present activity is not worth the trouble of carrying a very dormant program for ten months to serve people for two. . . . Children still represent the majority of users." Their colleagues in Idaho and New Mexico agreed. By June, ration boards were hearing that the heavyweight children's bikes from before the war were on their way back. "If this is true," the Baltimore office requested, "will you please confirm . . . whether these bicycles will be improved and much more substantial than the recent victory model bicycles."[60]

The Victory Bike program ended with a whimper, not a bang: on September 23, 1944, the rationing program was discontinued because, according to an internal report, the current and projected stock of bicycles was "too small to warrant maintenance of a rationing program."[61] Still, some in the bicycle industry wanted continued government intervention to ease the transition to peacetime. Since it was not one of the manufacturers chosen to build the Victory Bike model, Schwinn's factories had been turned to military purposes. In an undated report prepared for the WPB—probably in 1945—Schwinn wrote "on behalf of the Non-Operating Manufacturers of the Cycle Industry," urging the WPB to maintain some control over raw materials as the war wound down "to insure that all twelve manufacturers have an equal opportunity to compete" in the postwar market. Schwinn felt that such measures would compensate manufacturers for wartime service: "We do not feel that we, and others equally patriotic, who have maintained a high record of achievement in the production of materials of war for our fighting forces, should be abandoned and left helpless in the hands of competitors in the desperate struggle for survival in the postwar period."[62]

THE LEGACY OF THE VICTORY BIKE

The production of Victory Bikes was comparatively limited; the greater significance of the rationing program lies in the government decisions about privileging modes of transportation. Wartime rationing involved careful and rational debates over what later generations would call environmental impact, and impressive examples of government intervention in production, consumption, and manipulation of public attitudes and behavior. Leon Henderson's jaunty ride was memorable, but it was only the public face of a much more ambitious intervention in a market economy.

Wartime bicycling was a temporary aberration in the United States. As the strategic need to conserve resources abated, no significant conservationist arguments took its place. Indeed, writes the historian Carl Zimring, wartime frugality was a "temporary virtue": after the war, "Americans abandoned their salvaging ways and embarked upon the most conspicuous period of consumption the nation had ever seen." In particular, wartime propaganda encouraging Americans to limit driving to conserve resources had the somewhat perverse effect of reinforcing the desire to own and profligately operate an automobile after the war was over. The belief (reinforced by wartime policies) that personal travel symbolized American freedom fueled a vast expansion in automobile use and "created the perfect opportunity for car-related businesses to promote unlimited driving as the ultimate reward after years of sacrifice," according to the historian Sarah Frohardt-Lane.[63]

Decision makers before, during, and after the war followed the same general principle: the government avoided privileging any one type of vehicle on the road, even if it was more efficient or supportive of strategic interests. In the 1930s, auto enthusiasts had embraced this agnosticism because it allowed automobiles free access to urban streets, even if they were less efficient at moving people around than mass transit was. During the war, the system of rationing still allowed individuals to choose their method of transport, subject to the availability of materials and fuel. The rhetoric of choice was incredibly powerful: Harry DeSilva regarded it as an American birthright even while ostensibly arguing for the promotion of bicycling. Bicycling was not inherently patriotic. It became so only by virtue of the rider's choice to forgo another, preferred mode of transport. As a result, postwar Americans associated the automobile with affluence and freedom, and the bicycle with exigency and sacrifice.[64]

After the war, the Victory Bikes largely disappeared. Children returned to their gadget-laden, balloon-tired, heavyweight bikes. Even adults who continued to ride were unlikely to choose the remaining Victory Bikes. They were, by law and by design, undistinguished and utilitarian: they did not feature the names, paint schemes, or logos of their manufacturers. They were probably not very durable, and even the small number that survive in museum collections do not attract much attention today.

Once the war was over, bicycles were once again relegated to the status of a children's toy, and adult bicycle use plummeted. The wartime analysis that demonstrated the efficiency of the bicycle for personal transport was not enough to support its continued popularity. Children, on the other hand, still wanted bikes, and in postwar America their desires came to define bicycling culture.

CHAPTER 5

1950s SYNDROME

Excluding Bikes from
Suburban Streets,
Interstate Highways,
and Adult Lives

THE BEAV

In the spring of 1957, some American viewers saw the pilot of what would eventually become a wildly popular television series. That first episode had the provisional title of "It's a Small World," and it examined the adult realm from the perspective of a child, occasionally repositioning the camera to look up at authority figures. All of the action took place in an idealized suburban neighborhood. Appropriately for both the setting and the child's-eye view, the episode was about a bicycle: thirteen-year-old Wally and his younger brother Theodore "Beaver" Cleaver are tricked into believing that if they collect a thousand milk-bottle caps, they can win a coveted bicycle. Their efforts set off a comedy of flustered adults, childish subterfuge, and epic miscommunication as they guilt an unsuspecting middle manager into awarding a prize for a contest that doesn't exist. But for the boys, the bike is much more than a prize: it promises access to a wider world of interaction with other boys, traveling on their own throughout the town. In short, it symbolizes a path to adulthood. In the Beav's words, having a bike is about learning to be "'sponsible," a lesson learned at least temporarily when the boys have to return the ill-gotten prize. For the next six seasons, the Cleaver boys' lives were often depicted on two wheels—from taking up a paper route for a bike, to the awkwardness of winning a "beautiful English racing" model at a movie matinee while supposedly being grounded, to the childhood trauma of having a bike stolen.

Stories set in *Leave It to Beaver*'s suburban dreamland are evidence of the popular conception of the bicycle in the postwar culture: it is clearly a toy for children. Beaver invites his father to take a spin on a new bike but immediately regrets it: "Oh, I guess you kinda 'barrassed, driving a kid's bike," he frets. The bicycle is also associated with masculinity. The Beav wants to ride his bike to school, but Wally does not think he should take it up with his mother: "I don't know if women understand bikes too good. I think it would be better if you wanted to plant flowers or something." The laugh track swells. For the first four seasons, the bike is the boys' means of connecting to the outside world; Ward alone drives the family car, and the Cleavers' home is physically separated from shops, schools, and work.[1]

Beaver Cleaver's gap-toothed grin puts a cheerful face on a serious transformation in energy use and resource consumption that environmental historians have come to call "1950s syndrome." After World War II, Western economies benefited from an abundance of inexpensive petroleum. As one consequence, individuals, corporations, and governments vastly increased their use of fossil fuels and their by-products, building a society on assumptions of continued economic growth and petroleum consumption. Choices made in the grip of 1950s syndrome created an America based on the car and made previous modes of transport rare, complicated, and sometimes impossible.[2]

Wally and the Beav seem to be trapped in suburbia, unable to go anywhere on their own. An entire episode revolves around their asking for car rides. Wally thinks walking for recreation is fine:

Figure 5.1. Wally, Ward, and Beaver Cleaver (right to left) with the new bike that the boys earned by taking on a paper route in the first season of *Leave It to Beaver*, 1958. Many episodes revolved around transportation in the Cleavers' idealized suburb. Universal Studios.

"Oh, gee, Dad, I don't mind walking, if you're going on a hike or something." Beaver chimes in: "Sure, Dad, that's the fun kind of walking. But walking to get some place, that's no good." Beaver's annoying friend Gilbert complains that adults "sure squawk when they have to drive you someplace." Gilbert does a passable imitation of his own father's complaints about his car dependence: "Cub Scouts, playground, music lessons, library, over to Richard's, over to Beaver's! What do you think I'm running over here, a bus service?"[3]

By the fifth season, Wally's attention has been fully transferred from two wheels to four. Acquiring and operating a car becomes the focus of his late teens, with the legal driving age of sixteen or seventeen representing entry into adulthood in 1950s America. Wally needs a car in order to access the adult world, and many episodes revolve around that necessity. As Ward warns June after

Wally gets his driver's license, "This is the beginning: driving a car. Then off to college, then get a job, get married, children . . ." June blanches.[4]

In an energy-rich Cold War context, creating superhighways and emphasizing the freedom of personal automobile ownership were logical policy choices to drive economic expansion and decentralize potential urban targets of atomic warfare. Whether in cities or their suburbs, automobile use increased at the expense of public transit and pedestrianism in the 1950s. But the bicycle was again absent from the battle; as in the 1930s, almost no adults in the United States rode bikes, and thus cyclists had no political representation. As always, the bicycle was a signifier with multiple, conflicting meanings. At other times associated with high society, middle-class masculinity, vitality, the independent New Woman, modernity, technology, youthful exuberance, and patriotic sacrifice, in the 1950s the bicycle became primarily associated with childish things. For the cultural anthropologist Luis Vivanco, it was in postwar America that bicycles came to be seen "as technologically static and obsolete vehicles inferior to more 'advanced' vehicles such as motorcycles and cars." Therefore the bike was "not suitable for serious transportation but 'less serious' pursuits like . . . child's play."[5]

Because bikes were seen as toys for children, traffic laws and planning of the postwar decades increasingly devalued them, thus making it even more unlikely that adults would ride. Booming highway construction concentrated funding and engineering on automobiles. For the first time, bicycles were excluded entirely from certain public roads. Since cheap fuel supported the belief that all adults could own cars if they chose to, the sprawling designs of cities and suburbs came to assume personal automobile ownership as a precondition of adulthood, labor, and even citizenship. Bicycle-safety education focused exclusively on children, cementing the perception that only children rode bicycles, and only until something better came along. In the hands of small educational film producers rather than a national organization of bicyclists, the mission of postwar bicycle safety education was not bicycle advocacy but rather keeping children on bikes out of the way of adults in cars. A secondary concern was training children to be the drivers of the future.

But these developments were not in any way inevitable. On the other side of the world, as Japanese citizens began to rebuild their own economy and society after the war, they were coming to think of the bicycle in a very different way. Bicycle manufacturing was promoted in postwar Japan as a means of recovery and a symbol of hope, laying the foundation for a later influx of high-quality, inexpensive adult bikes to the United States that would revolutionize American cycling.

Although powerful forces were transforming transportation in postwar America, there was no explicit battle over bicycle policy for the simple reason that bikes were not a prominent part of adult lives, and no adults were fighting for their return. Beaver's childish obsession with his bicycle contrasted with the adult obsession with the automobile. Once he was old enough to drive, the Beav, like everyone else, developed 1950s syndrome.

LOSING ACCESS TO THE COMMONS

After the war, things initially looked good for the return of bicycling: as the *Wall Street Journal* put it in a front-page story in late 1945, "Bike makers see enough pent-up demand to keep them rolling several years." There was, in fact, a minor boom in bicycle production. The wartime Bendix Aviation Company, previously a maker of coaster brakes, predicted in 1945 that it would soon be producing two million bikes annually, more than the entire bike industry at the height of the 1890s bike boom. Although Bendix did not meet that goal, the industry at large got fairly close in 1947, reaching a new high in American bicycle production.[6]

But despite the postwar euphoria, sales were falling off precipitously by 1948. "The drunken spree in buying of all commodities . . . has ended," reported the *Wall Street Journal* dejectedly. Indeed, by the mid-1950s, American bicycle production had shrunk to the levels of wartime rationing.[7] The absence of adult riders spelled the end of political representation of cycling interests. After limping along for decades, the League of American Wheelmen finally disbanded in 1955.[8] While local clubs persisted, some of which kept the "Wheelmen" name, there was no national organization of cyclists to lobby legislatures, organize riders, or respond to legal threats. With advocates disappearing, the Bicycle Institute of America was created to represent the interests of a handful of industry groups, including the Bicycle Manufacturers of America and the National Bicycle Dealers Association. The group did not advocate for cyclists' rights and generally did not concern itself with specific state laws, but it did promote bicycling in journalistic stories and advertising campaigns.[9]

In this decline, the United States was exceptional. Although the number of personal automobiles increased in Europe two decades after the war, adult bicycling did not drop as much as in the United States. As the *New York Times Magazine* observed in 1949, the bicycle in Europe "is today the means of transportation used by many to travel to and from work each day . . . as much a part of the European scene and of its economy as is the automobile in the United States." By contrast, "Only in the Western Hemisphere are bicycles considered something only for the kids to play with."[10] In Britain in 1950, the Cyclists' Touring Club's membership hit its highest level since 1900. Although those numbers declined over the next decade, the organization remained politically active: in the words of the CTC's official history, nothing "diverted attention from the ever-present need to keep a watch for government or local authority proposals inimical to cycling and to rebut anti-cycling propaganda." The CTC was a steady and persistent advocate for adult cycling in Britain through the twentieth century.[11] In Japan, the bicycle continued to be a transportation mainstay for young and old alike. Indeed, throughout Asia the bicycle boomed after the war. But in America, the LAW withered away, children became the most visible riders, and the physical road was transformed to give priority to the automobile.

Excluded by Law

As bicycling declined, state laws across the nation were altered in ways that marginalized the bicycle further. These reforms did not eliminate the common-law assumption that bicycle riders had a legal right to the public road, but the increasing power and prominence of the motor vehicle led to language distinguishing motor vehicles from all other vehicles. Nineteenth-century case law had included the bicycle within the legal definition of *vehicle*, but statutory law was increasingly making exceptions.

Reflecting the ascendancy of the automobile and the widespread association of bicycles with childhood, model legislation had started to erode the bicycle's legal status even before World War II. For example, the definition of a vehicle in the 1926 Uniform Vehicle Code had included the bicycle only through a specific exemption. The UVC declared that anything that could travel on a highway, except a "device moved by human power," was a vehicle. That would seem to have ruled out bicycles had it not been for an additional provision that "for the purposes of . . . this act, a bicycle or ridden animal shall be deemed a vehicle." After declaring this limited exception, the 1926 UVC otherwise ignored bicycles and offered no specific regulations for their control.[12]

The 1944 version of the UVC dropped the exception entirely. It declared that a vehicle was "every device in, upon or by which any person or property is or may be transported or drawn upon a public highway, except devices moved by human power." Omitting the 1926 exception for bicycles and ridden animals, the 1944 revision for the first time offered a separate definition of a bicycle as a "device propelled by human power upon which any person may ride, having two tandem wheels." This separate definition could be construed to mean that the bicycle was merely a *device*, distinct from other vehicles, thus eroding bicyclists' claims to the public resource of the road.[13] In large cities, the 1946 Model Municipal Traffic Ordinance (MTO)—a product of the same effort to standardize laws that produced the UVC—likewise expunged bicycles from the definition of *vehicle*. In its first paragraph the MTO defined a vehicle as "every device . . . upon a highway, except devices moved by human power."[14] Those charged with crafting the laws governing automobiles had explicitly written bicycles out of the picture.

The UVC and MTO were guidelines for the individual states, not decrees, and the language of statutes varied throughout the country. Then as now, the bicycle laws were a patchwork. Some states continued to use the definition of *vehicle* established in 1926. Some adopted the 1944 UVC guidelines wholesale. And some, like North Carolina, tied themselves into knots trying to define both automobiles and bicycles as vehicles while applying some laws only to cars. According to North Carolina legislators, a vehicle was "every device in, upon, or by which any person or property is or may be transported or drawn upon a highway, excepting devices moved by human power or used exclusively upon fixed rails or tracks; provided, that for the purposes of this chapter bicycles shall be deemed vehicles, and every rider of a bicycle upon a highway shall be subject to the provisions of this chapter applicable to the driver of a vehicle except those which by their nature can have no application." In plain language, a vehicle was anything that traveled, except for some things, and those things would still be treated as vehicles anyway, except when they couldn't be. The lengths to which North Carolina legislators had to go to legally define a vehicle indicate the paradox of nominally including bicycles within the class of vehicles while providing ways to treat them as distinct.[15]

Across the nation, bicycles were increasingly being defined not as the equals of automotive vehicles but as their diminutive inferiors. A Missouri newspaper made the association obvious in 1948 when it called for "the regulation of the use of bicycles and other play vehicles on the public highways."[16] Like adolescents, the bicycle occupied a liminal state: not fully an adult, though no longer a child; not fully a vehicle, but not really a pedestrian. This perception had a corrosive effect on traffic-law enforcement and bike safety. As an encyclopedic traffic-engineering textbook put it in 1955, "Since many bicycle riders are juveniles and because of the attitudes of the public and the courts, police face a difficult situation in strict enforcement of bicycle laws."[17] This reasoning was recursive:

because of police discomfort with issuing citations to children, child bicyclists could easily flout the law, and thus they were treated less and less like rightful road users. When the inevitable conflicts between automobiles and bikes occurred, the crashes could be blamed on the immaturity and lawlessness of children.

Segregated Highways

As bicycles were increasingly marginalized on urban streets and state highways, they were about to be explicitly excluded from the new interstate highway system. The process began with the Federal-Aid Highway Act of 1944, which committed an unprecedented amount of federal money to existing road-building projects but also began planning for a proposed National System of Interstate Highways. The Highway Act of 1954 dedicated the first funds for this system. Two years later, with the explicit political support of President Dwight D. Eisenhower, the Federal-Aid Highway Act of 1956 created a vast and well-funded highway network that was designed to exceed demand. In other words, the new superhighways would be built even where there weren't a lot of cars, on the assumption that they would come later. The cart was now before the horse: the highway would create new traffic flows rather than respond to existing patterns of use.[18]

The mid-twentieth-century interstate highway system was the first legally segregated public road. In the late nineteenth century, legislative attempts to exclude bicycles from public roads had mostly failed in the courts, and successes were limited to privately owned or managed toll roads. Except in rare instances where no alternative route existed, the interstate denied access to several types of vehicles that could not maintain the mandated minimum speeds, including motor scooters, farm tractors, and bicycles. Unlike all other previous public roads, the postwar interstate highway system would consist of "controlled access" roads, meaning that both their users and their connections to abutting property would be limited by law. The farmer and the cyclist—for whom the Good Roads movement had built state highways in the early twentieth century—were both excluded from the interstate system by midcentury.

This was a fundamental departure from the existing rules of the road, and it required some legal jujitsu to get around the commons philosophy that a road could make demands on public funds only when it allowed equal access to all. David R. Levin, a federal Public Roads Administration lawyer, grappled with the issue in 1945. The problem was the centuries-old legal principle that abutters had a right to access their property from any streets or highways that crossed it. Levin claimed that the police power to regulate traffic in any way—such as stop signs, one-way streets, and divided lanes—was a sufficient legal precedent to support this new type of exclusion. But ultimately, it seemed that ability to control access to a highway would rest not on a legal argument but on a political

Figure 5.2. A child's bicycle under the rear wheels of a heavy truck in Van Nuys, California, December 1951. The eleven-year-old victim, Billy Snell, has already been taken away by ambulance; his mother and nine-year-old brother look on in this *Los Angeles Examiner* photo. EXM-N-9406–021–3, University of Southern California Libraries Special Collections.

one: "No one can doubt any longer that we need to control access to some of our streets and highways," wrote Levin, "to accommodate the free movement of large numbers of motor vehicles safely and conveniently." The new highway was a legally distinct concept, something that Ross De Witt Netherton could look back on in an exhaustive exploration of the controlled-access highway published in 1963. Summarizing two decades of transformation, he declared that "each era of highway history has seen a reexamination of its highway needs and a reformulation of its highway concept," and that the postwar interstate system was not just a new road network: it was a whole new idea, one that diverged from older philosophies of the public highway.[19]

Many historians, including Mark Rose, Raymond Mohl, and Christopher Wells, have pointed out that the funding mechanism for the interstate highway system was its masterstroke. It was a radical experiment in redistributive national taxation, and one that gave the road over to the exclusive use of the internal combustion engine. Since the early decades of the twentieth century, states had earmarked gas taxes to pay for road construction. This model effectively hid the cost from taxpayers because the tax was paid at the wholesale, not the consumer, level. As Wells puts it, out of this tax model, "a powerful, self-replicating system emerged: gas taxes funded more and better roads, more and better roads generated new traffic and longer trips, new traffic and longer trips consumed more gas, higher gas consumption created more tax revenue, and more tax revenue funded more and better roads." Once this model was enshrined at the federal level in the 1956 Highway Trust Fund, it drove the expansion of highways, automobiles, and gas consumption. The Trust Fund was an example of what historians call the postwar liberal consensus: a broadly popular tax collected revenue from all buyers of gasoline, irrespective of location, and redistributed it across the nation through federal spending in order to spur economic growth. Because it was largely invisible, this system entirely bypassed the turn-of-the-century objections to general taxation for the public good. Furthermore, when state constitutional amendments were introduced linking gas taxes to road construction, making it impossible to divert the proceeds for any other use, governments came to see the purpose of roads as solely to accommodate the internal-combustion automobile that funded them.[20]

Federal action thus strengthened the idea that automobiles were the sole proper users of roads. As state highway departments hired more and more engineering experts and construction firms to meet federal specifications for auto-only highways, an assumption of monomodal transport solidified in the minds of the profession and the public. A Disney cartoon from 1950 illustrated the transformation of mild-mannered Goofy into road-hogging "Mr. Wheeler":

> **Driver:** Hey, you think you own the whole road?
> **Mr. Wheeler:** Hmph! Of *course* I own the road. My taxes pay for them. I voted for road bonds. I pay for the roads and I'll use 'em! . . . (*later, yelling at passing cars*) Get off *my* road! Move over! Lemme pass!

This new concept, that roads were solely for cars because they were funded by fuel taxes, became axiomatic, even though it wasn't true. Most municipal funding, a great deal of state budgets, and even some of the cost of the federal interstate system continued to come from the sources they had always drawn upon—municipal bonds, developer fees, and sales, property and income taxes. Then as now, these funds were contributed by all citizens, regardless of whether they drove or not. But the neat linkage of the Highway Trust Fund came to overshadow this reality in the minds of the public, advancing a powerful myth. As one crotchety newspaper columnist could put it by 1965, "Auto owners pay taxes which are used to construct streets and highways. Strictly speaking, the bike riders do not pay for any of the highways and therefore should give the autos the uncontested right of way." Looking back, present-day observers have called this the finishing touch of the "modal divide," by which city streets that were once filled with multiple public and private transport options eventually came to be perceived as the preserve of only one.[21]

Commuting from Suburbia

Fast, autocentric highways paved the way for suburban living, and *Leave It to Beaver* was meant to be a representation of that new world. The Cleavers lived for the first two seasons on the generically named Mapleton Drive, before moving to the even blander Pine Street. Different episodes suggested that their imaginary city of Mayfield might be in Ohio, Wisconsin, or Pennsylvania, but it did not really matter: Mayfield was a generic town in a generic state in generic Middle America. Mayfield reflected the racial exclusivity of real-life suburbia as well as the demographics of baby-boom America: suburban schools and neighborhoods were bursting with (white) children, and *Leave It to Beaver* focuses on a home life preoccupied by the concerns of child rearing. Wally and the Beav were perfectly timed boomer children: Ward is a war veteran, and in the show's chronology, Wally would have been born in 1944 and Beaver in 1950.

Built on the Universal Studios back lot, the Cleavers' neighborhood was a microcosm of low-density, single-use suburban design. The house itself was a middle-class dream, with two stories, a front lawn, a driveway, and a garage. That garage, and the car inside, was the centerpiece of many episodes. In the sixth season, the title sequence depicts the family piling into the car for an outing, the Beav grinning through the rear window as the car reverses into the street. In this suburban setting, the automobile was a necessity: the cul-de-sacs and curving streets of Mayfield had no visible public bus stops and certainly no trolley tracks. Ward needed a car to travel to work; Wally and Beaver could not walk to school but had to travel by school bus, bike, or car. Beaver's surroundings were symptomatic of a transformation of American cities that made the personal automobile indispensable.

From interpersonal relations to the long-term impact of subsidized mortgages to political behavior and consumerism, the transition from densely populated, compact, demographically diverse cities to ethnically homogeneous, physically spread out, and affordable single-family housing left almost no aspect of the American experience untouched. Present-day urban planners lament the legacy of the suburbs, arguing that "we live today in cities and suburbs whose form and character we did not choose. They were imposed upon us, by federal policy, local zoning laws, and the demands of the automobile."[22]

Suburban tract construction was a response to postwar housing demand, creating huge numbers of identically built homes in developments largely outside city limits. With federal regulatory support, along with the economic advantages of mass production, suburbia became a vast and undifferentiated collection of homes, sprawling across once-empty fields at a distance from employers, businesses, and city centers.[23]

The most important form of government involvement was financial: the Federal Housing Authority, or FHA, offered insurance to back what had previously been prohibitively expensive mortgages and eased access to capital for huge developments. In order to qualify, developers and cities were motivated to follow FHA design standards, which promoted the big lots of the car-dependent suburbs and eliminated the mixed-use designs that placed walkable destinations among residential blocks. Because suburbs of the mid-twentieth century rarely offered public transit, and cities were replacing streetcars with buses and personal automobiles, the only way to get to work, shops, and cultural centers was by car. The road was becoming solely the province of the internal combustion vehicle.[24]

KIDS ON BIKES

While adults required cars to get around, suburban children needed bikes; it was in these postwar American suburbs that the strong cultural association between childhood and chainrings was set for marketers and the general public alike. As the *Wall Street Journal* noted in late 1945, "The bicycle industry is hustling to put the nation's small fry and teen-agers back on wheels. . . . A renewed appeal to adults may come later." For the present, the industry was "not forgetting, as one Midwestern manufacturer put it, that bikes are still 'glorified toys.'"[25]

By the 1950s, the bike was the exclusive property of the children of the baby boom. A 1956 publication on import tariffs from the Council of Foreign Relations summed it up best: "Since adults in the United States no longer use bicycles as a means of transportation or for recreation, American machines for the past 25 years have been sold almost exclusively to boys and girls between the ages of 5 and 14. Some 15-year-olds continue to ride, but social custom, especially strong among adolescents, taboos the bicycle after its user becomes eligible, usually at 16 years of age, for an automobile driver's license." More recently, the scholar Zack Furness has agreed, declaring that in postwar suburbia it could be "put simply: bikes are for kids, cars are for grownups." Frank Berto, a historian of bicycle technology, observes that the postwar bike was "used almost exclusively by children or teenagers too young to get a driver's license," and that it was the focus of manufacturers for decades: "Children's bicycles made up the majority of the U.S. bicycle market until the 1970s. Adult bicycles were a sideline."[26]

Leave It to Beaver was not the only postwar television show that linked bikes with childhood. The one time adults ride bikes on *I Love Lucy* is during a visit to Europe in the fifth season, aired in 1956. In a 1959 episode of *Father Knows Best,* bicycles are potent symbols of childhood, and the adults Jim and Margaret go bicycling only in order to relive some of their youth. Bicycles showed up more often on the *Andy Griffith Show.* In 1960, Andy dealt with a misbehaving boy on a bicycle: "There ought to be a law against riding on the sidewalk," complains the shopper he has run over. "There is," Sheriff Andy reassures her. Barney Fife nips it in the bud by quoting municipal ordinance to the offending kid before impounding his bike: "You're not allowed to ride on the sidewalk. . . . Bike riding on the streets only!"[27]

The association of children and bicycles showed up in popular periodicals, too. Throughout the 1950s, countless newspaper stories recounted safety schools, bike rodeos, and kids' traffic courts, but they never reported on safety training for adult cyclists. The *Rotarian* presented a vignette on a children's bicycle traffic court from Middletown, Ohio: "It seeks to impress upon bike riders that

they are not pedestrians on wheels, but rather are controlling a potentially dangerous vehicle." Created in 1949, the experiment "recognizes that today's bicyclist is tomorrow's motorist."[28]

With such a focus on cyclists as future drivers, it was logical that children's bicycles themselves came to resemble automobiles. As one observer writes, children had begun to ride "lavish art-deco style bicycles in the 1930s, largely mirroring

Figure 5.3. Ten-year-old David Paepke of Sauk City, Wisconsin, with the new Sears, Roebuck, and Company bicycle he won for his Madison Bicycle Safety Week slogan, "No hands today may mean no life tomorrow." With its wide tires, streamlined front headlight, and faux motorcycle-style gas tank—with completely superfluous engine exhaust detailing—this was a typical bike for American kids in the 1950s. Wisconsin Historical Society, WHS-78010.

the sleek lines, large frames, chrome highlights, and whitewall balloon tires found on automobiles of the same period." After the brief triumph of functional design during the war, the bike had returned to heavyweight form in the 1950s. When asked to describe Beaver's stolen bike, June Cleaver can recall only that "it had all kinds of little doo-dads on it!" Where bicycles had echoed motorcycle design in the first several decades of the century, now they emulated automobiles: one 1948 ad described a "sparkling two-tone beauty Roadmaster with its shining embossed chrome—a big searchbeam headlight—a combination tail and automotive type stop light—the Shockmaster fork and automotive type rims that make an easier cushioned ride." The accompanying image showed a bike with everything but tailfins. The next year's model of the Roadmaster, "the BICYCLE with Automotive STYLE and Safety Features," actually had tailfins: "Chrome fenders in beautiful Gothic design as seen on new automobiles," and "an automotive-type, brake-operated stop light."[29]

The 1950s Safety Film

Because adults were not riding, bicycle safety education in the postwar years was exclusively targeted at kids, and its principal medium was the cheesy educational film. By and large, in the absence of adult riders and bike advocacy organizations, bicycle safety was taught by noncyclists. Safety films were produced by small, regional production companies that sold completed films to schools or police departments for use in health classes or community outreach programs. These were the same companies that made driver's education, social hygiene, and public health films for use in schools. Their messages varied, but in most cases the acting was poor, production values were dismal, and the focus was exclusively on children.[30]

Many films attempted to appeal to children by emphasizing bicycle riding not as an end in itself but as training for the adult responsibility of automobile driving. This approach was visible immediately after the war in a 1946 national bike-safety campaign intended to address secondary-school students "in a manner which they consider to be adult." Bicycling, however, was not really the point: "This over-all program should include normal activities such as riding a bicycle, operating a motor-bike, and should lead to safe driving of an automobile."[31] As the National Education Association put it in 1950, "Bicycle safety instruction . . . will influence the young student to take an interest in other problems of traffic safety including that of becoming a good driver."[32]

No less a figure than Jiminy Cricket declared the bicycle rider to be the larval stage of the automobile driver. "Remember," said Disney's animated conscience in a 1956 short film, "a bicycle is to you what a motor car is to a grown-up." This rhetorical tack flattered young cyclists by equating them with adults, while simplifying traffic interactions for riders and drivers alike: "You follow the same rules . . . the same arm signals to let people know which way you are going; . . . [you] ride on the same side of the street: the right side, next to the curb. Obey the same traffic signals and all other rules of the road." This Disney short was one of many in which Jiminy sang the chorus, "I'm no fool, no sir-ee, I'm going to live to be 103!"[33]

The Boy Scouts of America took the same approach in their cycling merit-badge pamphlet, revised in 1949: "The first thing you should learn *and remember* about your bicycle is that it is not a toy. It's a machine. It's as much a machine as Dad's auto." *Bike Safety*, shot in Lawrence, Kansas, in 1950, dwelt on this theme. Like most such films, it showed only children and adolescents riding bicycles, while emphasizing their future responsibility: "You are now an operator of a wheeled vehicle," declared the narrator. "You are the automobile driver of tomorrow. And good, safe bicycle riders often turn out to be the best drivers." This depiction of bicyclists as future drivers explicitly reinforced the long-standing legal philosophy that bicycles were vehicles: "Cars, trucks, buses and bicycles; all are vehicles: all must obey the traffic laws." Still, cyclists needed to know their place. "Keep to the right side of the road or street," directed the narrator. "That side is for the slowest-moving vehicles." *Bicycle Clown* (1958), possibly the most boring of all the safety films, made it clear that bikes belonged on the right, driving with traffic and following signs and signals; poor Jimmy, who starts the film being loaded into an ambulance, had previously been instructed by a motorcycle policeman that "a bicycle rider must ride on the right side of the street, just like a car."

Jimmy, sadly, thought, "Oh, traffic signs—they're for cars," and thus became the bicycle clown of the title.[34]

Drive Your Bike (1955) reinforced the theme of cycling as training for driving an automobile and asserted that the best way to ride was by behaving like other vehicles. The film starts with a shot of three preteen boys in the front seat of a car, turning the wheel and bouncing along as the car sways from side to side. Eventually the camera pulls out to reveal that they are actually still sitting motionless in the driveway. An unidentified father figure steps to the driver's side window to ask, doubtfully, if they are really ready to drive. They reassure him that they have been taught the traffic laws at school: "We call it learning to drive our bikes. Coach tells us that we have to follow all the same traffic regulations as the cars, so that if we learn all our regulations when we drive our bikes, we'll be ready to drive when we're old enough." Dad is incredulous: "Just exactly what do you mean, 'drive your bikes?'" The boys have an answer: "Well, when we ride our bikes in the street, we're just as much a part of traffic as the cars."

Drive Your Bike emphasizes the incipient manhood of the boys; the purpose of bicycle riding is proclaimed to them by the ultimate male role model, the athletic coach. As the boys relate, "Coach says we should always drive our bikes like we would drive a car, and never do anything we wouldn't do if we were driving a real car." In a reversal of roles, the boys teach the father figure. Dad concludes that the boys are doing "a good job of 'driving' your bicycles. You're learning a lot of valuable and important things that will be very useful to you when you learn how to drive a car."[35]

You and Your Bicycle, an educational film shot in Oakland, California, in 1948 and re-released in 1959, also illustrates the emphasis on children. As in most films of the genre, no adult is shown on a bike anywhere in the film. Repeated shots are framed— rather unnervingly—through the windshield of a car that is closely following a lone child on a bike. The windshield perspective serves to depict children on bikes as an "other" on the road—viewed by adults only from within their cars, never as equals. At the same time, the film instructs children to ride in the roadway with automobile traffic. Even if they are permitted to ride on some side-walks in residential areas, the narrator warns cyclists, "You must be careful and sound a warning when approaching anyone near the sidewalk." The bicycle belongs on the road and is portrayed as an intruder on the sidewalk: "If a person is on the sidewalk, dis-mount, walk your bicycle around them, and then go right ahead with your ride."[36]

The theme of children on bikes as future drivers persisted into the sixties, paradoxically reinforcing the immaturity of riding even while implying that bicycles were legally vehicles. *Bicycle Today, Automobile Tomorrow* (1969), a rare color film produced by the inimitable Sid Davis with the Inglewood Police Department and the Los Angeles School District, flatters children by comparing them to the adult operators of exciting machines. "What do the pilot of the helicopter, the motorcycle rider and the bicycle rider have in common?" asks the narrator, as a traffic cop on a Harley-Davidson and a child on a bike pull up next to a police helicopter with spin-ning blades. "They should know the safety rules and traffic laws that must be followed before riding on the streets," is the answer. Bicycle and automobile are explicitly shown as equal: "In general, the rules for the bicycle rider are the same for the motorist," intones the narrator, while a line of bicyclists follows a van in signaling and making a right turn. The concluding lines drive home the theme: "Remember, the bicycle rider of today is the automobile driver of tomorrow."[37] It was apparently inconceivable that the bicycle rider of today might also be the bicycle rider of tomorrow.

Licensed to Ride

The municipal bicycle license was another mainstay of the 1950s bicycle safety films. The word *license* can, of course, be construed as conferring the right to use the road on either vehicles or their operators. The municipal bicycle license of the 1950s might also be confused with the turn-of-the-century bicycle sidepath tag, issued by a public-private partnership as proof of payment for the use of a separate path. But the municipal bicycle license was unlike all of these other expressions of state authority. It was not required for the use of public roads, it could not be revoked by the courts, it was not used to raise funds, it was not part of the state-level traffic-management bureaucracy, and it was not proof of a rider's competence or maturity or a bicycle's mechanical fitness. It was instead a haphazardly maintained property-registration system by which some municipal governments and police departments attempted to manage one type of petty larceny. Bicycles have always been targets for theft and joyriding. They are portable, easily sold, comparatively valuable even when used, and largely untraceable. The municipal bicycle license was intended as a voluntary registry of ownership that would help the police deal with a persistent nuisance that burdened taxpaying citizens.

At one point it appeared that the municipal bike license might acquire greater significance: the 1946 MTO was written in a way that seemed to require licenses, declaring that "no person . . . shall ride or propel a bicycle on any street or upon any public path . . . unless such bicycle has been licensed and a license plate is attached."[38] A commonly-used driver's-ed textbook urged in 1949 that "experiments" with required skill tests for bicycle licensing be continued, as "there does not seem to be much value in the mere sale of license plates, except as a better check against theft." But few cities adopted the MTO's language, and fewer still enforced it against the children who rode bicycles. Despite various proposals, the bike license never became a means of managing traffic or guaranteeing the bicycle's place on the public road.[39]

Police departments began licensing bicycles in the 1940s, and the practice spread in the following decade. The police of San Jose, California, reported licensing around six thousand bicycles a year in 1939 and 1940. "Each city has an emblem which is punched on the frame," noted a newspaper story. "This makes it easier to identify a stolen bicycle." The patrolman in charge recalled that "before licensing began, the police station was full of unclaimed vehicles, and . . . an auction was held each year to clear the place out;" but licensing bikes made it easier to reunite them with their proper owners. While the licensing requirement was backed up by fines for noncompliance, it still proved difficult to enforce. *Life* reported on the practice in 1947, emphasizing both the difficulty of adult police strictly enforcing the law and the fact that the bicycle license was a childlike version of reality. "California Children Run Bike Court" is the headline of a story describing a boy fined fifty cents for a missing license by a juvenile traffic court. "The judge on bench is Jon Applequist, 14."[40]

The childhood anguish of bike theft was common enough to merit an appearance in *Leave it to Beaver*. When the Beaver's bike is stolen, a policeman is summoned to the Cleaver residence. As it becomes clear that the family cannot describe the bike, the cop falls back on an alternative solution: "Well, of course," he says, "the best thing we have to go on is the registration number." As Ward realizes his failure the officer asks: "Didn't you take it down to police headquarters and have it registered and they gave you a little license tag? It's a city ordinance, you know." Ward tries to save face: "I *meant* to register it, I guess we just didn't get around to it, eh, Beav?" But the damage was done: "It's pretty difficult to track down a bike that's not registered," sighs the patrolman, resigned to Ward's incompetence.[41]

The bike license conveyed a mixed message. On the one hand, it seemed to give the bike equal status with the automobile. "In most cities you can license and register your bicycle, just like the licensing of an automobile," explained an educational film in 1969. On the other hand, a municipal bicycle license clearly did not have the same purpose as a license issued by a state department of motor vehicles. *Bicycle Today, Automobile Tomorrow* promised only that the bicycle license was "cheap insurance, and it helps the police to return lost and stolen bicycles."[42]

In the battle over whether or not the bicycle had a place on the American road, the municipal bicycle license was a smokescreen: it had all the trappings of officialdom and could have been a step towards figuring out a way to share the road, but it actually had nearly nothing to do with the public streets. It was merely an inventory system for stolen bikes. Like the safety films of the era, the bike license effectively treated the bicycle as the diminutive, child's version of the car. Despite the earnest efforts behind these initiatives, they continued to erode the status of the bicycle, associating it with children and making it easier to dismiss.

THE JAPANESE OCCUPATION AND AMERICAN BICYCLING

Postwar American popular culture had firmly categorized the bicycle as a child's plaything. On the other side of the planet, however, the bicycle represented hope for better days and a means to self-sufficient adulthood. Because the Japanese thought of and used the bicycle differently, a different type of bicycle was built in Japan after the war: inexpensive, lightweight, and equipped with European-style derailleur gears. When that design eventually came to America in the late 1960s, it would revolutionize American cycling. Understanding the bike battles on America's public roads requires traveling to Japan.

Japanese dramatic films portrayed the bicycle in ways unthinkable in American popular culture of the same era. In the critically acclaimed 1949 Yasujiro Ozu film *Late Spring*, the film star Setsuko Hara rides to the beach with her suitor, an expression of unparalleled joy on her windswept face as the two pedal past English-language speed-limit signs. A Coca-Cola ad points the way to a more Westernized Japan. Setsuko's character, encouraged by a loving father, is on the cusp of choosing her own independent life.[43] The bicycle as a vehicle of hope was also the central theme of the popular novel *The Green Mountains*, made into a film by Imai Tadashi in 1949. The historian M. William Steele describes it as a film "in which bicycles (branded with the name 'Hikari' or Bright Light) allow young men and women to love and to hope for a new life." The film's title evokes nostalgia for youthful potential—possibly for the characters and possibly for the nation as a whole. The popular theme song echoed this hope. The film itself captures striking images of two-wheeled freedom. Riding their bicycles on an outing to the beach, a group of young adults are captured with dramatic cinematography: shot from below, outlined against a wide sky, cheerful in the sun, they ride heroically into their future.

As the characters plan their lives together, their bicycles sit in the sand dunes nearby.[44]

For postwar Japan, the bicycle represented the promise of the future. As Peter Hoffman observed in 1969, "When the war ended, Japan lay in ruins. . . . [T]he people were plunged into extreme despair. . . . [C]onfusion reigned." Writing in the American magazine *Bicycling!*, he declared that "the people had little hope until the bicycle came to their rescue." More recently, William Steele has drawn an analogy with the Italian postwar film *The Bicycle Thieves:* "In the depressed economy of immediate postwar Japan . . . to have a bicycle was to have hope."[45]

American Occupation officials in Japan, however, brought with them their own view of the bicycle: they saw it as a developmental tool for an immature nation. They regarded bicycle manufacturing as an appropriate industry to encourage Japanese reconstruction; moreover, it appeared to be a low-skill endeavor that would serve as a step toward developing more complex manufacturing processes. Because of this, bicycle manufacture and export became an American-approved mainstay of Japanese industrial development during the seven years of occupation and a bulwark of economic recovery planning for decades after.

Before the War

The Japanese people had been early adopters of the bicycle and serious participants in the 1890s bicycle boom. Rapid adoption of European technological developments and social fads was consistent with the ideology of post–Meiji Restoration Japan, and the bicycle provided a solution for navigating Japan's notoriously underdeveloped rural roads. Japanese consumers initially purchased their safety bicycles from Europe and America, but domestic producers soon appeared. American bicycle manufacturers were nervous about price competition from Japan as early as 1896: "The merchants of San Francisco have been so alarmed by the wild statements . . . as to how cheaply everything could be made in Japan," noted the *LAW Bulletin*, "that they have got the impression that all American industries were to be closed." A Japanese correspondent debunked wild rumors in the story, such as the claim that bicycles could be made in Japan for as little as twelve yen: in 1896, European imports were still cheaper than domestically produced bicycles (which had an average price of $110 on the Japanese market). Though it could not compete on price, the Japanese bicycle industry was already producing bikes in high volumes.[46]

As the 1890s bicycle boom faded in the United States, bicycling became immensely popular as a utilitarian transportation choice in Japan. Companies that would eventually become cornerstones of the Japanese electronics and manufacturing industries began to produce bicycles to meet domestic demand. Panasonic, for example, was founded in 1918 to make bicycle lamps but eventually grew into a singularly Japanese expression of capitalist production known as the *zaibatsu*.[47] Encouraged by government policies that effectively subsidized capitalism, the *zaibatsu* were conglomerates, united by a central holding company or bank, that drew on the technical expertise of government-sponsored Japanese universities.

By comparison, the automobile did not have a great impact on early twentieth-century Japan: the scarcity of resources needed to build and fuel cars, unpaved roads, and the high population density of the island nation made the bicycle a much more logical choice. The Japanese manufactured a million bikes a year in 1920 and a million and a half in 1929, rivaling total American production at the height of the 1890s boom and vastly outstripping it in per capita production. The Japanese bicycle-component manufacturers Shimano and Suntour were founded in this period, exporting components and bikes to markets throughout Asia from their factories in Sakai.[48]

"Japan is passing through the bicycle stage," wrote the *Wall Street Journal* in 1922, implying that, like adolescence, bicycle transportation was a developmental phase. The *Journal* argued that the bicycle was an improvement over the two-wheeled rickshaw cart, though still inferior to the automobile. But the automobile wasn't an option: the "state of the highways, taxes and other conditions have limited the number of automobiles in the empire to less than 8,000 . . . including trucks." Bicycles filled in where autos could not: the *Journal* reporter estimated that there were nearly 2 million bikes in Japan in 1921. Subsequent accounts reported the total number of bikes owned in the nation doubling by 1925 and doubling again to nearly 8 million (in a nation of only 73 million people) by the end of the 1930s. By that time, Japan was also the world's third largest exporter of bicycles, supplying much of Asia.[49]

The Japanese bicycle exports of the 1930s did not do well on American shores for a variety of reasons. In response to a 1938 inquiry from a Montana distributor, the Seattle office of the Mitsubishi Trading Company summed it up apologetically: "Up until the present, there have been very few bicycles brought into this country, primarily, because price was a little high, as well as the styles were not right." A protectionist tariff added at least 30 percent and occasionally a great deal more to the cost, and Japanese bikes were built with lightweight British frames. Not only was this style unfamiliar to American buyers, but the British standards for threads and tire sizes made them incompatible with American-made parts. While "there has been some consideration given to the manufacture of American style bicycles," explained the importer, "none of these have yet been offered." Military and diplomatic issues resulting from Japanese imperial expansion were also now impeding trade, as the importer acknowledged euphemistically: "Right now, the unsettled condition in the Orient makes it difficult to handle merchandise of this kind." While the Seattle office had high hopes that business conditions would soon improve, it was not to be.[50]

While there were few large bicycle factories in Japan, the many small and medium manufacturers added up to a significant production base. As industrial observers later recalled in the English-language Japanese publication *The Oriental Economist*, "Japan had 717 bicycle plants at the end of 1938, of which more than 60 percent was occupied by factories employing . . . between 5 and 10 [workers]." By 1941, recalled that publication, "most of the bicycle manufacturers converted to subcontracting for munitions productions," as the light tooling of bicycle production was easily repurposed. Transformed to military production, small manufacturers at first soared but then suffered: like much of the rest of urban Japan, the bicycle manufacturing centers of Osaka and Sakai were heavily bombed in World War II, leaving most prewar production capability in ruins by 1945.[51]

SCAP and the Bicycle Recovery

The bicycle made a comeback in postwar Japan for complicated reasons. Although Japan was officially occupied by all the Allies jointly, in practice the occupation was largely an American project overseen by General Douglas MacArthur and his staff at the General Headquarters (GHQ) of the Supreme Commander for the Allied Powers (SCAP). SCAP had multiple, conflicting tasks. The first priority was to feed the large numbers of Japanese who were literally starving in the ruins. Next it aspired to build a functioning domestic economy, generate exports, purge the nationalists blamed for wartime aggression, and create a demilitarized nation with a new, Western-style democratic government. At the same time, SCAP attempted to provide trade opportunities for American companies while quashing incipient socialism. It was a ridiculously contradictory list of goals—but the bicycle seemed to offer a path to accomplishing many of them.[52]

Article 9 of the postwar Japanese constitution apparently eliminated the military, stating that "land, sea, and air forces, and other war potential, will never be maintained." As a result, approved industries could not have any direct military application. Swords were to be made into plowshares: in 1946, Japanese newspapers reported on former bomb manufacturers who built braziers or hibachi out of bomb casings, improvised rice containers from artillery shells, and used old searchlights to make window glass and lampshades.[53]

The very first SCAP directive shuttered all military production, and many of Japan's engineers, tool operators, and designers immediately turned to bicycle manufacturing for employment.

Bicycle production seemed an ideal postwar industry. It was non-military, an aid to internal transport, suitable for export, and capable of raising foreign funds. Because the bicycles could be produced in traditional small shops, work could begin without significant capital investment or physical facilities. SCAP noted that one of the first bicycles produced in these shops used a greatly simplified frame and steering tube to simplify production and limit the use of scarce metal.[54] *The Oriental Economist,* founded by the political economist, journalist, and budding politician Ishibashi Tanzan, supported this use of the small-scale bicycle manufacturing; encouraging domestic bicycle production accorded with his vision of nationalist reconstruction. One article argued in April 1946 that under SCAP direction, "a role of considerable importance is imposed upon bicycles as a suitable sort of collateral goods," capable of being traded with other nations. The magazine noted that in 1946, following SCAP directives, nearly 150,000 bicycles were designated for export, a remarkable accomplishment for the first year after the war.[55]

Recognizing the bicycle's importance to postwar reconstruction, the authorities tracked manufacturing numbers closely. From June 1946, SCAP directed all bicycle and parts manufacturers to report their monthly production to the national Bicycle Association. There was some practical difficulty in obtaining data from the more than nine hundred small producers, who had very good incentives to avoid official reporting. The price set by the government was so low and demand so high that many producers sold them at higher, black-market rates. By May 1947, SCAP was figuring out the obvious: that "the blackmarket-makers are not reporting to the Ministry of Commerce and Industry [nor] the Bicycle Association about their activities." The Japanese took advantage of black-market demand by altering the official rationing policy to create powerful production incentives: "The Ministry of Commerce and Industry agreed with members of the Bicycle Association to sell part of the 'official' production at blackmarket prices" but required manufacturers to use the proceeds to increase production.[56]

Figure 5.4. It didn't catch on, but this Japanese prototype bike combined readily available components with a vastly simplified frame and steering tube to offer an inexpensive and utilitarian bicycle immediately after the war. Allied and Japanese leaders alike saw the bicycle as a means of rebuilding Japan's domestic and export economy. "Bicycle Technical Data," Reconversion Civilian Production 1945–6, RG 331, NARA II.

A plan by SCAP economists to eliminate the *zaibatsu*, which they saw as monopolistic, never came to full fruition, but SCAP did move to "deconcentrate" these large conglomerates. Small bicycle component manufacturers benefited from this policy, as they were "more flexible and less vulnerable to being designated for reparations or deconcentration," according to the historian John Dower, and thus "were able to respond creatively to the postwar crisis." This elbow room allowed for fledgling or recently revitalized companies like Maeda, Suntour, and Shimano to expand bicycle-component production and make their own, much less expensive versions of French and Italian derailleur components by the 1950s. Partly because the European technology was relatively expensive, it was rare in America before the late 1960s.[57] SCAP-enabled postwar reconstruction in Japan was about to put inexpensive, advanced technology and components in the hands of American cyclists.

Betting on Recovery

Bicycles helped boost the postwar Japanese economy not only through manufacturing but also through spectator sport. The innovation of Japanese *keirin* racing, in which individual cyclists race around an outdoor track before sprinting the final lap, combined sport with state-sanctioned betting to raise funds for the bicycle industry and for general recovery. It is the only bicycle racing form to have been developed outside the West, and its physical form reflects its origins: taking place on an oval track built from earthworks, it did not require an enclosed, banked wooden track, a financial impossibility in the postwar years. Its legal form likewise reflects its goals of reconstruction: as a state-controlled betting pool, "its purpose was to give the masses a healthy moral impetus and a dream of fortune," according to an American observer in 1969.[58]

In a nation where private betting is punishable by long prison sentences, *keirin* is today one of a small number of legal—though heavily regulated—forms of sports betting.[59] In July 1948, the Japanese Diet passed the Bicycle Racing Act to make *keirin* a nationally recognized forum for betting and a means of raising funds for reconstruction. Prefectural governments and municipalities could set up meets and collect the betting proceeds. Overseen by a national association—the Nihon Jitensha Shinkokai, or NJS—the proceeds were dedicated to a short list of approved expenditures. The 1948 act primarily approved "advancing improvements in bicycle (and other machine) technology and rationalizing related manufacturing industries." Among other projects, the betting proceeds funded the "Open Research Center for Bicycle Production Techniques" in 1954, later known as the Japan Bicycle Promotion Institute. In its first thirty years, *keirin* betting raised nearly 38 billion yen, or roughly $187 million at 1978 exchange rates, to subsidize the bicycle industry.[60]

The American planners at SCAP specifically reviewed and approved the Bicycle Race Law when it originally came up in the new House of Representatives in March 1948. The Japanese law was subject to approval by the Americans, and while the Governmental Powers Division of the Government Section seemed concerned, other Americans in GHQ judged the proposed law acceptable. The internal GHQ document summarizing the discussion literally bears an American "O.K." penciled in next to the Japanese law. Not so for the next proposed law on the list: the "Dog Race Law Bill" was marked as "Disapproved" by three of the four American offices passing judgment, and indeed dog racing never became one of the approved public betting forms in Japan. It would seem that bicycling was viewed differently from dog racing by the American occupiers; betting on bicycling seemed to be less morally hazardous.[61] Through *keirin*, bicycles became integral to Japanese public policy. "Japan's antituberculosis and anticancer programs have been directly dependent on Keirin racing," observed the American Peter Hoffman in 1969. In only three years, "Keirin racing provided 330 million yen for the development of national sports" while "social and welfare corporations and fire and police departments received another 330 million yen during the same period," he noted. According to present-day observers, proceeds were "to be applied in funding projects for the advancement of the public good," which could include "advancing social welfare; upgrading medical care; developing education and culture; and promoting physical education and other programs beneficial to society."[62] It was a long way from the handlebar streamers and cards in the spokes of American bikes: in Japan, the bicycle made meaningful, measurable contributions to society.

With subsidies from *keirin*, some of the companies supporting domestic bicycling eventually became enormous multinational conglomerates. Honda got its start in 1946, when Soichiro Honda produced a motor that purchasers could mount on their own bicycle frames. Panasonic had begun making bicycle lamps before the war; Sanyo and Matsushita started out in bicycle accessories after it.[63] Japan's Ministry of International Trade and Industry (later combined with the Japan External Trade Organization) made concerted efforts to export the bicycles and components to the United States and the rest of the world.

A crucial export opportunity came in 1963, when the newly

reestablished Columbia bicycle company in the United States was under pressure to replace the English manufacturer Raleigh, which had pulled out of a deal to supply bikes to an American retail chain at the last moment. Columbia could fill in for the English firm by producing American-made bicycles for the domestic market, but only if it used Japanese hubs, shifters, and derailleurs. Selling Japanese components to American markets was an untested and risky business model, but Columbia's president went to Japan to look for components and bought everything in sight. According to the bicycle historian Frank Berto, this arrangement transformed the American bicycle market: "Every one of the eight American bicycle makers went back the next year and started buying Japanese parts. In no time, [the Japanese] were selling $100 million worth of parts in the U.S."[64] The Japanese gears and components kicked off a revolution in American cycling, making lightweight, multispeed bicycles for adults accessible and affordable and contributing to a 1970s bike boom that was the largest in America since the 1890s.

Differences of Opinion

The key to understanding this series of events is the bicycle's cultural associations in the minds of the SCAP functionaries. The bicycle was perceived to be nonthreatening, pacifistic, and linked to childhood. While other manufacturing segments with military applications were dismantled after the war, bicycle manufacturing was encouraged. Just as the bicycle was seen as a premodern, adolescent stage of industrial development, American occupation officials saw the Japanese as an immature people. In 1951, General MacArthur famously observed in testimony before the United States Senate: "The Japanese, . . . [m]easured by the standard of modern civilization . . . would be like a boy of 12 compared to our own development of 45 years." Although the Japanese felt betrayed by MacArthur's words, they went unchallenged in the United States, according to the historian Naoko Shibusawa, "for Americans and Europeans had long believed that there was something immature and undeveloped about the 'small' Japanese and their 'toylike' nation."[65] This view reflected a long-standing attitude among Western nations toward their colonies and non-Western nations, and it was bolstered by the pseudo-science of race and rationalizations of the civilizing mission of empire. In the Japanese context, it linked a "childlike" people with a vehicle that the American occupiers associated with childhood, and SCAP's actions occurred against this backdrop.

This cultural association was deeply ironic, as during the war the bicycle was not a toy but a weapon. The bicycle enabled imperial Japan's military campaigns in a way that Western armies had contemplated since the 1890s but never implemented on a large scale. In Burma, in New Guinea, and on the Chinese mainland, bicycles were an important part of military success. When Japanese forces invaded the Malay Peninsula in 1941, the rapid movement of troops to Singapore took place on two wheels. The invading troops commandeered Japanese bikes owned by civilians, eventually amassing around six thousand for each division and easily picking up spare parts from the bikes that Japanese industry had been exporting to the region for decades. Historians have come to call this rapid mounted attack the "Bicycle Blitzkrieg," and a popular anecdote claims that Allied forces mistook the sound of thousands of advancing bicycles—perhaps the clatter of bare rims on roadways—for tanks.[66] Back in Japan, small-scale bicycle manufacturing, equipped with machine tools designed for making small, precise metal components out of steel tubes, was readily transformed into arms and munitions production. Either way, the bicycle was not a toy in the hands of the Japanese during the war.

For environmental scholars, the phrase *1950s syndrome*, coined by Christian Pfister, is a handy catchall for a variety of interconnected trends: cheap energy, a lockstep commitment to GDP growth, a vastly expanded consumer economy, and development of a transportation infrastructure that depended upon all of the above. The short postwar period of inexpensive gasoline "is the main reason why the Northern type of industrial society became so wasteful," according to Pfister. "The anomaly lasted long enough to effect structural changes, such as relocating firms and residential areas in a manner predicated on car transportation."[67] It locked Western industrialized nations into an automotive existence.

It was in the fever dream of the 1950s syndrome that the peculiarly American association of internal-combustion automobiles with adulthood, and of bicycles with childhood, became dominant. Yet this distinction was neither inherent in the material objects nor historically predetermined: the bicycle had been associated with technological modernity, upward mobility, adulthood, and masculinity in the American bicycling boom of the 1890s.

As the cultural anthropologist Luis Vivanco has said, "It turns out that there is very little that is self-evident about bicycles." Instead, "bicycles are heterogeneous, multidimensional, and contextual objects, enmeshed in specific technological conditions, practices of life, social relations, cultural meanings, and political-economic dynamics."[68] With all of those forces at play, the meaning of the bicycle is constantly changing, and always up for renegotiation. While there was very little public debate over bicycling in the 1950s United States, the possible meanings of the bike were contested in the minds of Americans. In the 1970s, new conceptions of the uses and meanings of the bicycle would prompt new battles, and this time they would be fought in courts, legislatures, and newspaper opinion pages.

CHAPTER 6

BIKES ARE BEAUTIFUL

The Bike Boom, Bikeways, and
the Battle over Where to
Ride in the 1970s

Before he appeared as America's sweater-wearing father figure on *The Cosby Show*, and before accounts of his behavior tarnished that nostalgia, Bill Cosby played a high school coach on the *Bill Cosby Show* in the early 1970s. It was in this role that Cosby appeared as the host of a groovy 1974 educational film, *Bicycles Are Beautiful.* According to the film, adult bicycling was back, fitness and ecology were key, and the action was on the West Coast. People were rediscovering the "healthy fun" of bicycles, said Cosby: "Getting out in clean fresh air is good for your heart, your lungs, and your circulation, and your figure." As the film shows a cyclist riding past a Chevron station crowded with cars, he narrates: "You don't have to stand in any lines to fuel up a bike, because the only fuel the bike burns is what your body provides. And you're not polluting the air either, and that's beautiful."

Emphasizing a new word for bicycle infrastructure, Cosby declares, "There are now over 25,000 miles of *bikeways* in use in the United States," including "bikeways that range from paths exclusively for cyclists, to street routes to be shared with autos." Much

Figure 6.1. Bill Cosby narrates *Bicycles Are Beautiful* (1974), an educational film that reflects the complexities of the 1970s bike boom: although the film acknowledges that more adults are bicycling for new reasons of health and sustainability, it still focuses on children. Like the safety films of the previous decades, it was not made by cyclists or addressed to adults.

of the film covers West Coast developments. In one scene, the mayor of Santa Ana, California, outlines that city's intention to build "a bike-trail system" for students to ride to school "away from automobile traffic or in a separate lane, just for bicycles."

Standing at a bike-shop bench, Cosby underscores another idea: "The National Safety Council and the new concept in bicycle safety education recognizes the bicycle as a full-fledged vehicle, just like a car or a motorcycle, so you're bound by most of the same traffic laws." Emphasizing his words, the Cos proclaimed: "National standards *now* call for all cyclists to drive on the right-hand side, *with the traffic.*"[1]

The National Safety Council was an independent group dating from the Progressive Era that was focused on professional safety standards and certification, but was for some reason now teaching bicycle etiquette. Why was it doing so, and why did it feel the need to hire a star like Bill Cosby to get viewers' attention? Why were California mayors pledging to reshape their notoriously autocentric cities? Where had these new bikeways come from, and why did anyone think that the old concept of treating the bicycle as a vehicle was somehow new? The answer to all these questions is that the bicycle boom of the 1970s had revived unresolved conflicts over sharing the public road. Bill Cosby was hired by safety advocates to educate new cyclists partly because there was no organized group of riders to do the job for themselves. Management of the new bike boom was left in the hands of disparate, sometimes conflicting groups that did not agree on how to accommodate the increased number of cyclists. As a result, the 1970s bike boom was another missed opportunity to solve the problems of managing the common resource of the public road.

THE RETURN OF THE BIKE

Observers have never fingered any single dominant cause for the late-twentieth-century return of the bicycle. They have identified contributing factors, such as improved bike technology, a wave of environmental consciousness, and policy actions. One 1972 study identified "physical fitness, recreation, and 'protect the environment' programs" as themes that "directly tie in with the bicycle boom and give it . . . vitality." Two years later, an industry spokesman credited "the renewed popularity of bicycles" to "ecology-minded young people and Federal subsidies for bicycle paths," noting that "the recent energy crisis was only 'the crowning touch.'"[2]

Policy responses to the increase were as diffuse as the perceived causes. The surprising resurgence of adult bicycling was defined as a problem to be solved by governments through a sense of crisis, not as the goal of any group or individual, and only made it onto the agenda of policy makers as an emergency to be managed. Some of the national initiatives that that seemed to be related to the bike boom—like the Department of the Interior's mid-1960s push to build scenic trails or the National Safety Council's focus on protecting children—were really focused on other goals to which biking was secondary. Concerns about the environment and energy shortages provided impetus but not clear paths of action. Instead, partially shaped by the era's philosophy of New Federalism, policy innovation occurred at the state and municipal levels, leaving a patchwork legacy of infrastructure, law, and financial mechanisms that petered out as the boom subsided.

Cycling advocates and industry actors were similarly unprepared to cope with the increase in biking. The national LAW was missing in action at the beginning of the boom and divided at the end. It lacked the useful political connections that political scientists call social capital, did not represent all the new riders of the boom, and had no unified position to guide its responses. Bicycle manufacturers were surprisingly unprepared for the increase in adult bicycling that they had been trying to promote for most of the century.

The 10-Speed in America

One cause of renewed interest in cycling was the availability of new and different types of bicycles, partially a result of a change in complicated government regulations. Since the beginning of the twentieth century, the federal government had charged a hefty tariff on imported bicycles. This meant that the lightweight, multi-speed adult bikes being developed in Europe were expensive and rare on the American market, and the heavy, single-speed style of children's bikes prevailed. After World War II, the Eisenhower administration altered the tariff structure considerably in an attempt to help rebuild the British manufacturing sector. The net effect of the tariff changes was to create a new category of bicycle, with associations of high technology and class status that made it an appropriate possession for adults. This was the design that Americans came to refer to as a 10-speed, regardless of how many gear combinations it actually had. The name just served to distinguish lightweight adult bikes that used European-style derailleurs to change gears from the heavier American bikes, which often featured coaster brakes and used technologies other than the derailleur to shift between three gears—if they even had more than one gear. One minor change to the tariff provisions in 1970 was critical to the success of the domestically built 10-speed: it allowed the importation of the necessary components duty free until 1973, as long as those parts weren't also manufactured by competing American firms.[3]

There is no better symbol of this transformation than the Schwinn Varsity, a bike with hand-operated (rather than coaster) brakes and multiple gears. It wasn't a particularly lightweight or speedy bike, but the name evoked a college-going upper class, and the design was perfect for baby-boom children now enrolling at sprawling college campuses. It was introduced in 1960 with European components and eight speeds, but Schwinn later changed the design to offer ten speeds. The bicycle historian Frank Berto declares it "was designed for the average inexperienced young American cyclist accustomed to a balloon-tire bike," easing the transition to lighter frames, drop handlebars, and derailleur technology. In its first years on the market, the comparatively inexpensive Varsity outsold all other derailleur-equipped bikes on the American market combined, preparing the public for the coming 10-speeds with Japanese-made components. According to Berto, "Schwinn's network of franchised dealers spread the Varsity's success, and soon 10-speed bicycles were found throughout America."[4]

Observers realized that the potential effects of this design trend on adult bicycling were enormous. In 1972, a California academic study stated that "the multi-speed cycles have made the bicycle a potentially viable alternative mode of transportation. To those who have not ridden the 'new' bikes the concept of bicycling is purely as a recreation or exercise activity probably based on childhood memories." A wire-service report in 1972 evocatively described the impact of the new designs: "In the heavy traffic of New York's Fifth Avenue a well dressed executive, striped tie fluttering over his shoulder and briefcase strapped on behind, weaves his 10-speed bike around cars and buses on his way to his downtown office."[5]

Steady sales of adult bikes increased during the 1960s and peaked in 1973 with 15.2 million bikes sold, a total never surpassed before or since. Manufacturers struggled to meet the demand. A 1972 wire-service story claimed that bicycle dealers were "losing money because manufacturers aren't turning them out fast enough." It quoted a dealer in Boise, Idaho, who claimed that adult multispeed bikes were "like mail order brides—they're spoken for before they arrive."[6]

Fitness Evangelists and Advocates

Along with the increased availability of lighter, faster bicycles came an increased interest in bicycling for fitness and health. Most famously, Paul Dudley White, President Eisenhower's cardiologist, prescribed cycling to adults in the early 1960s. *Life* magazine emphasized adult fitness and recreation in 1963: "There are 30 million bikes in the U.S. today, and proud owners use them both to limber up and to satisfy a gypsy urge."[7] (The "urge" referred to touring, or multiday recreational group riding.) The closest American equivalent to the British Cyclists' Touring Club (CTC) in these years was American Youth Hostels, Inc., which promoted bicycle tourists who might stop overnight at its affiliates' locations.

This trend spurred a new appeal to adults by bicycle enthusiasts. Fred DeLong explored the engineering of bicycles in the pages of *American Cycling, Bike World,* and *Bicycle Business Journal* throughout the 1960s. The American Richard Ballantine self-published the first edition of *Richard's Bicycle Book* in 1972 to great acclaim in both the United States and the United Kingdom. He advocated for cyclists' rights, presented a new philosophy of adult bicycle riding, and promoted the revolutionary power of alternative transportation. He also tried to disabuse Americans of the belief that the new 10-speeds were solely for racing and fitness. That sort of connection appeared in advertising; Schwinn promoted "a smart sophisticated 10-speed lightweight for a fitness-conscious adult."[8]

In a minor way, bicycle advocacy also returned. The LAW held a meeting in Chicago to reorganize in 1964, supported by the Chicago-based Schwinn. But at the beginning of the 1970s the group still had only a few scattered chapters, no national leadership, incredibly low membership, and no major publications. It also had no full-time employees until 1973. The Bicycle Institute of America (BIA) and the Bicycle Manufacturers Association (BMA) were both more active on policy matters. They represented the industry more or less interchangeably, producing promotional brochures and educational programs. Much of the advocacy work nationwide was undertaken by just two men, Bob Cleckner and Keith Kingbay, who worked at various times for Schwinn, the AYH, the BIA, and the LAW.[9]

Environmentalism and Appropriate Technology

Although individuals and groups promoted adult bicycling, they did not offer new arguments for taking to two wheels. It was not until the birth of the modern environmental movement that people found a novel reason to ride. Even then, the early strains of environmental thought and rhetoric did not really promote individual actions like cycling for transportation. Instead, throughout the 1950s, the main concerns were the conservation of natural spaces, managing population growth, and understanding pollution. But the language and logic of environmentalism developed many different modes, and following the first Earth Day in 1970, bicycle use was increasingly encouraged as a sustainable, nonpolluting form of transport.

In 1970 the *Whole Earth Catalog*, a unique combination of practical back-to-the-land advice and psychedelic futurism, introduced a "Bicycle Page for You" (alongside plans for building your own biosphere). "Bicycles are small, inexpensive, require little maintenance, pleasurable to use, and smogless," wrote a contributor. "If America traded in all their [D]etroit iron for bikes, a lot of problems would be solved." This argument for cycling was new in the American experience: it did not prioritize fitness or personal gain but addressed environmental and sustainability concerns.[10] By 1974, the publication featured four pages on bikes alongside information on communal living and blacksmithing. "Not only is bicycle travel human-scaled, healthful and non-polluting," observed the catalog, "but it turns out to be more efficient than jetplanes, salmon or seagulls." Promoting bicycling fit with the publication's motto, "Access to Tools," and reflected the counterculture's emphasis on self-sufficiency.

The *Whole Earth Catalog* and its successors promoted bicycles as "appropriate technology," a concept attributed to E. F. Schumacher. His 1973 book *Small Is Beautiful* promoted low-impact and efficient machines and systems. Mixed in with R. Crumb cartoons and Thoreau anthologies, bicycles were featured in the catalog not only as transportation but also adapted to drive grain mills, railroad hand cars, and other "homestead bicycle technology." The concept was embraced by California's Office of Appropriate Technology, created by Governor Jerry Brown. The state architect Sim Van der Ryn recalls the mandate that the bicycle should replace short cab rides for state employees around the capital. In 1976, fifty used bicycles were purchased, painted white, and adorned with the state seal.[11]

This environmentalist rhetoric rapidly entered mainstream bicycle culture. A bicycle guide from 1950 that had focused on health and vitality was rereleased in 1972 with a completely different emphasis. Its revised first sentence read: "With the current concern in trying to save the world from various forms of pollution, it is little wonder that the bicycle is now enjoying a renaissance." The *Chicago Tribune* printed an advice column in 1975 under the heading *Mother Earth News*, with one entry suggesting that readers who wanted to get back to the land should instead open a bike shop in a small town. By 1979, *Bicycling* magazine's technical editor, Fred DeLong, was describing the boom as an "ecologist's dream" and noting that "states are beginning to realize that the bike might be a partial solution to the energy crisis."[12]

The Energy Crisis

An even more persuasive reason to ride emerged after October 1973, when the Organization of Petroleum Exporting Countries (OPEC) imposed an embargo on oil exports to nations supporting Israel. The price of oil quadrupled within a few months. Even before the embargo, inflation and a stagnant economy had driven up the costs of fuel in the United States. The "continuing increase in the price of gasoline is causing more and more people to switch to pedal power," wrote a member of the West Palm Beach bicycle club in 1973, and a wire-service story had argued for the practicality of the bicycle and the transportation savings it allowed: "The idea that the bicycle is a toy is as outdated as the five-cent cigar."[13]

Partly for these reasons, for the first time ever, the Federal-Aid Highway Act of 1973 included mass-transit funding and even bicycle infrastructure as possible uses of highway funds. This change gave states the option of using funding derived from gas taxes and earmarked for roads to build bike lanes, signs, and paths. This was a typical piece of New Federalism—the idea that the federal government would devolve some power to the states to decide what to do with federal monies granted to them. President Nixon signed the highway act mere months before the OPEC oil embargo.

The shift to the bicycle was evidence of a tectonic shift in the postwar American attitude toward energy consumption. The historian Mark Fiege has called the return to the bike a "major socioeconomic reversal." He points out that some Sunoco gas-station franchisees started selling bicycles in 1973, offering bike maintenance in converted auto garages. When the 1979 Iranian revolution created renewed volatility in the oil market, the interest in cycling was reinforced. "With the gas situation—hey—this is the only way to travel these days," observed one participant in a 10,000-strong bicycle tour around New York City.[14]

WHERE TO RIDE?

Despite the much-touted benefits of cycling, legions of new cyclists created logistical problems, as one Connecticut journalist pointed out in 1973: "These millions are going to have to have more space to ride and a greater share of the current road and highway system." The bike boom also created a sense of crisis, as a Minnesota government report argued in capital letters in 1976: "A MAJOR BICYCLE SAFETY PROBLEM EXISTS concerning the existing and increasing use of bicycles on the public roads."[15] Yet another bike battle was looming.

The major problem was that nobody seemed certain about where cyclists should ride. Conflicting constituencies and philosophies confused the matter. The Stanford Environmental Law Society summed up the situation in a 1976 pamphlet: "Governmental response to the bicycle revolution has generally been unplanned, ill-informed, and underfunded, where there has been any response at all."[16] For much of the twentieth century, it had been comparatively easy for governments and courts to apportion the road between disparate users, simply because the low numbers of cyclists minimized or masked possible conflict. But now that cyclist numbers were increasing, someone needed to manage competing demands for a limited public space.

Ride on the Left?

With its emphasis on treating bicycles as vehicles, Bill Cosby's film challenged a bizarrely persistent myth that the proper place for the bicycle was on the left of the leftmost road lane, facing oncoming traffic. In 1939, a letter to the editor of the *Pittsburgh Press* asked, "Would it not be possible . . . to get cyclists classed as pedestrians, and have them travel on the left side of the road facing traffic? . . . It is strange that this obvious precaution has been neglected for so long by the traffic authorities." Although the myth was rarely endorsed by safety experts, there are still a few examples of authorities retelling the tale. One Maine newspaper in 1940 advised children heading back to school: "When bicycling: Always ride facing oncoming traffic and off the main road."[17] In 1942, the Detroit Public Schools recognized the longevity of these bad ideas, writing in a school textbook that "for years there has been . . . disagreement as to whether or not [bicycles] should be ridden on the left-hand side of the road facing oncoming traffic." Offering only a weak refutation of the left-side argument, the misguided text directed young bicyclists off the road and onto the sidewalk. In a 1951 newspaper story, an irritated Connecticut state policeman blamed the perpetuation of the myth on parents: "Some kids told me their parents taught them to ride on the left side, facing traffic, like pedestrians. That's wrong and it's dangerous. The right side of the road is the only side of the road for anybody operating any kind of vehicle, I don't care what it is."[18]

This argument was revived as Americans returned to the bike in the late 1960s. Although safety literature consistently taught that the appropriate place to ride was on the right side of the right lane, the left-lane myth persisted in letters to the editors of small-town newspapers, a few novels, some court proceedings, and a seemingly ineradicable oral tradition. In 1965, a crotchety columnist in Sarasota, Florida, responded to the bike boom in an article titled "The Danger of Bike Riders" and proposed a solution: "Why shouldn't the bike riders be required to ride on the left so that they, too, can see approaching autos and act accordingly?" The next year in Ocala, Florida, Pete Negri, a Chamber of Commerce safety committee member, argued that mixed messages were confusing children. He was quoted as saying that although police and authorities taught children to ride on the right, "parents and teachers tell children to do just the opposite." Negri argued for a revised ordinance "permitting bike riders to face traffic."[19]

These views were not restricted to Florida. In 1973, a city alderman in Nashua, New Hampshire, tried unsuccessfully to direct cyclists to ride into traffic: "As a driver . . . he felt more comfortable about having bicyclists headed in his direction." A letter writer in Bangor, Maine, agreed: as "one who has been dodging bicycle riders for the past 50 years," Ernest Southard felt that it was past time to "put the bike rider where he belongs on the left side of the road, facing traffic." To Southard, "a bicycle is not and cannot be considered a motor vehicle," so it should be demoted to the status of a pedestrian. In Wisconsin, Ernest Williams suggested a ride-on-the-left statute to his state representative in 1977, prompting a weak reply: "There is presently no statutory provision for bicycle operators to ride facing traffic as suggested by Mr. Williams," responded the Wisconsin Department of Transportation. "If such a statutory provision were implemented, it could cause other types of problems.

For example, few of the newer types of bicycles could be operated on gravel shoulders without damage and additional hazard."[20]

The sorts of letters which appeared in small-town newspapers throughout the decade sometimes became a bit overheated. A 1975 letter excoriated cyclists as entirely responsible for traffic conflicts: "The law-makers in trying to cope with the increasing number of bicycles have made an irresponsible blunder when they specified that bicycles shall travel with the flow of traffic," wrote a citizen of Youngstown, Ohio. "Suddenly it has become acceptable and even stylish to mingle with the flow of traffic, right there on the pavement with the cars and the trucks and the busses." The sight of young children riding with traffic outraged the writer: "Their parents and then the lawmakers out [sic] to be horsewhipped," he declared, and then offered his solution: "The law shoudl [sic] read: 'Thou shalt ride your bike facing traffic and get off the road every time a motor vehicle approaches you. You are a pedestrian and you shall act like a pedestrian or die like a pedestrian."[21]

As late as 1978, letter writers kept it up, declaring that existing laws requiring bicycles to ride with traffic were "gross stupidity." T. A. St. Clair of Venice, Florida, declared that "a bicyclist facing traffic has the perfect opportunity of avoiding collision, being able to take to the ditch or whatever, where danger is imminent. With his back to oncoming traffic, he has no chance. . . . God gave us the law of survival," and the writer recommended that the law of man should be changed to allow children to see oncoming traffic and choose to dodge it.[22]

Such correspondence typically sparked a deluge of incredulous responses from cyclists. A 1974 rebuttal from Palm Beach, Florida, is representative: "The writer's proposal to have bicycles ride facing traffic is enough to cause every rider I know to wake up screaming in terror."[23] But if it was never endorsed by cyclists, what explained the persistence of this view? Part of the confusion might have been the changes in laws applying to horse riders: once considered vehicles, by the 1970s equestrians were urged to ride on the left of the road, facing traffic. Another reason might have been the enduring association of bicycling with children, which had the effect of discounting bicycles as vehicles in the public perception.

Some cyclists clearly took the advice to ride on the left. A pair of young women, injured in a collision while riding a tandem bicycle on the left-hand side of the road, tried to include "testimony from the investigating police officer as to the custom and usage of riding bicycles against traffic in Michigan" when their case came to trial. The court thought it was ridiculous for the young women to introduce in defense of their actions evidence that they were doing something illegal, and the appeals court decided that such testimony should be excluded. But when the case went to the Michigan Supreme Court, the justices ruled that if Trooper Ackerley wanted to testify "that it is safer to ride a bicycle on the left side of the roadway facing oncoming traffic, even though such conduct violates a Michigan statute," then his testimony should be permitted. Even some state troopers, apparently, were dissatisfied with the law.[24]

All national-level safety curricula taught the exact opposite of the left-hand myth for the better part of a century. Even more explicitly, since WWII, all bike safety curricula had emphasized that bicycles were vehicles, and moved with traffic. The entire premise of the safety film *Drive Your Bike* was that the best way to ride your bicycle was to operate it exactly as one might drive a car. In the film, one boy was briefly tempted to ride against traffic, "but then he thought how dangerous it would be to drive a *car* down the wrong side of a busy street."[25]

The left-hand argument resembled an urban legend—a tall tale that, despite its implausibility, held some essential shape that satisfied the prejudices of both teller and audience. In 1975, the bicycling advocate Donald Pruden called it "an unfortunate popular mythology of bicycle riding." Following the common structure of urban legends, sources often invoked some unspecified law, somewhere, that required riding bikes on the left. Knowledge of that law was always second- or third-hand. "But I was brought up to ride facing the traffic," wailed the author and bike advocate Bibs McIntyre in 1972, prompting a response from a patient BIA representative: "That myth is going to kill some more bicyclists every year . . . and it is a myth. . . . Every time we try to run down the report of such a law, either the person who told us is remembering wrong (perhaps recalling a pedestrian rule) or else the law's been changed since." One 1974 law review article declared that Wisconsin was working on a statute requiring bikes to ride on the left, but there is no evidence from Wisconsin legislative or advisory-board records that any such law was ever proposed.[26]

For decades, letters to the editor referenced these nonexistent laws, as in this missive from Ludington, Michigan: "Years ago we were taught to ride facing traffic in order to see what was coming at us, thus avoiding being hit. That law was changed approximately 20 years ago." There was no such law. A different letter writer incorrectly remembered that "back in the 1940s or '50s, California had a law" requiring cyclists to ride on the left. Another writer claimed that telegraph boys were the source, relating that "the first job I ever had was shagging telegrams for postal telegraph in Wichita, Kan[sas,] in 1925. We were always instructed to ride facing traffic. We never lost a messenger."[27]

The myth showed up in fiction, too. A 1947 novel captured a mother's instructions: "Take yourselves a ride and be back a little before five. Don't go too far or on lonely roads and stay well off side and ride facing traffic." Decades later, in the first edition of Judy Blume's young-adult novel *Tiger Eyes*, a conspiring protagonist agrees to the safety requirements of adults, no matter how nuts: "'Remember . . . ride facing traffic,' Walter tells me. 'That's a rule we observe on The Hill.' 'Facing traffic,' I repeat."[28]

Wherever it came from, the myth endured throughout the decade. A Minnesota government report from 1977 observed that "some parents tell their children, 'I don't care what anybody says, ride facing the oncoming traffic.'" The report's authors were unequivocal: "Out of sheer ignorance, many parents are placing their children's lives in unnecessary danger." That same year John Heering of Bethel, Connecticut, wrote to *Boys' Life:* "I found a mistake in the Bicycling Column. The safety quiz answers say you should ride on the right side of the street. I always thought you should ride on the left side." For his trouble, John was publicly chastised by the cartoon donkey in charge of the letters column: "Wrong, John. Always ride with the traffic." The Associated Press offered a widely reprinted article in 1979 chronicling the efforts of an eleven-year old boy to "change the law that requires bicyclists to ride with the flow of traffic." To Jeff, it seemed more logical to ride facing traffic: "If you're riding facing traffic and see that a car is out of control, you can see it and get out of the way," he is quoted as saying. As late as 1982, a debate in a newspaper in St. Petersburg, Florida, featured three letters suggesting bikes ride on the left and three arguing they ride on the right. "Cyclists *should* be required to face oncoming traffic," said one writer, and another agreed: "There ought to be a law."[29]

Ride on the Bikeways

In response to yet another letter instructing cyclists to ride on the left, one rider in Florida patiently corrected the myth, and then seemed to sigh with resignation: "Let's face it, we bicyclists are at the mercy of the auto regardless of what side of the road we're riding on. The best way to prevent car-bike collisions is to separate cars from bikes by building and maintaining sidewalks and bike paths and requiring cyclists to use them."[30] But this letter merely traded one problem for three more: bicycles weren't legally allowed on many sidewalks, separate paths did not exist, and even if they were developed, requiring cyclists to use paths might lead to denying them their rights to the road.

In the early years of the bike boom, advocates had hope that these problems could be overcome, and dreamed of a bikeway-riding future. Peter Hoffman was intrigued by the new possibilities in 1968: "The idea of bikeways and trails set aside for the safety and enjoyment of cyclists is recognized as a dynamic new dimension in community and recreational planning," he wrote in the pages of *Bicycling*. "Bike paths and trails exist or are being built in nearly every state," enthused Bibs McIntyre in 1972, with emphasis: "Within the next decade, officials estimate there will be *two hundred thousand miles* of Bikeways."[31]

It is tempting to equate the 1970s demand for separated paths with the earlier sidepath boom. But there were major differences: the 1890s sidepath movement was an alternative to unpaved roads, whereas the 1970s bikeway movement sought an alternative to roads full of cars. The funding mechanisms, philosophy, and proposed designs of the two movements were completely different. Indeed, bikeway supporters seemed to be unaware of the existence of the earlier sidepath movement. And although the word *sidepath* had a specific meaning, the word *bikeway* could have varying and sometimes contradictory meanings. What the two movements did have in common was the potential to create conflict. The bike boom fueled "public pressure for bikeways and routes where bicycles can be ridden with relative safety," according to one California study from 1972. But building bicycle facilities ran into familiar difficulties related to public conflicts over a commonly held resource.[32]

Many observers agree that Homestead, Florida, "started the current bicycle renaissance," laying out on-street bicycle routes with blue and white signs as early as 1961. Local cycling clubs promoted recreational riding, and several celebrities, including Dr. Paul Dudley White, helped push things along. Their campaign eventually led to an off-street path that they called a *bikeway*. Mae West—a Hollywood star who ascribed to the bike some of the credit for her famous figure—was there to dedicate the bikeway in February 1962. The BIA promoted Homestead-style trails and on-street lanes through the 1960s, producing a self-described "newsletter of the bikeways explosion" and underwriting a trail-construction handbook.[33]

Tantalizingly, the federal government also started supporting urban bike infrastructure in the 1960s, though from an unlikely quarter. The Department of the Interior—generally associated with the management of scenic national parks and of resource extraction and recreation on federal lands—began to eye the cities as well. The department provided $2 million in matching funds for national park trails for hiking and biking in 1960. Four years later, "Interior Secretary Stewart L. Udall, deploring 'the tyranny of the automobile,' endorsed . . . a call for more bicycling space" while speaking to industry groups and the AYH. The next year, Udall commissioned the two-year study that eventually yielded the "Trails for America" report, a remarkable document promoting not only hiking trails in national parks but also bike paths and lanes in cities: "To avoid crossing motor vehicle traffic, bikeways would be located along landscaped shoulder areas on frontage roads next to freeways and expressways, along shorelines, and on abandoned railroad rights-of-way," or "along quiet back streets and alleys."[34]

The report was the basis for 1967 congressional hearings that led to the National Trails System Act. Along with projects related to the Appalachian and Pacific Crest trails, one version of the bill included "the metropolitan areas of the Nation" as a venue for bicycle-trail building. As Udall pointed out, the Department of the Interior had already provided $365,000 for "urban trail development in or near 12 large cities." It wasn't much money, and Udall didn't envision more federal funding beyond this pilot project: "We would encourage the States . . . and the cities . . . to spend more money on this type of project," said Udall in the hearing, implying that no one should hold their breath waiting for more federal support.[35]

Keith Kingbay spoke on behalf of the Chicago LAW (one of the few clubs still using the name) in favor of urban bike trails at the 1967 hearings. "In each and every case where bikeways, bike trails, have been established in heavily populated areas, they have proven eminently popular," Kingbay testified, promoting the experiences of Chicago, New York and Coral Gables, Florida. The problem was that Kingbay hadn't had a chance to read the bill, which drew the ire of the committee chairman, Colorado's Wayne Aspinall, a legendary enemy of Udall's conservationist philosophy: "This is a very important matter that this committee is engaged in now, my friend," he lectured Kingbay. His dismissive remarks concluded with the observation: "There was one time when I liked to bicycle also. I got that out of my system, though, in about 16 months."[36] Because of the representatives' greater interest in recreational hiking trails, the bill that eventually passed made reference to urban bicycle trails but provided little money for them.

Among other proposals, the Department of the Interior urged the reuse of abandoned railroad rights-of-way as recreational trails. This idea had come up sporadically as passenger rail travel declined in autocentric postwar America. While the DOI supported the idea in the 1966 *Trails for America*, a 1971 follow-up noted that "little has been done by States and municipalities" to convert rights-of-way into trails. But that report merely listed abandoned railways and didn't indicate how states could find funding to purchase them. By the end of the decade, the department had launched a $5 million pilot project to fund rail trails in ten Eastern states, but according to one Washington State newspaper, "Congress has failed to provide more money for the Rails-to-Trails program," leaving the Northwest out of that round. Many remarkable trails would be built on abandoned rail lines in the coming decades, and some features of railroad engineering—gentle grades, tunnels, and bridges—made them especially attractive and accessible routes for cyclists. "To build a bike route like this would cost a fortune," enthused one advocate in Spokane, Washington.[37]

But the rail trail was not an immediate solution to the needs of cyclists in the 1970s. Converted trails were suitable mostly for recreational use, not as part of a commuting or transportation network, and abutting property owners sometimes opposed such projects by any means necessary. Meanwhile, some cycling advocates argued that diverting bicycle traffic onto converted rail trails was not a solution to sharing the roads; it was just a means of avoiding the conflict.

Although federal funding for urban bike trails was scarce during the 1960s, one city was becoming the utopia of cycling, a laboratory for studying bikeway design and bicycle transportation. Described by the experimenters as "a semi-isolated academically-oriented community of 24,000 people," Davis, California, became "probably the most spectacular example of the re-birth of the bicycle in America." Climactically pleasant and congenially flat, Davis furnished an excellent small-scale laboratory for practical bicycle transportation, watched intently by significant audiences in the nearby state capital of Sacramento and slightly more distant San Francisco.[38]

Figure 6.2. The University of California pioneered separated bicycle paths on its Davis campus in the 1960s, developments that expanded into the surrounding city of Davis and made it a frequently cited utopia for American bicycle infrastructure. But the specific designs developed at UC Davis were not widely adopted. AR-013, University Archives Photographs, Special Collections, University of California Library, Davis.

The Davis cycling network came into being as a result of the transportation crisis that arose when the University of California system expanded the Davis campus to meet the demands of the baby boom. Administrators banned automobiles from the central campus, counting on the bicycle to provide a viable transit alternative. As *Sports Illustrated* put it, "Bicycles became so numerous they virtually forced automobiles off the streets." Because Davis was unusually spread out, there was enough space on existing roadways "to park cars and run bicycle paths between the sidewalks and the parked cars." In other words, Davis had the room to create physically separated bicycle paths. The trend extended from the campus to the rest of the city: after significant community organizing ousted the existing city council in 1966 in favor of a pro-bike coalition, "a citywide system of bicycle paths was constructed," at least partially inspired by European models.[39]

The Davis initiatives attracted national attention. A summary was published in the *Congressional Record* in 1971, ending with a slightly overheated ultimatum: "Our research has led us to the conclusion, that at least in the cities—*no bicycle paths, no bicycles.*" The authors meant it as "an urgent call for action to create and maintain a viable bicycle support system." Later that year the California State Assembly passed a resolution affirming that "bicycling is becoming the principal sport and recreation of ever-increasing numbers of Californians of all ages, and serves as an important mode of basic transportation." But since sharing the road in auto-centric California seemed "sometimes hazardous," the assembly directed the transportation department to "study the most feasible and least expensive methods by which existing and future public streets and thoroughfares can more safely accommodate bicycle riders," deftly summarizing many bike battles throughout history.[40]

The resulting 1972 study was mostly the work of engineering and urban planning faculty from UCLA and UC Davis. Since the 1890s bicycle boom, read the preface, "a great network of roads, streets, and highways have been built to accommodate the private automobile with only marginal provision for bicycle use (predominantly by schoolchildren who as soon as possible put aside their bikes for cars)." The guidelines offered a hierarchy of bike infrastructure, class I being entirely separated bicycle-specific paths on the Davis model, and class III being road lanes with painted boundaries or signs reminding drivers to share the road. The report acknowledged that "Class III bikeways offer very little to the would-be cyclist and are not generally recommended." For these planners, "an 'ideal' bikeway in urban and rural areas is one that is completely separated from motor vehicle and pedestrian traffic, thus having a minimum number of interactions and conflicts with other travel modes."[41]

By 1971, the rest of the nation was taking notice of the Davis experiment. A headline in New York's *Village Voice* criticized Mayor John Lindsey in light of Davis's progress: "Start Pedaling, John, You're Falling Behind." One journalist wrote in 1974 that "the network of bikeways in Davis, Calif., has become a model for bike-conscious towns." Davis was described to incredulous Americans as if it were a different planet: "Many of the city's broad, tree-lined avenues have two of their four lanes marked for bicycles. Shoppers with wide baskets mounted on their bicycles glide silently into the main business district from sprawling suburbs." By 1976, law professors at Stanford described it as "a bicyclist's utopia."[42]

While the Davis experience was informative, however, it wasn't definitive: the distinctive features of its bike network (protected lanes between parked cars and sidewalks, and certain intersection designs), were not widely copied elsewhere. Standards for bike infrastructure design instead came from the Federal Highway Administration in 1976. These "proved to be the template for the next two decades of American bicycle planning, not the more exotic of the Davis designs," points out the historian Bruce Epperson.[43] But while Davis-style bikeways did not proliferate, the example spurred other innovations.

While California was designing bicycle infrastructure in 1971, Oregon was figuring out how to pay for it. The Oregon Bicycle Bill worked around the iron triangle of auto interests, legislators, and state highway departments to mandate spending on bicycle infrastructure from gasoline-tax revenue. The rationale combined the long-established popularity of recreational cycling with new concerns over environmentalism and practical commuting. As *Sports Illustrated* put it, "The bicycle bill squeaked through the legislature in the midst of an environmental uprising that centered on the more famous bottle bill." The article was referring to Oregon's law requiring a deposit for recyclable glass bottles, the first in the nation. Like that legislation, the 1971 Bicycle Bill was unique, leading the urban studies scholar Steven Reed Johnson to declare it "the first designated state funding for bicycles in the country." Sponsored by Don Stathos, a Republican representative from the southernmost region of Oregon, it required 1 percent of the state's gas-tax revenue to be spent on bike facilities. The bill's support did not come from the traditional transportation lobby but from the college town of Eugene and the Bike Lobby (an advocacy group) of metropolitan Portland, leading a supportive state senator to declare that the "legislature overrode the Highway Commission, the cities, and the counties, and ordered that the funds be spent for bicycle trails because 'they have been grossly behind the times.'" As *Sports Illustrated* pointed out, Oregon had the money but not the expertise: county road planners had to travel down to Davis to find ideas for bicycle-specific infrastructure.[44]

The law came under attack in the following years, both from transportation interests and agricultural counties to the east of the Cascade Mountains. One editor claimed that "State Highway Commission members have recently expressed disgust about Western Oregon bike routes," claiming low ridership in 1972. But while cities and counties had varied levels of commitment to building bicycle infrastructure, Oregon bicycle advocates beat back the challenge to the funding law. One advocate chided the *Sports Illustrated* reporter in 1975 for not figuring out that Oregon's "program also provides for basic intercity and intracity transportation," not just recreation. He continued: "One state has made a tangible and public commitment to bicycles as a transportation alternative," and, even more incredibly in auto-obsessed America, "a state highway department is being redirected" by the will of the people.[45]

The result gave Oregon a source of stable financing that, while imperfect, provided more support for bicycles as transportation than existed anywhere else in the nation. Early in the decade, various states had attempted to legislate funding for bikeways but largely failed; Governor Ronald Reagan vetoed California's bill in 1972. Although bills similar to Oregon's were proposed in Nebraska, Maryland, Washington, New York, Michigan, and Arizona, they weren't identical successes. Opponents of a proposed Massachusetts bicycle bill appealed to the state supreme court in 1976; the justices were "asked to determine whether a bill to establish such bikeways and parking facilities out of funds derived in part from the gasoline excise tax is permissible" when the state constitution earmarked gas taxes solely for road building. The court found once again that bicycles were vehicles, and that even though the state constitution "restrict[ed] the use of specified funds to certain 'highway purposes,' bicycles were a part of the legitimate vehicular traffic on our highways."[46] The decision, however, was moot, because the bill was never passed.

While states were floundering in their attempts to finance bicycle infrastructure, the 1973 Federal-Aid Highway Act seemed to promise $120 million in funds. But there was a catch: reflective of New Federalist philosophy, the 1973 act allowed states the discretion to spend the money either on bikeways or on roads. There was no direct link between funding and bicycle infrastructure. According to Bruce Epperson, the results were predictable: "States were loath to divert funds from roadway projects unless they were specifically earmarked to alternative transportation projects."[47] Some states set aside federal money for particular projects, but the results were spotty and scattered.

Ride on the Bike Routes

The word *bikeway* was flexible, allowing bicycle advocates to muster support for development without specifying what they meant—which could be anything from dedicated, separate urban bicycle paths to rail trails to sparsely signposted, long-distance bike touring routes on existing roadways. The word could mean almost anything. Godfrey Frankel had first used the term "Bike-Ways" in his 1950 guide of the same name, but he appeared to mean "ways of riding your bike," such as touring, hosteling, racing, and club rides. In the late 1960s, the Department of the Interior used the term to refer to recreational trails in parks, on former railways, or alongside urban roads. Peter Hoffman, writing in *Bicycling* in 1968, meant exactly the opposite, supporting "a plan for utilization of secondary, lightly traveled streets, designated as 'bikeways,' to be shared by careful bicyclists and considerate drivers." But four years later Bibs McIntyre used the term for *both* off-street paths and on-street routes. At one extreme, the word meant purpose-built bicycle paths physically separated and protected from traffic; at the other, it might just mean a sign added to an existing road, or even just a map picking out roads for bicycles to travel on. According to a Washington, DC, paper, the term included "sidewalk routes with curb cuts, special bicycle lanes in the roadway, and separate bicycle paths." But in their grandest moments, the bikeway proponents sounded like the advocates of the forgotten sidepath movement. If the bikeway revolution was successful, "you could ride a bicycle coast to coast, on special bike roads connecting every state," enthused a *Christian Science Monitor* news service story in 1973.[48]

The category of bikeway did in fact include cross-state touring routes, but they weren't necessarily special or bicycle-specific. One observer spoke approvingly of "the sprawling milk and cheese land of Wisconsin," where "residents of the Badger state and their guests have a 320-mile state bicycle trail" crossing the southern part of the state. The thirty-two-mile Elroy-Sparta portion of this route, conceived in 1965, was a ground-breaking trail built out of a converted railroad bed, probably the first of its kind. But the cross-state route dedicated in La Crosse in 1966 wasn't actually a single, contiguous 320-mile bicycle-only path; instead, it was made up of a route stitched together through paths and low-traffic rural highways. The route had signs, maps, and some new trails; but it mostly just directed cyclists to ride on roads, as they always had.[49]

Of all the innovations, the most visible—though perhaps least effective—legacy of the bikeway revolution of the 1970s was a sign still common on American streets: a green rectangle with the words *Bike Route* in white lettering accompanying a simplified outline of a bicycle. These were "guide" signs, meant to be followed by cyclists like breadcrumbs along quiet streets. Tellingly, the new design did not come from traditional transportation engineers; well into the 1960s, the *Manual on Uniform Traffic Control Devices* did not include any sign referring to bicycles. The push for the new design came, once again, from Stewart Udall's Department of the Interior, which (along with the Bureau of Public Roads) introduced the green guide sign and a now-familiar, diamond-shaped yellow

Figure 6.3. The word *bikeway* meant different things to different people. A separated, bicycle-specific trail on an electric utility right-of-way like this one in Racine, Wisconsin, in the late 1970s was a rare piece of infrastructure. Much more common was the addition of the recently developed bike-route signage, like the sign at the left, to existing streets. RG 368 G, Heritage Conservation and Recreation Service, Still Pictures Branch, NARA II.

bike-crossing sign in 1967. According to the press release, the signs "serve both to guide the cyclists on a predetermined bicycle route consisting of a combination of trails, secondary roads and other suitable surfaces, and as a warning to motorists."[50]

The bike route served as a budget bikeway, requiring only signage on the existing road, without any new construction. Salt Lake City's 1973 proposal for a 44-mile bike route, for example, involved no more than putting signs on low-traffic streets. Bike routes could also be a fallback option: in response to a community survey in 1974, whose responses emphasized the preferences of drivers, St. Petersburg, Florida, chose to build bike routes instead of a previously planned system of recreational trails: "A network of short neighborhood routes, marked to alert motorists of bicycle traffic on designated streets, will now have a higher priority." Unlike Davis-style paths, the signage was so cheap and so accommodating to motorists that it was readily adopted across the nation, and not just in the traditional bicycle boom areas. "A dozen bright green reflective signs will be erected today to mark the route of the city's first bike path," wrote a Kentucky newspaper in 1975.[51]

The bike route made such marginal accommodations for cyclists that it did not qualify for even the lowest of the 1972 California Bikeway guide's three existing categories, necessitating the addition of new class IV (painted lanes) and class V (signage) specifications. A Eugene, Oregon, group emphasized in 1974 that bike routes were bottom-rung options: "merely placing 'bike route' signs along low-traffic roadways" was less preferable than "marking off bike lanes either between traffic lanes and parked cars or up against the curb or roadside, and constructing completely independent off-street bike paths." While he supported separated infrastructure (calling class I and II bikeways "the only meaningful type"), the advocate Richard Ballantine mocked New York mayor John Lindsay's opening of a new bike route in 1974, with "little signs posted along the avenues . . . practically speaking, these make absolutely no difference whatsoever." The Stanford Environmental Law Society agreed that they were paltry attempts to "appease cyclists."[52]

Traffic engineers in Prescott, Arizona, were aware of this problem in 1974, but the city planning director, Ed Mollring, didn't have an answer: while acknowledging that a bike route "is nothing more than usually a stripe," as opposed to the "actual bike way or bike path which is usually constructed behind the curb," Prescott found problems with both options. It "seems rather difficult sometimes to mix bicycle traffic with high speed automobile traffic. . . . [I]f you mix them by just painting a strip on the road it sometimes isn't that adequate of a separation. And sometimes it can give the bicyclists a sense of false security because the strip is really a boundary line that doesn't really afford any actual physical separation or protection."

Figure 6.4. A citizens' group in Colorado, one of many local organizations representing adult cyclists, inspects a newly painted bike lane on a residential street in Littleton in the mid-1970s. Several things demonstrate that this is an early experiment, including the fact that the lane is marked on only one side of the road, and the cyclists are thus riding against traffic. But some things never change: a truck is parked in the bike lane behind them. RG 368 G, Heritage Conservation and Recreation Service, Still Pictures Branch, NARA II.

But two years later, the bike route's deficiencies were described as an advantage by Prescott journalists: "The bike route, as distinguished from a bike path, will have no physical separation from vehicular traffic and would not eliminate any parking spaces."[53]

The same attitude prevailed in Wilmington, North Carolina: though conveying no actual benefit to cyclists, the signs were attractive because they did not disrupt auto traffic or city budgets. Though the city boasted of its new bicycle route in 1979, "cyclists will have little to assist them other than a series of signs," the newspaper observed. City councilor Rupert Bryan "questioned whether posting . . . signs did much to protect cyclists," pointing out that there was no provision for painted lanes, markings, "or other safety features." While city planners tried to reassure him that they had fully scouted the route, Bryan observed, logically enough, that he would "feel a lot more comfortable if they'd checked it out on a bicycle rather than in a car." In the end, other city council members argued successfully that painted lanes would just give cyclists a false sense of security: signs were all that was needed.[54]

For some, bike routes were the dead end that brought the bikeway movement to a disappointing halt. After their son was killed while riding on the road in 1975, Gary and Annette Mix committed themselves to building paths with charitable donations in Daytona, Florida, but by 1977, "after thousands of dollars in lost wages and hundreds of hours of often futile meetings," they gave up, building only a single path that was essentially made up of existing sidewalks. They were "surprised at the complexity of government and disappointed that the many pledges of support so eagerly made by politicians and hundreds of local citizens, many wealthy and influential, rarely were fulfilled."[55]

For others, the bikeway movement reinforced existing environmental injustices. Bikeways were held up in 1978 as one among many examples of institutionalized racism when African American residents of Jackson, Mississippi, sued for relief. They pointed out that "blacks are underserved in the provision of bikeways inasmuch as none of the 13 miles of trails for the exclusive use of cyclists is located in black areas and only roughly 20 miles of the

108 miles of bikeways are located in predominantly black areas." While the court dismissed the overall claim of electoral discrimination that produced such injustice, it did acknowledge that "there is no question that a majority of the bikeways are located in predominantly white areas."[56]

In a handful of cities, however, the bikeway moment paved the way for future success. Minneapolis and St. Paul began building bicycle-specific infrastructure that helped transform the Twin Cities into a model of alternative transportation and livability in the following decades. In a remarkable 1974 report, St. Paul planners called for more bike education, enforcement of bike laws, and registration of bicyclists, but they also proposed miles of paths and on-street routes. These were to be built following the 1972 California bikeway standards, connecting existing paths in city parks with business areas and reaching toward Minneapolis. The map included with the plan echoed the routes laid out by the sidepath movement seventy years before and foreshadowed the network of bicycle lanes and paths that makes the Twin Cities unique in the nation today.[57]

Ride on the Right

If urban planners had to scramble to deal with the demands of the 1970s bike boom, the legal domain was presented with a similar problem. Ninety-nine years after the decision in *Taylor v. Goodwin* established a common-law precedent for bicycles as vehicles, the U.S. Department of Transportation published a report complaining that "the legal status of the bicycle and the bicyclist in relation to motor vehicles and pedestrians needs to be defined more precisely in order to avoid confusion over rights-of-way and legal liabilities associated with traffic laws."[58] A century of legislative developments had further confused rather than clarified matters. It was not clear where bicycles should travel, or even whether they should be on the road at all.

The DOT partly blamed children for the confusion, arguing that "the whole impetus behind the existing bicycle regulations in the code is to avoid applying harsh criminal laws to children." Before the 1970s, the UVC had been crafted to allow for the exclusion of children's bicycles from the ever-increasing number of laws controlling automobiles. But "substantial use of bicycles by adults, both as a transportation and recreation device, may have rendered [the UVC as written] inadequate." Among many deficiencies, allowing bicycle vehicles to mix with pedestrians meant "the bicyclist on the sidewalk is virtually in a legal vacuum," according to the DOT. Similarly, the MTO had allowed cyclists to ride on sidewalks except where explicitly prohibited, but it had not clarified their rights and responsibilities on them, and a 1975 revision of the UVC had to add a line that bicycles "shall have all the rights and duties applicable to a pedestrian under the same circumstances." Confusingly, model legislation now considered the bicycle sometimes to be a nonvehicle, equivalent to a pedestrian. The 1975 revision added a new line, endorsing the view that bicycles impeded "real" traffic: "Persons riding two abreast shall not impede the normal and reasonable movement of traffic and, on a laned roadway, shall ride within a single lane."[59] It is against this background that the state of California judged its own laws a mess. A statewide Bicycle Committee found in 1975 that the failure to clearly designate whether a bicycle was a vehicle, and where it should be on the road, "has caused more confusion and frustration among motorists, bicyclists and law enforcement agencies than any other bicycle section" in state law.[60]

One persistent legal question, debated since the nineteenth century but more urgent once standardized lanes were painted onto roads in the 1930s, was exactly how far to the right the bicycle was expected to travel. While theoretically treating bicycles as equal vehicles under common law, statute law had increasingly created controls that applied only to bicycles. Under UVC 11–1205(a), the majority of American states required bikes to "ride as near to the right side of the roadway as practicable, exercising due care when passing." According to the Stanford Environmental Law Society in 1976, "This is the worst provision in the vehicle codes. It is confusing, subject to varying interpretations, and would appear to restrict cyclists to the right curb even in situations where it is both safer and more convenient to move left." The statute was an extension of the legal language governing "overtaking" and "impeding," by which legislatures since the beginning of the twentieth century had intended to allow faster vehicles of all types to pass slower ones on the left. But there was also confusion: where was the actual physical space described by this language? Were cyclists meant to stay to the right part of the lane, inside its boundaries? Were they supposed to stay out of the lane entirely and ride on the right shoulder? Were they allowed to swerve to avoid obstacles, over-take on the left, or shift to the left half of the lane to turn? Why had the legislatures chosen the awkward *practicable* instead of *practi-cal, plausible,* or *possible*—did they mean something different? More difficult yet, who determined what was practicable: cyclists, drivers, police, or the courts?[61]

The definition of *practicable* was significant because it could be used by the courts to assign fault, negligence or liability after tragedy. One California case from 1970 involved an appeal by a fourteen-year old paper boy "permanently and totally disabled by injuries he suffered in the collision" with a truck driven by a cus-tomer. The trial jury had originally been reminded of the state vehicle code's instruction that "requires bicycles to be operated 'as near (to) the right side of the roadway as practicable.'" Among other issues, they found the mere possibility that the paperboy might have been anywhere but the far right of the lane enough to imply some negligence on his part, and the appeals court agreed.[62]

In the patchwork legal world of American federalism, laws gov-erning bicyclists changed whenever they crossed state lines. By 1979, thirty-two states had adopted the UVC "practicable" wording closely, but another twelve jurisdictions had substantial excep-tions or reinterpretations, and the remaining eight didn't have any comparable law at all. California state law—the most bicycle-friendly in the nation, and later a model for others—adopted the general UVC instruction but added a welter of exceptions allowing bicyclists to avoid obstacles and make turns. In a simple solution to a nationwide problem, Maryland added two important words in 1979, responding to rider input by stipulating that cyclists ride as far to the right "as practicable *and safe.*"[63]

One problem with the "practicable" standard that Maryland was trying to solve was that the far right of the road was often pitted with storm-drain gratings that were designed and installed before the bike boom. The mid-century grating designs generally had slots that were oriented parallel to the direction of travel and were just wide enough to trap a wheel, stopping the bicycle instantly and sending the rider over the handlebars. A 1975 Louisiana case provides one example among many. The appeals court found that while a storm drain "was a standard type . . . which had been used by the Highway Department for many years," it had gaps of $1\frac{1}{8}$ inches—a problem for fifteen-year old Rory Townsend. Rory was "riding on his Kabuki, 10-speed bicycle" along with his friend Julie. "The tires on these foreign made racing bicycles were . . . less than $1\frac{1}{8}$ inches wide, and they would easily drop into any of the slots or spaces," observed the court. That's exactly what happened, and thus Julie "saw Rory flip over his bike," sustaining injuries serious enough for his mother to file suit. The appeals court found Rory liable. Only one justice dissented: "This bicycle rider . . . had the right to expect that the street was reasonably safe for his use, and he had all the 'rights' of a motor vehicle in availing himself of that use. . . . [T]he Department of Highways breached its duty to this bicycle rider when it designed and installed the grate," which was "highly dangerous to bicycle riders." An Ohio court later agreed with this dissent, deciding that since the state had adopted the UVC "practicable" language in 1975, bicycles "no longer have a right-of way to the entire right lane of a highway as do other vehicles." If the cyclists were supposed to ride to the right, they could therefore assume that storm grates in their path would be made safe for their travel. The legal solution directing cyclists to the right paradoxically created an engineering dilemma for cities, which now had to remake the right side of the road so it did not actively threaten cyclist safety. It has taken some time for engineers to catch up.[64]

The "practicable" standard created additional confusion, as one Idaho case demonstrated in 1979. After a driver was found liable for running over and killing eight-year old Randall Owen on his bicycle, the driver appealed on a number of grounds, claiming that if Randall was hit by a car, he could not, by definition, have been riding as far right as was practicable: getting hit was proof that a rider was not sufficiently out of the way. The state Supreme Court disagreed, arguing that determining a practicable distance required understanding what was "reasonable" given constantly changing conditions at the side of the road. This was the crux of the problem: "as far right as practicable" was not a place, it was a state of mind.[65]

This confusion over laws is obvious in the educational films of the 1970s. Like the films of previous decades, they were not produced by riders themselves; but unlike the locally made educational films of previous years, the best-financed and most widely distributed educational films of the 1970s were produced by third parties. While Bill Cosby's narration in *Bicycles Are Beautiful* was quite supportive of bicycles, the fact was that no bike advocates could afford to make such a film themselves. Schwinn was listed as a supporter, but the production was dominated by the National Safety Council. The film addressed only children and recommended practices that adult cycling advocates deplored, like walking across an intersection rather than turning left in traffic. Such contradictions are even more evident in the bizarrely conflicted safety film *I Like Bikes* of 1978, financed by General Motors. Speaking to young cyclists while encouraging them to quickly graduate to the automobile, the film features an anthropomorphic bike declaring that "safety-wise, please realize, you *never* should trust me." In a display of paradoxical self-hatred, Ike the Bike declares, "I like bikes, *but* they're so hard to see," "Little things upset 'em," and, most tellingly, "Why can't they pay attention?" Ike concludes, grudgingly, that "though the biker may be wrong," drivers still had to live with bikes.[66]

The American Automobile Association's *Only One Road: The Bike-Car Traffic Mix* (1975) was something of an exception, and a

Figure 6.5. In the AAA film *Only One Road*, Larry Wuellner demonstrates practical skills for adults riding in traffic, including this panic stop in response to a car door thrown open in his path. Unlike the bike-safety films of previous decades, this film is specifically directed at adults, recognizes practical uses of bicycles for commuting, and promotes the philosophy of sharing the road and understanding the concerns of all road users.

remarkable record of changing attitudes. The film was focused on adult bike commuting, supportive of bicyclists' rights, and aware of driver concerns. "There's a complex mix of vehicles on the road today," begins the narration, declaring the new bicycles of the boom to be "a realistic choice for serious transportation." Over footage of adults and senior citizens riding with traffic, the narration affirmed that "these people, like motorists, have a legitimate use for the road." The film demonstrated practical behaviors for adult cyclists interacting with other traffic, including making left turns from the leftmost lane rather than walking their bikes through intersections.[67]

The attitude on display in *Only One Road* reflected signs of change across the country. For the first time in the century, groups of riders gained meaningful representation in the legislative process, as many states created bicycle advisory groups. Among many others, Minnesota established a State Bicycle Committee in 1976. With representation from around the state, the committee proposed a top-down revision of laws, education, enforcement, appropriations, and planning. Wisconsin followed suit in 1977, creating a Governor's Advisory Bicycle Coordinating Council charged with encouraging citizen participation in reshaping roads and traffic laws.[68]

By the end of the decade, the UVC had again revised the bicycle's legal status. The model law once again defined a bicycle as "every *vehicle* propelled solely by human power upon which any person may ride, having two tandem wheels." But revising the UVC didn't change laws uniformly: many states, including California, continued with the definition in use during the previous quarter century, relegating bicycles to the status of "device" rather than "vehicle."[69] Even today, the legal status of a bicycle in the United States depends on what state it is in.

Take the Lane

While legislators and courts were encouraging bicyclists to ride as far to the right as practicable, while city planners were dreaming of bikeways separated from the road, and while crazy people demanded that cyclists ride facing traffic on the left, a newly activist message pushed back against all these instructions. A number of bike advocates in the 1970s recommended that adults ride their bicycles like the vehicles the law had often declared them to be and take the lane as theirs.

Treating bicycles as vehicles had been a mainstay of bicycle education for decades: even Bill Cosby directed his 1974 message to bicycle "drivers." The historian Bruce Epperson highlights the opinion of the California transportation engineer Harold Munn, who argued that the solution to mixing traffic was to encourage more skilled, assertive cyclists to lay claim to their space in the lane. While approaches to this concept have varied, it has broadly come to be known as vehicular cycling.[70]

The most vocal of its advocates was John Forester. During his appearance as an expert witness, a federal court described Forester as "an industrial engineer by profession, and a bicycle enthusiast, author, professor and consultant in the area of bicycle traffic engineering."[71] His self-published guidebook, still in print today, presented an assertive and iconoclastic view of the bicycle that proved immensely attractive to many cyclists.

Vehicular cycling rhetoric argued that statutes incorporating "practicable" language were meaningless, unenforceable, and inimical to cyclist safety. Forester acknowledged the existence of the "practicable" standard but declared that "nobody knows what it means." Therefore, it "is never enforced as such. There are so many reasons one should not obey it . . . that it is practically inoperative." Instead, he urged competent and adult riders to do what has come to be known as "taking the lane": that is, riding steadily in the center of the lane, like a vehicle, to avoid the dangers of the right-hand side of the road, to increase visibility, and to demand the attention of drivers.[72]

Forester's activism was sharpened when he took the city of Palo Alto, California, to court over a bikeway system that included a section of sidewalk. Forester railed against separated paths as a conspiracy by motorists to erode bicyclists' rights and remove them from the road. "These people wouldn't succeed if they said openly that they wanted cyclists cleared off the roads," he claimed. "They have got as far as they have only because they are able to use arguments that mislead the public into thinking they are pro-cyclist." Forester argued that his observations of traffic accidents and intersections had "completely demolished the logical foundations for the bikeway propaganda. There is no argument for bikeways that has not been refuted. We have been able to do this because effective cycling is so right and cycling in the bikeway manner is so wrong."[73]

This argument was persuasive enough to start appearing in official pronouncements elsewhere in the nation. A Minnesota government report in 1977 argued that "bicyclists may encounter greater danger on separate facilities than would be encountered riding on the roadways with the other traffic." Barring fixes, it said, "the desirability of separate bicycle facilities on or alongside a roadway would clearly be questionable."[74]

The vehicular argument was a logical and cost-effective solution to the problem of managing distinct users on a commonly held resource: simply treat all users alike, thus simplifying rules and reinforcing the principle of equal access for all. As one American observer wrote about the 1895 *Taylor v. Goodwin* case, "The object of the existence of a highway is public travel. All citizens have the right to its use; not alone those using horses . . . but others as well." Eighty years later, Forester reiterated the idea, saying, "The highways are public highways, built and maintained for the use of the people." Separate paths allowed the exclusion of bicycles from that public space.[75]

The vehicular argument also bolstered the adult, masculine qualities of cycling, which had been dismissed as childlike behavior for most of the century. Emphasizing confidence, self-control, assertiveness, technical knowledge, and skill, the rhetoric appealed to male cyclists who had ridden in cycling clubs before the boom. Once it was adopted as an educational curriculum by the LAW, journalistic coverage found it newsworthy: one 1980 Associated Press story declared that an adult rider was "practicing competent bicycling." According to Paul Norris, a forty-six-year old army veteran and bicycle educator, riders should "take your position on the road as a vehicle, obey the rules of the road and signal what you're going to do." If you were going to ride, Norris said, "ride decisively, positively, Teutonically, if you will."[76]

In its valorization of assertive, skilled cyclists, vehicular cycling could be dangerously dismissive of the new and untrained cyclists of the boom and thus corrosive to political unity among riders. As Bruce Epperson has argued, Forester employed "a polemical style that frequently alienated potential friends and allies." He demeaned young, old, or inexperienced cyclists who did not fearlessly face down autos thousands of pounds heavier as "incompetent" and implicitly questioned their courage and manhood. Bikeways, in Forester's language, were "based on the idea that the best way to increase the number of cyclists is to attract the people who are too frightened to cycle on the road." He accused bikeway supporters as being blinded by emotion: "These people have emotional problems which they think bikelanes will solve." Motorists, he thought, were more easily explained: "They just look on cyclists as the niggers of the roads. You can't expect them to ask for psychological treatment for it, any more than you expected the old-time racist to do so." Obliviously, Forester sighs: "Each group honestly believes that their view is the only correct and normal view, and that anybody who disagrees with them is either foolish or crazy. . . . No, my saying this about them is not a case of the pot calling the kettle black."[77]

Vehicular cyclists feared that new bicycle infrastructure would be accompanied by laws forcing all cyclists to use off-street paths, possibly increasing the complexity and danger of intersections. This concern helped sink a Pittsburgh bikeway plan. A proposal called for putting up bike-route signage on less-traveled routes but also banning bikes from downtown's busy Fifth Avenue. When cyclists judged it a bad deal, the plan was shelved. In St. Petersburg, Florida, a newspaper reported that a strong minority of cyclists opposed "special lanes on city streets for bike traffic. They say the designated lanes are not needed." Instead, the members of the St. Pete Bicycling Club said that "teaching people how to ride bicycles in auto traffic would be a better investment."[78]

Confirming these fears, language mandating use of separated facilities, sometimes known as "mandatory sidepath" laws, did appear in Oregon and other states. (Despite the terminology, the bikeways these laws referred to were philosophically, legally, and fiscally different from turn-of-the-century sidepaths.) Actually, there had been just such a provision in the UVC since 1944, declaring that "wherever a usable path for bicycles has been provided adjacent to a roadway, bicycle riders shall use such path and shall not use the roadway." While these laws were rarely enforced, their mere presence on the books was galling to many cyclists. By 1979, twenty-seven states had adopted this language, and another eleven had alternative versions.[79]

Bizarrely, when combined with mandatory sidepath laws, a few bikeway plans forced bicyclists to use sidewalks, from which bicycles had been banned nearly a century before. Bike advocates argued that these laws actually were "leading to an anti-bikeway backlash among skilled cyclists." A group of Ohio riders brought suit against the city of Avon Lake when it banned bicycles from three major streets and directed them onto the sidewalks in 1975. But the appeals court ruled that the city "acted within their legislative discretion by confining bicycle riding to the sidewalks." The bike was really just a toy to the court, not a tool for transportation: "Plaintiffs' enjoyment of bicycling as a recreational activity is due respect and protection, but we suggest that this wholesome activity is not crippled by its removal from congested urban streets."[80]

Vehicular cyclists also came to criticize on-road bike lanes painted on the street, one of the cheaper solutions to the bike boom, and eventually a more common solution than separated paths. "I am now questioning the benefit and safety of bicycle lanes," wrote Frederick Wolfe in 1979. "Many bicyclists, including myself, will simply avoid bicycle lane travel whenever possible." Forester agreed, advising that "cyclists are better off without bikelanes."[81]

This was a remarkable split, worthy of Bruce Epperson's nickname "the Great Schism." Put simply, some adult riders had become philosophically opposed to the only kinds of bicycle infrastructure on offer and discouraged traffic engineers from contemplating most bicycle-specific developments, including off-street paths and painted lanes. The split pitted some cyclists against the DOI's trail building, cities that were building bikeways, and many advocacy groups. The most benign action could trigger disagreement. While the AAA's *Only One Road* was arguably even-handed and supportive of bicyclist rights, it still fragmented advocates: the veteran advocate Keith Kingbay called it an "excellent film," while the newcomer Forester called it "defective."[82]

The split was exacerbated when the federal government moved to regulate bicycles through the new Consumer Product Safety Commission (CPSC). Originally created by California safety advocates,

Figure 6.6. *Sprocket Man*, a comic book issued by the Consumer Product Safety Commission, was originally created by bikeway advocates and Stanford University with art by Louis Saekow. It was intended to educate the children of the new bike boom, but this 1975 version includes a legalistic defense of the CPSC's power to regulate adult bicycles. The perceived threat of CPSC action alarmed and angered many experienced cyclists.

the comic book *Sprocket Man* was reissued and widely disseminated in 1975 by the CPSC to spread the word about new federal safety standards for bike manufacturing, including a requirement that bikes be equipped with reflectors. But adult cyclists were indignant because the proposed regulations seemed to treat their 10-speed bicycles as toys, and terrified that design standards would eliminate lightweight adult designs entirely. The strangely legalistic text of *Sprocket Man* defends the CPSC's right to regulate "nearly all bicycles that are toys or other articles intended for use by children (but may also be used by adults.)" Sprocket Man himself is a bit conflicted about the new bike boom, urging strict enforcement in response: "The sheer NUMBER of bikes in use these days shows that the days when bikes were merely TOYS for kids are BYGONE . . . and that the ANARCHY of the cyclist can be afforded NO LONGER!" Some adult cyclists felt beset on all sides: bikeway advocates were urging them off the road, and now the federal government was declaring their bikes toys and mandating their design. The implications infuriated Forester, who took the CPSC to court. His case was partially successful, but largely moot: manufacturers had already worked out accommodations with the CPSC. By the end, Forester and the manufacturers seemed to be on opposite sides.[83]

These debates racked the reborn League of American Wheelmen, disrupting strategic alliances and sowing the seeds of disagreements that divide cyclists to this day. The split weakened support among cyclists for the only nationwide plan for bicycle facilities—the bikeway movement initiated by the Department of Interior. It undermined city-level plans for painted bike lanes. It also divided skilled recreational cyclists from their longtime political allies, the bicycle manufacturers. Forester himself served as a regional director for the LAW for several years and as president in 1979. Although his teaching material became the basis of LAW educational efforts for some time, there was no peace between the camps, and Forester would leave his leadership role amid much rancor, spending the following decades as a vocal critic.[84]

LEGACIES OF THE BIKE BOOM

By the 1980s, the impetus for creating separate infrastructure had diminished. "Bikeways are not the ultimate answer to the problems faced by bicyclists," wrote a Pittsburgh columnist in 1981, instead recommending road improvements and resurfacing that would benefit motorists and cyclists alike. "Bike Lanes Remain Unrealized Dream," read a 1983 headline in a Spokane paper.[85] The promise of the bike boom seemed to be put on hold. In the end, only three modes of bicycle infrastructure from the 1970s remained in widespread use: bike routes in cities, state "bicycle route" designations, and rail trails. The first two consisted mostly of inexpensive signage or maps, and the third removed bicycles from the roads entirely.

Once again, money was the central obstacle to developing bike infrastructure. In 1972, a federal brochure had enthused that "money will become available as more States, following Oregon's lead, pass legislation providing funds for bikeways along highways."[86] But bills emulating Oregon's diversion of gas taxes failed all over the nation, leaving the bikeway revolution unfunded. While the 1973 Federal Aid Highway Act promised money, in reality funding was spotty, consisting mainly of small sums from the Department of the Interior's Land and Water Conservation Fund and state-level agencies. One bill, the Bikeway Transportation Act of 1977, would have earmarked $45 million a year specifically for bikeway construction. Cosponsored by New York's Ed Koch, it died in committee as some representatives criticized its use of highway funds for "recreational" purposes. Parts of that bill lived on in the Surface Transportation Assistance Act of 1978, but that law offered only $20 million annually over four years; moreover, it was optional, and funding was contingent on availability. Cities were largely left on their own to pursue individual projects, and they generally chose the cheapest options: bike-route signs or nothing at all.[87]

While bicycles surged in number during the 1970s, their presence exposed long-standing conflicts about their use. By the end of the 1970s, more Americans were bicycling for recreational purposes, and bicycle commuting was becoming slightly more common. But urban design that catered to bicycles was scarce and controversial, laws were contradictory, and the embryonic culture of adult cycling for transportation withered as energy prices stabilized during the 1980s. The unresolved battle of the 1970s about whether bikes belonged on public streets set up a return to the fights over the commons in the present day.

CONCLUSION

The Road as a Commons

The road is a commons. More specifically, it is a common-pool resource. Any member of the public can use it to their advantage, but any unchecked use might hinder or rule out use by another. Those exposed to the philosophy of modern environmentalism might think of this as a tragedy of the commons: a disaster in the making, requiring the common property to be either directly owned and managed by the state or split into private shares so that individuals might be motivated to manage the resource themselves. But in the decades since Garrett Hardin warned environmentalists of the *tragedy* of the commons, multiple avenues of research have instead demonstrated its *triumph:* for millennia, humans have successfully figured out ways to manage access to resources through collective action. Humans are not disconnected atoms: for thousands of years, they have lived within traditions, communities, cultures, and nation-states that have worked fairly successfully to apportion, manage, and maintain desirable resources. In moments of crisis and rapid change, those human institutions created to manage and control resource use are often damaged; but periods of calm can allow for repair.[1]

The shared resource of the road has limits, just like other resources we value: a breathable atmosphere, unpolluted rivers, untapped forests, self-sustaining fish populations, and healthful cities. The road is shared, communally funded, and exhaustible. Its philosophy declares that no just user may be banned; case law, statutes, and constitutional precepts allow for the regulation of users but not their unfair exclusion. Freedom of movement is a constitutional right, and the courts generally accept that road users cannot be denied the use of the transportation method of their choice, given certain restraints. This philosophy predates later controls: a corporation cannot be entirely restricted from driving trucks on a public road, though their number and size might be regulated, and their drivers licensed. Similarly, communal tradition would not allow the exclusion of a bicycle rider from the public streets in her neighborhood, even if she is not required to be licensed or inspected by the state. But every new appropriation adds strain, particularly with high-demand users; the large delivery truck cannot occupy the same space at the same time as the young bicycle rider. Too many users of one type make other uses unfeasible: many buses or huge numbers of bicycles might slow drivers. Masses of fast cars can make walking unpleasant and risky. Steps taken to regulate users may become impractical as technology and use patterns change: requiring hand signals of cyclists made more sense before hand-operated brakes became common, and painted lanes created to manage automobile traffic in the early twentieth century ironically caused difficulty when bikes returned a half-century later.

Despite the carefree and innocent connotations of the bicycle, debates over its place on the road are actually divisive fights over a scarce resource, and can quickly descend into paranoia, derision, criticism of minority group rights, macho chest-beating, and bloody-mindedness. These conflicts are evidence that managing the commons is a constantly renegotiated problem of communal action. The vehemence of the recurring battles since the bicycle's arrival demonstrates that even the smallest alteration of perceptions, policy, or physical construction may be perceived by competing forces as a new front in a war over a scarce resource.

While this book's examination of selected bike battles demonstrates their similarities, the language is seductively wrong. Despite the overheated rhetoric, it's not really a war out there, and using the term *battle* unduly dramatizes what is really just political negotiation. The title of this book was chosen to communicate that it contains only some episodes out of many recurring conflicts, not to make a claim of militant combat; it also sounds better than "Selected Cycling Policy Debates." But even that title might have promoted a dangerously choppy understanding of the past, as pointed out by the historian Paul Pierson: "The shaping of public policy is more than a matter of 'policy choice' at a particular moment in time," he argues. "That moment of choice is framed by prior and later events and processes that we exclude from our analyses at considerable cost." Pierson reminds us that "we need to see what happened after the dust settled."[2]

Rising above the recurring debates, we can see that the concept of the road as a commons is based on thousands of years of tradition, law, and legislation. Roads have been held as a public trust that has successfully provided access to many competing users. In the way that historians think of time, this pattern of use has only recently been disrupted by crisis. The needs of urbanization, industrialization, and the growing power of the nation-state in the late nineteenth century led to a century of new road construction, debates over financing, and competition between new technologies.

The resulting waves of closely-packed crisis triggered sporadic episodes of debate and policy formation. First, the increasingly crowded streets of the late nineteenth-century city—overflowing with competing modes of transport, from streetcars and carriages to human-powered vehicles—required swift management by courts and legislatures. Urbanization and travel then drove multiple groups to support taxation to build a paved "Good Roads" system, briefly overcoming social and political divisions to unite road users in support of combined infrastructure. Cyclists, politically split by racial and social divisions, were unable to argue for a separate system, and their visible contribution to the compromise was obscured.

In the first decades of the twentieth century, expanding use of the speedy personal automobile necessitated completely new engineering and policing institutions. The temporary crisis of World

War II briefly changed the equations of resource use, although this shift resulted in little more than a demonstration that alternatives were indeed possible. After the war, an unprecedented and unmatched period of inexpensive energy called for massive road building to meet the needs of automobile drivers. Then, when the limits of energy supply were briefly exposed in the 1970s, another crisis was touched off as human-powered transportation returned to the road, exposing the weaknesses of the half-century-old legal, political, and physical systems that gave priority to the car. Attempts to respond to the return of the bike were piecemeal, contradictory, and leaderless, making it impossible for any single group to bring about substantive change.

This perspective on American transportation emphasizes the contingency and confusion of policy development. Today's rules of the road and the physical road itself are the legacies of crisis response: they betray a century-long history of patchwork fixes, abandoned initiatives, good intentions, and obsolete reasoning. They resemble what computer programmers call a *legacy system:* designed in previous ages for prior needs, its logic shapes our actions in ways not of our choosing. Scholars of what has come to be known as automobility have already identified the many modes of the "systemic domination" of automobiles.[3] But similar things can be said about cyclomobility: the likelihood that any individual will choose to travel by bike depends on a complex history leading to a system of economics, politics, culture, and physical infrastructure that might support or discourage that choice. The system that we are left with might enable us to share the road for a while, but any change in the makeup of road users, shift in available funding, or reconsideration of fundamental goals would destabilize the whole shebang. All three of these things have happened, once again, in the first decades of the twenty-first century.

THE BIKE IS BACK

Counting the original fad of the 1890s and the 1970s bike revival, the twenty-first century might be witnessing the third great age of bicycling. The National Bicycle Dealers' Association reported that the approximately 14 million adult bikes sold in 2005 represented the largest total since 1973. But the phenomenon goes beyond the number of bikes on the roads. Examining demographics, surveys, and policy, John Pucher and others have instead declared that a bicycle "renaissance" is now underway.[4]

Since the bike boom of the 1970s first put adults on affordable 10-speed imports, other designs, such as mountain bikes and hybrids, have encouraged even more adult riders. But economic causes might be the most important factor in the resurgence of the bike: increasing energy costs, particularly since 2008, have made automobiles slightly less desirable. Throughout the Western world, the number of vehicle miles traveled per capita is on the decline. Automobile ownership among younger adults has also declined, perhaps as the result of economic pressures on a generation with limited employment opportunities and hefty student-loan debt. This transition could be a part of a seismic shift in transport: the news that fewer young people are getting driver's licenses has confused the autocentric United States. Most improbably, the bike renaissance is cool, not a childish fad. The hipster's fixie is a sign that twenty-first-century biking culture is associated with urban young adults.

Physical changes in the city have also put more Americans back on their bikes. One of the most important sources of the renaissance is a philosophical change, visible in the Congress for New Urbanism, founded in the early 1990s. New trends in urban planning promote sustainability, denser and more walkable cities, removal or calming of urban highways, and multimodal transportation. The most relevant expression of this type of thought is found in "Complete Streets" policies that specifically seek to physically rebuild streets for pedestrian, transit, bicycle, and automobile users. It began in the 1990s, when federal legislation began requiring "routine accommodation" of many different types of users in road design. Since then, many states and cities have gone further, passing ordinances specifying that the goal of streets should be to accommodate a diversity of users.[5] Complete Streets advocates sometimes point to Oregon's 1971 Bicycle Bill as the origins of their legal and policy approach, and in some ways their designs can be seen as a return to the unfulfilled promise of the early bikeway movement.

THE BIKE NEVER LEFT

From one perspective, the bike is back. From another, it never left; for the last century and a half, observers have repeatedly hailed yet another return of the bicycle. While some of these returns were wishful thinking, others were real but quickly forgotten. What is certain is that the interest in practical bicycling has persisted. "This eminently useful employment of the bicycle is rapidly increasing in all countries," ran an article in *The Wheelman* in 1882. "From all parts of the country of late indications point, seemingly, to a boom in the bicycle business," observed the *Spokane Press* in 1904. "The bicycle of today has staged an amazing comeback," argued *Popular Mechanics* in 1935. "More people are riding bicycles these days than ever before," pronounced the *Wall Street Journal*'s front page in 1941. "The Bike Boom is on," said Godfrey Frankel in 1950. "The nation's adults are proving to be a major factor in a bike sales boom that is setting records," wrote the *Wall Street Journal* in 1965. "As you probably know, a 'bike boom' is underway," noted the *Chicago Tribune* in 1975. "An annual census shows bicycling continues to boom," declared the *San Francisco Chronicle* in 2013.[6] Though media attention and numbers have varied, people have never stopped thinking about the bike.

Stepping back from the view of bicycle use as a fad or a response to crisis allows us to reconsider this century and a half of transportation policy. From this perspective, the bicycle is amazingly resilient. It just never went away, even when the road and its rules were not designed for it. And the twenty-first century bicycle renaissance might be bigger and more lasting than its predecessors: since the 1990s, adult cycling has been fairly steady, the bike industry is more stable, and evolving multimodal design philosophies are likely to create streets with space to sustain cycling in the future.

Earlier periods of increased interest in bicycling inevitably led to attempts to redesign the roads to support multiple, divergent uses. In 1900, unpaved roads prompted cyclists to imagine a network of paths allowing them to "go from New York to any point in Maine, Florida or California on smooth roads made especially for them." In 1941, a journalist worried about bicycle safety called for "the proper conditioning of the shoulders along State highways so that automobile and bicycle traffic can be physically separated." In 1965 one letter writer wondered if "officials could work out some type of program of making paths for the bikes along the heavy traveled roads." And in 1972, Bibs McIntyre enthused prematurely that "there will be *two hundred thousand miles* of Bikeways," occasionally with "a special lane or lanes . . . [where] cars are not permitted."[7] While these dreams were persistent, they went largely unfulfilled in the twentieth century.

Today, support for bicycle-specific infrastructure has returned. An incredible plethora of names has been invented for a variety of forms: bikeways, green lanes, quietways, bike boulevards, Dutch lanes, grade-separated paths, cycle tracks, and more. Most of these designs go beyond simple paint on the pavement to restructure the physical roadway. The Green Lane Project of People for Bikes, an industry-connected advocacy group, declared in 2014 that "we focus on protected bike lanes, which are on-street lanes separated from traffic by curbs, planters, parked cars, or posts."[8] The bikeway, it would seem, is back.

With the popularity of bicycle-specific infrastructure today, the bikeways opposition of the late 1970s looks politically shortsighted, a missed opportunity to secure funding for infrastructure improvements and thus encourage new riders. Bicycle advocates of today are finally creating the separated, protected infrastructure that was envisioned and partially built more than a century ago, proposed in the bikeway movement of the late 1960s, and thwarted by the conflicts of the following decade.

It's not just the physical road but also its rules that are being changed as state legislatures are urged to make up for past omissions. "Idaho laws," also known as "stop-as-yield," exempt cyclists

Figure C.1. The corner of 9th Avenue and 20th Street in New York City in 2012, with a lane marked solely for bikes and physically protected from vehicle traffic. This newly added lane is part of a wave of new, bicycle-specific infrastructure, coming after a century's worth of attempts to accommodate shared use of the same roadway. Green Lane Project, People for Bikes Foundation.

from having to come to a complete stop at stop signs, thus modifying rules designed in the early twentieth century to control motor vehicles. Laws mandating a three-foot minimum distance when passing cyclists are attempts to reduce collisions and clarify the still-confusing "as far right as practicable" placement of riders. Following Oregon's 2007 passage of "vulnerable user" legislation, several states have enacted laws that carry heavier penalties for careless driving that harms a cyclist or pedestrian.

Today bicycle advocacy is far better organized and more diverse than ever before. Even the League of American Bicyclists, heir to the complicated history of the League of American Wheelmen, is now committed to equity and inclusiveness as a bedrock principle. This commitment is visible not only in the gender-neutral name but also in the rhetoric and strategy of the organization. The group now promotes an image of bicycling diversity and explicitly supports both on- and off-street bicycle infrastructure. And advocates in the bicycling community and the bike industry are joining forces with walkers, public-transit advocates, and transportation planners.

POLICY ANALYSIS AND THE BICYCLE

The history of the bike battles demonstrates that transportation choices are not simple questions of personal choice and emotion. Americans do not drive solely because of an imagined love affair with their cars, and their dismissal of the bicycle was likewise not simply the result of changing fashion. The tools of policy analysis, when applied to what many describe as fads or crazes for the bicycle, instead reveal the influences of institutions, constituencies, path dependency, and crisis-driven agendas. Understanding bicycle history as being shaped by urban and environmental policy reveals a complicated and rich past and explains the wild mix of traffic on the streets today. The road might be a common-pool resource, but its competing users have uneven histories of access and claims to ownership. Applying the concept of path dependency, our current decision space has been constrained by past transportation, access, and funding choices. We are philosophically committed to accommodating diverse types of users in a road network that has been designed for only one.

What didn't happen is just as important as what did. Interurban and interstate sidepaths were not built at the turn of the century. The paths that were built were later paved over, committing all to a shared road network before the implications of that decision were clear. If sidepaths had succeeded, a radial network of bicycle-specific paths might have extended from American cities into their hinterlands, linking downtowns with future suburbs. Similarly, pivotal discussions in law and politics excluded bicycles: if a powerful LAW could have placed a representative in the rooms in which the UVC and MTO were written in the 1930s, later confusion over the status of the bicycle might have been avoided. Missed opportunities in the 1970s could have capitalized on significant funding streams from Oregon-style bicycle bills and the Department of the Interior's trail-building philosophy. Together, they could have funded the sort of separated infrastructure or inclusive systems that Complete Streets advocates are still dreaming of four decades later. These scenarios reflect the concept that historians call contingency. It requires imagination to see that even though history turned out one way, events could easily have taken another direction.

A PATH FORWARD

A powerful example of path dependency is the structure of the Highway Trust Fund, which is dependent on gasoline taxes. It is stunningly ironic that this source of funding is drying up just as much of the highway infrastructure is nearing the end of its life. Decreased travel, increasing fuel efficiency, and a lack of political will to raise gas taxes mean that the compromise agreement that created the highway system is in trouble. Increasingly, governments will do what Wisconsin's governor, Scott Walker, proposed in 2013: make up for the shortfall in gas taxes by increasing the portion of highway funding that already comes from general taxation and other revenue sources to subsidize road construction and maintenance. In the summer of 2014, the U.S. Congress proposed turning to pension funds, of all things, to prop up the system. These actions break the logic of linkage that has fueled the myth that cars pay for roads themselves. Now more than ever, everyone—no matter whether they walk, drive, ride the bus, or stay at home—will increasingly be aware that they are financing the construction of roads. These dramatic changes indicate that whatever the future road will be, it will be different from the roads of the second half of the twentieth century.

History that recognizes the road as a commons can help prepare us for that change. Urban planners, administrators, and decision makers should conceive of the road as a commons, working best when it supports diverse and divergent constituencies. Lewis Mumford warned of the dangers of a highway system that promoted autos alone: "The fact is that each type of transportation has its special use; and a good transportation policy must seek to improve each type and make the most of it," he wrote in 1963.[9] His warning was missed half a century ago, but we might have another chance. It is not just about the bicycle: making the decision now to structure the road as a commons future-proofs it against any unforeseen technology development, resource crisis, or funding mechanism. The inevitability of change should prompt us to rethink how we use the road now. Looking at the confused legacy of a century and a half of crisis management should motivate us to design cities and streets that can better accommodate that change.

Bicycle advocates could benefit from the same viewpoint. Our arguments work better when they define the road as a public good: a long-standing commons with multiple users. With that approach, advocacy could be more inclusive, collecting a wider base of supporters of shared goals. In any era, "bikelash" aims to diminish diversity, stereotyping cyclists as a privileged, selfish minority. Emphasizing cyclists' contributions to the public good and managing the road as a shared resource defuses that tactic. With a shared road—designed to include all users—bicycling will increase naturally.

The bike battles show what matters most of all is money. In a democracy, public support for expenditures must be based on a broad consensus of what constitutes a public good: this is what makes it a common property. Many of the best-managed commons, lasting for thousands of years, have mechanisms that make the contributions and claims of competing groups easily visible to each other and subject to public monitoring. Bike advocates would benefit from any institution or development that makes visible their contributions to and relative claims on the common-pool resource of the road.

Finally, managing the production and equitable use of a common-pool resource requires experimentation. Armed with the historical knowledge of a constantly-reshaped road, urban planners, legislatures, and communities should feel free to experiment with the form, funding, and rules of the road to accommodate shifting demands. But the public doesn't need to wait for heroic experimenters to overturn entrenched highway departments. Disruptive technologies and shifting economic realities will force change even without them. Autonomous vehicles, insurance-company black boxes in cars, wireless toll-collection systems, lightweight vehicles, and gas-sipping power systems will further destabilize the model of an autocentric road funded by gas taxes. The road has never been a rigidly defined form, and it's going to continue changing beneath our wheels.[10]

Thinking of the road as a commons highlights the problems of overuse and managing competing demands, but it also reminds us that comparable common-pool resources have been managed perfectly well. As Elinor Ostrom points out, "Communities of individuals have relied on institutions resembling neither the state nor the market to govern some resource systems with reasonable degrees of success over long periods of time." These have included communal land management in Switzerland, traditional Japanese village assemblies, Spanish *huerta* irrigation systems, and Philippine *zanjera* networks.[11] Like these systems, the road as a commonly held thoroughfare—whose purpose is to accommodate the travel of all users—has existed over millennia, with or without institutional support, whether as the Roman *viae publicae*, the King's Highway, or the public streets. To paraphrase Georges Clemenceau, the road is too important to be left to the engineers. The road is ours to manage, and communities can lay claim to it to serve our local needs, no matter what decisions may be made by state highway departments.

The road resembles many other difficult problems of environmental management and sustainability. Individual actions—like recycling, conserving water, or advocating meaningful responses to climate change—are taken within the long-standing constraints of both the natural world and the human systems of technology and politics. Choosing to ride a bicycle on a road long built for cars reveals the pressures in our systems of property ownership, transportation policy, and resource consumption that can push humans into unsustainable circumstances. In some ways, reconsidering the bicycle is part and parcel of the environmental moment in modern America: the 1970s bike boom was part of a forceful confrontation with the very real limits on available oil resources, and the twenty-first century renaissance comes with a reappraisal of the principle of designing cities around the personal automobile. Such strategic thinking is required of all environmental topics; the bike battles of today, with competing rhetoric of individual rights and communal responsibility, look very much like the environmental politics of the past forty years.

As I write this conclusion, the morning is slipping by, and I need to get to work. I'm considering riding my bicycle, but it's been a harsh winter here in Wisconsin, and the streets are crowded and slippery, with little space for my bike. Cabin fever is making it likely that I'll choose to ride anyway. In the coming years, I imagine that road users like me will choose between many existing and still-unforeseen modes of competing transportation, according to their needs and resources. In the future, more than ever, we'll need to share the road.

ACKNOWLEDGMENTS

This work could not have been completed without the financial support of two University of Wisconsin–La Crosse Faculty Research Grants, a College of Liberal Studies Small Grant, a University of Wisconsin Libraries Research Fellowship, and reassigned time from the UW-L Department of History. I thank all of these sources and particularly Charles Lee, Ruthann Benson, and my colleagues in the department.

A long list of readers commented on early drafts and versions of this work. Presentations at the Urban History Association, the Social Science History Association, the International Association for the History of Transport, Traffic and Mobility, the History Roundtable Discussion Group at the Heinz History Center in Pittsburgh, the Minnesota Environmental History Conference, and the UW-L History Authors Writing Group all helped me clarify my thoughts. Chris Wells, George Vrtis, and Michael Egan read and commented on specific chapters. E-mail correspondence and conference-hallway discussions with Silas Chamberlin, Bruce Epperson, Clay McShane, Glen Norcliffe, Ruth Oldenziel, and Carl Zimring steered me in the right directions. Two readers for the University of Washington Press assisted immensely. Ranjit Arab, who has actively edited this work, reined in many of my worst writing habits and was a tireless supporter. My closest reader and most thoughtful critic is always Jennifer Trost.

Moni McCarty and Jenifer Holman at UW-L's Murphy Library made this project possible: Holman's discovery of rare holdings of *Sidepaths* started the whole thing, and McCarty worked miracles with interlibrary loan. Paul Beck and Laura Godden at the Area Research Center put up with my nonsense; Roger White at the Smithsonian Institution was very helpful at an early stage; and Holly Reed explained the complexity of the Still Pictures Branch at NARA II at a late one.

Some of the research that eventually became chapter 2 previously appeared as "The Sidepath Not Taken: Bicycles, Taxes, and the Rhetoric of the Public Good in the 1890s," *Journal of Policy History* 25, no. 4 (2013): 557–86.

Although this work would not exist without the assistance of these people and groups, all opinions and errors in this work remain my own.

NOTE ON CITATIONS AND SOURCES

Since the overall purpose of this book is to bring often-inaccessible scholarly history to a wider audience, I've balanced simplicity and thoroughness in documenting my research. Primary and secondary sources are cited following the *Chicago Manual of Style*, 16th edition, with the exception that first as well as subsequent citations of published secondary sources are in shortened form. Full citations of scholarly and secondary sources appear in the select bibliography, and other sources are fully cited in the notes. Legal sources follow the *ALWD Citation Manual*, 4th edition, for non-court documents, allowing for a simplified citation to one reporter and year, while British sources follow the *Oxford Standard Citation of Legal Authorities*. Newspaper dates are presented in numerical format, and newspaper headlines and the titles of some nineteenth-century works have been shortened to the first phrase or four to five words. Some of these sources were located through online databases or services. These include the Prelinger archive of ephemeral films, Google's archive of scanned newspapers, Tom Tryniski's Fultonhistory.com website, the Library of Congress "Chronicling America" archive of newspapers, the Hathitrust Digital Library, the Digital Public Library of America, the Lantern database of the Media History Digital Library and the University of Wisconsin–Madison, and the magic that is YouTube. Many legal sources were accessed through the WestLaw collections, the HeinOnline database, and the Public Access to Court Electronic Records (PACER) service.

ABBREVIATIONS

AAA	American Automobile Association
AASHO	American Association of State Highway Officials
AASHTO	American Association of State Highway and Transportation Officials
BIA	Bicycle Institute of America
BMA	Bicycle Manufacturers Association of America
BSA	Boy Scouts of America
CDT	*Chicago Daily Tribune*
CPSC	Consumer Product Safety Commission
CTA	Cycle Trades of America
CTC	Cyclists' Touring Club, United Kingdom
DOI	United States Department of the Interior
EPA	Environmental Protection Agency
GDN	*Genesee Daily News* (New York)
GHQ	General Headquarters of the Supreme Commander for the Allied Powers
LAB	League of American Bicyclists
LAW	League of American Wheelmen
LOC	Library of Congress
MSHS	Minnesota State Historical Society, St. Paul
MTO	Model Municipal Traffic Ordinance of the National Conference on Street and Highway Safety
NARA I	National Archives and Records Administration, Washington, DC
NARA II	National Archives and Records Administration, College Park, Maryland
NCSHS	National Conference on Street and Highway Safety
NCUTLO	National Committee on Uniform Traffic Laws and Ordinances
NMAH	National Museum of American History, Washington, DC
OPA	Office of Price Administration
NRA	National Recovery Administration
NYS	New York State Archives, Albany, New York
NYT	*New York Times*

RG   Record Groups of the NARA
RPL   Local History and Genealogy Department, Rochester Public Library,
            the Central Library of Rochester and Monroe County, New York
SCAP   Supreme Commander for the Allied Powers
TLA   NCUTLO, *Traffic Laws Annotated*, Washington, D.C.:
            U.S. Government Printing Office, 1979
UCTD   United Cycle Trades Directorate
UVC   Uniform Vehicle Code of the NCSHS
WEC   *Whole Earth Catalog* (counterculture periodical published 1968–72
            and irregularly thereafter, in several different formats)
WHS   Library-Archives of the Wisconsin Historical Society, Madison,
            Wisconsin
WPB   War Production Board
WSJ   *Wall Street Journal*

NOTES

INTRODUCTION

1   See William Cronon's foreword to Wells, *Car Country*, x, xii, 75, 193, 289; McShane, *Down the Asphalt Path*, xii; Bijker, Hughes, and Pinch, *Social Construction of Technological Systems*, xli–xliv; Bijker, *Of Bicycles, Bakelites, and Bulbs*, 45–50.

2   Andrews, *Managing the Environment, Managing Ourselves*, 9.

3   Hardin, "Tragedy of the Commons," 1243–48.

4   Ostrom, *Governing the Commons*, 30–35; Disco and Kranakis, *Cosmopolitan Commons*, 13–25; Wall, *Commons in History*, 4–37.

5   S. P. Scott, *Civil Law* IX (Cincinnati: Central Trust, 1932), Title XIII.

6   *Smith against Shepherd* [1599] Cro. Eliz. 711, 78 ER 945; *Pelham v. Pickersgill* [1787] 1 Revised Reports 350.

7   Nathan Bailey, *An Universal Etymological Dictionary*, 5th ed. (London: Knapton, 1731), s.v. "Via Regia"; *Pelham v. Pickersgill*.

8   *Oxford English Dictionary*, s.v. "thoroughfare," www.oed.com; William Blackstone, *Commentaries on the Laws of England*, book 3 (Oxford: Clarendon, 1768), 5; see also William Hawkins and Thomas Leach, *A Treatise of the Pleas of the Crown* . . . , vol. 1, 6th ed. (Dublin: Lynch, 1788), 365; Blomley, *Rights of Passage*, 74–79.

9   Wilhelm, "Freedom of Movement," 2461–97; *Smith v. Turner*, 48 U.S. 283, 492 (1849). Of course, this right was not extended to slaves; Clementson, *Road Rights*, 9, 16. The court eventually found that even "the air is a public highway." *U.S. v. Causby*, 328 U.S. 261 (1946).

10 McShane, *Down the Asphalt Path*, 62–63; McShane and Tarr, *Horse in the City*, 72.

11 Troesken and Geddes, "Municipalizing American Waterworks"; Troesken, "Water and Urban Development"; Platt, *Electric City*.

12 Vivanco, *Reconsidering the Bicycle*, 25–26; see also the many essays in Horton, Rosen and Cox, *Cycling and Society*.

13 "Vive la Révolution," *Economist*, 9/9/2012; Tanya Snyder, "Census: American

Bike Commuting Up Nine Percent in 2012," http://usa.streetsblog.org/2013/09/19/census-american-bike-commuting-up-nine-percent-in-2012, accessed October 2014.

14   LAB, "Where We Ride: Analysis of Bicycling in American Cities," 2013, http://bikeleague.org/sites/default/files/ACS_report_forweb.pdf, accessed July 2014.

15   J. David Goodman, "More Than 200,000," *NYT, City Room* blog, 4/26/2010, http://cityroom.blogs.nytimes.com/2010/04/26/more-than-200000-a-day-now-cycling; Ashley Halsey III, "What Drivers Should Know," *Washington Post*, 9/15/2012.

16   LAB, "ACS: Bike Commuting Continues To Rise," www.bikeleague.org/content/acs-bike-commuting-continues-rise, accessed 3/26/2014; Ronald D. White, "Fewer Teens Getting Driver's Licenses," *Los Angeles Times*, 12/6/2011.

17   The Complete Streets approach is best summarized in McCann, *Completing Our Streets*, 22–25; McShane, *Down the Asphalt Path*, 79–80; National Association of City Transportation Officials, *Urban Street Design Guide* (New York: Island Press, 2013); National Association of City Transportation Officials, *Urban Bikeway Design Guide*, 2nd ed. (New York: Island Press, 2012).

18   Hurst, *Cyclist's Manifesto;* Wray, *Pedal Power;* Blue, *Bikenomics;* Penn, *It's All about the Bike;* quote from Mapes, *Pedaling Revolution*, 7.

19   Furness, *One Less Car*, 8; Henderson, *Street Fight;* Pucher and Buehler, *City Cycling*, xiii, xi; Pucher, Buehler and Seinen, "Bicycling Renaissance In North America?," 451–75.

20   Mapes, *Pedaling Revolution*, 8; J. David Goodnam and Sean Patrick Farrell, "As Bike Lanes Proliferate," *NYT, City Room* blog, 8/25/2009; Terry Tyler, "It's Time to Outlaw," *Lubbock Avalanche-Journal*, 5/19/2010; Jason Blevins, "Colorado Supreme Court Overturns," *Denver Post*, 2/4/2013; *Webb v. Black Hawk*, No. 11SC536 (Colo. 2/4/2013).

21   Nick Wilson, "Republicans Ridicule Bike Lanes," Courthouse News Service, 3/17/2010; *Departments of Transportation . . . Appropriations for 2011: Hearings, Part 4, before House Appropriations Subcommittee*, 111th Congress (Washington, DC: U.S. Government Printing Office, 2010).

22   Matthew Shaer, "Not Quite Copenhagen," *New York*, 3/28/2010; see also Robert Sullivan, "Bicyclists vs. Pedestrians: An Armistice," *NYT*, 9/27/2009; John Cassidy, "Battle of the Bike Lanes," *New Yorker, Rational Irrationality* blog, 8/3/2011; J. David Goodman, "Expansion of Bike Lanes in City," *NYT*, 11/22/2010; Michael Grynbaum, "Lawsuit Seeks to Erase," *NYT*, 3/7/2011; Grynbaum, "Judge Rejects Groups' Effort," *NYT*, 8/16/2011.

23   "Bike-Lane Bloodbath," *New York Post*, 9/21/2011; Shaer, "Not Quite Copenhagen"; "Bill de Blasio Wins the Bike Vote," *New York Daily News*, 9/3/2013.

24   Courtland Milloy, "Bicyclist Bullies Try to Rule," *Washington Post*, washingtonpost.com, online column, 7/8/2014; Stu Bykofsky, "Bikes: True Confessions," *Philadelphia Daily News*, 12/13/2013. See also Randy LoBasso, "Why Disre-

spect Festers," *Philadelphia Weekly*, 8/28/2013; Scott Rowan, "A Critical Mess," *Chicago Tribune*, 10/11/2011.

25 Jordan Michael Smith, "Conservatives' New Enemy: Bikes," *Boston Globe*, 12/16/2013; P. J. O'Rourke, "Dear Urban Cyclists: Go Play in Traffic," *WSJ*, 4/2/2011; Christopher Caldwell, "Drivers Get Rolled," *Weekly Standard*, 11/18/2013; "Why Walking Leads to One-World Government," *Economist*, *Democracy in America* blog, 6/26/2012.

26 "Opinion: Death by Bicycle," *WSJ*, http://live.wsj.com/video/opinion-death-by-bicycle/ 5/31/2013, accessed July 2014; Andrea Bernstein, "Wall Street Journal Editor," *Transportation Nation*, WNYC, 6/7/2013, http://www.wnyc.org/story/297726-wall-street-journal-editor-has-even-more-say-bike-share.

27 Caldwell, "Drivers Get Rolled"; Will Doig, "Are Urban Bicyclists Just Elite Snobs?" *Salon*, 12/4/2011; Daniel Duane, "Is It O.K. to Kill Cyclists?" *New York Times*, 11/9/2013.

28 Kaya Burgess and Rhoda Buchanan, "10,000 Pedal for Action," *Times* (London), 5/9/2012; Nick Squires, "More Bikes Sold Than Cars," *Telegraph*, 10/2/2012; Amelie Herenstein, "Crisis Hit Italians Swap Cars for Bikes Despite Perils," Agence-France Press, 5/27/2013; Philip Pank, "Welcome to the Age of the Bike," *Times*, 11/6/2012; BBC, *War on Britain's Roads*, 12/5/2012; Peter Walker, "Even More Fake," *Guardian Bike Blog*, 12/13/2012.

29 Christopher Hume, "What Goes around in Ontario," *Toronto Star*, 8/10/2011; Jason Margolis, "Cyclists Accuse Toronto Mayor," *BBC News Magazine*, 5/2/2012.

30 Ford quote from Margolis, "Cyclists Accuse"; Duane, "Is It O.K."

1. GET OUT OF THE ROAD!

1 *View on Boulevard, New York City* (American Mutoscope and Biograph Company, 1896), from EYE Filmmuseum, Amsterdam, The Netherlands.

2 C.K., "'Left': Or How the Bicycle Saved My Client," *Wheelman* 2, no. 3 (1883): 214, 212; "He Stopped Tooting," *Washington Post*, 11/8/1908; Michael Martin, "Bike Touring Builds Character," *Bangor Daily News*, 8/21/1978; "Riding a Bike," *Nacogdoches Daily Sentinel*, 9/20/2008.

3 Balogh, *Government Out of Sight*; Novak, "Myth of the 'Weak' American State."

4 Hall and Karsten, *Magic Mirror*, 4.

5 Thomas Blount, *Glossographia Anglicana Nova* (London: Dan Brown, 1707), n.p.; Thomas Blount, *Glossographia* (London: Thomas Newcomb, 1656), n.p.; Bailey, *An Universal Etymological Dictionary*, 5th ed. (1731), is very similar to Blount's 1707 work.

6 "Feast of Wit," *Sporting Magazine* 14 (April 1799): 276; McShane and Tarr, *Horse in the City*, 60–113.

7 Statute of Marlborough, 1267, 52 Hen. 3, c. 15.

8 *Pelham v. Pickersgill* [1787] 1 Revised Reports 348.

9   Blackstone, *Commentaries on the Laws of England* 3, 5; see also Hawkins and Leach, *A Treatise of the Pleas of the Crown* . . . , vol. 1, 365; Blomley, *Rights of Passage*, 74–79; Clementson, *Road Rights*, 16; McShane, *Down the Asphalt Path*, 62–63; McShane and Tarr, *Horse in the City*, 72.

10 Street, *Pedestrian Hobby-Horse*, 76–79; *Gibbons v. Ogden*, 22 U.S. 1, 153 (1824); McShane, *Down the Asphalt Path*, 54.

11 Dunham, "Bicycle Era," 137; see also Petty, "Impact of the Sport."

12 "Velocipedes and Turnpikes," *Bench and Bar* 1, no. 2 (1869): 92; Dunham, "Bicycle Era," 142, 111; "Obstructions," *Local Courts and Municipal Gazette* 6 (December 1870): 178; *R. v. Plummer*, [1871] 30 U.C.R. 41.

13 Dunham, "Bicycle Era," 145–46.

14 *Polite Athletics, CDT*, 4/17/1881, 6/27/1881; "Some Odd Bike Suits," *CDT*, 5/1/1895.

15 Dunham, "Bicycle Era," 194; Stanley Lebergott, "Wage Trends, 1800–1900," in Conference on Research in Income and Wealth, *Trends in the American Economy in the Nineteenth Century* (Princeton, NJ: Princeton University Press, 1960), 462.

16 E. A. P., "The Price of Bicycles," *Wheelman* 1, no. 2 (November, 1882): 111, 112.

17 S. L. Gracey, "The Minister: Mental and Muscular," *Wheelman* 1, no. 3 (December, 1882): 214; Robert P. Scott, *Cycling Art, Energy and Locomotion* . . . (Philadelphia: J. B. Lippincott, 1889), 7; Dunham, "Bicycle Era," 255, quoting Gracey, "The Minister," 214.

18 Philip G. Hubert Jr., "The Wheel of Today," in Dudley Allen Sargent, et. al., *Athletic Sports* (New York: Scribner's, 1897), 179.

19 Fein, *Paving the Way*, 27; T. S. Miller, *Bicycle Tactics* . . . , 3rd ed. (Chicago: n.p., 1887), song no. 5; see also Dunham, "Bicycle Era," 201.

20 Herlihy, *Bicycle*, 127–81.

21 *Taylor v. Goodwin* [1879] 4 QBD 228; this decision was available to American readers by 1881 at 28 Moak Eng. Rep. 748.

22 Ibid.

23 Dunham, "Bicycle Era," 273–75, 279–88.

24 Ibid., 289–94.

25 Taylor was himself aware of this conundrum: see his letter to the editor, "Are Bicycles Carriages?" *Evening Standard* (London), 3/31/ 1879, in response to a story published on 3/29/1879.

26 Clementson, *Road Rights*, 89–90.

27 Charles E. Pratt, "Regarding Rights of Bicycles in Streets, Parks, &c.," Broadsides and Ephemera Collection, Duke University Digital Collections; reprinted in *The Bicycling World* 2 (5/6/1881): 409.

28 Luther H. Porter, *Wheels and Wheeling* (Boston: Wheelman, 1892), i; Mionske, *Bicycling and the Law*, 10–11; *Holland v. Bartch*, 16 Am. St. R. 307, 314 (Ind. 1889).

29 Charles Sumner Lobingier, "Bicycles," in David S. Garland and Lucius P. McGehee, eds., *American and English Encyclopaedia of Law*, 2nd ed., vol. 4 (Northport, NY: Edward Thompson, 1897), 15–16.

30 Clementson, *Road Rights*, 26. *Richardson v. Danvers*, 176 Mass. 413 (1900) also found that a bicycle was not a carriage.

31 Charles J. Babbitt and Arthur W. Blakemore, *The Law Applied to Motor Vehicles . . .* , 2nd ed. (Washington, DC: Byrne, 1917), 3–4; "Notes on Recent Decisions," *Cincinnati Law Bulletin* 5 (1880): 518.

32 *Holland v. Bartch*, 120 Ind. 46 (1889); Clementson, *Road Rights*, 93; discussion of importance of *Taylor* at *Holland v. Bartch*, 16 Am. St. R. 307, 314 (Ind. 1889).

33 1887 N.Y. Laws 184, ch. 704; General Ordinances of Pittsburgh (Pa.) § 2590 (1889). On the distinctions between case law and statutory law, see Petty, "Impact of the Sport," 188, 202–3.

34 *State v. Yopp*, 97 N.C. 477 (1887).

35 *Macomber v. Nichols*, 34 Mich. 212 (1876); Clementson, *Road Rights*, 31, 90.

36 *Holland v. Bartch;* Clementson, *Road Rights*, 93.

37 Epperson, *Peddling Bicycles to America;* for the technological history, see Clayton, "SCOT: Does it Answer?" and responses in the same issue. Herlihy combines these approaches in *Bicycle*, chapter 11.

38 *Thompson v. Dodge*, 49 Am. St. Rep. 533 (Minn. 1894). Five years later, a state law was proposed in Minnesota to force cyclists to dismount when encountering other traffic; reportedly "this bill died a natural death in its infancy." A. B. Choate, "The Bicycle on Roads and Streets," *LAW Magazine* 1 (July 1900): 10.

39 *Swift v. Topeka*, 23 P. 1075 (Kan. 1890); *Lindsay vs. Winn*, 12 Lancaster L. Rev. 61 (Common Pleas Court of Lackawanna County, 1894); *Taylor v. Union Traction Co.* 184 Pa. 465 (1898).

40 *Schimpf v. Sliter*, 46 N.Y. St. Rep. 225, 64 Hun 463 (N.Y.S. 1892).

41 "Car-Track Nuisance," *LAW Bulletin* 24, no. 1 (1896): 2–3.

42 *Mercer v. Corbin*, 117 Indiana 450 (1888); discussion at Clementson, *Road Rights*, 146; "Bicycles and Vehicles," *Rochester Weekly Republican*, 3/7/1889; "Wheelmen Must Keep Off Sidewalks," *CDT*, 2/24/1889, 9; "Bicycles and Vehicles," *Weekly Republican*, 3/7/1889, 3.

43 *Swift v. Topeka*. See also Elliott and Elliott, *A Treatise on the Law*, 635. On the constitutional right to travel, see Mionske, *Bicycling and the Law*, 11–13.

44 *Gagnier v. Fargo*, 88 N.W. 1030 (N.D. 1902); *Knouff v. City of Logansport* 59 N.E. 347 (Ind. App. 1901).

45 "Recent Humorous Cases," *Albany Law Journal* 19 (1879): 368; see also "Bicycles," *American Law Review* 13 (1879): 748.

46 Porter, *Wheels and Wheeling*, 22; Choate, "Bicycle on Roads and Streets," 10; on the unsuccessful legal challenge, see *In re Wright*, 29 Hun. 357 (N.Y. 1883); this was not a U.S. Supreme Court case. Cf. Herlihy, *Bicycle*, 205; Clementson, *Road Rights*, 138.

47 For example, Pennsylvania Act of 1889, P. L. 44; Dunham, "Bicycle Era," 286–89.

48 Novak, *The People's Welfare;* Novak, "Police Power and the Hidden Transformation of the American State," in Dubber and Valverde, *Police and the Liberal State,* 54–73.

49 *State v. Yopp;* "Important to Bicyclists," *Rochester Union Advertiser,* 7/5/1887.

50 Clementson, *Road Rights,* 135.

51 "The Scorcher," *Rochester Post Express,* 5/5/1896.

52 "Scorcher Must Go," *Buffalo Morning Express,* 5/9/1896.

53 "Rules Laid Down," *CDT,* 10/6/1890; Robert G. Steel, *Bicycle Routes in Michigan . . .* (Grand Rapids: Seymour & Muir, 1896), n.p. See also "Rights of Wheelmen," *CDT,* 5/24/1896, 38.

54 Quotes from "Rights of Wheelmen," *CDT,* 5/24/1896. On lack of streetlights, see Platt, *Electric City,* 144–47; "Bicyclists Retaliate on Police," *CDT,* 5/19/1895.

55 Clementson, *Road Rights,* vii.

56 H. Noyes Greene, *The Highway Laws of New York* (Albany, NY: Matthew Bender, 1902), §162.

57 "Law for the Wheelman," *CDT,* 6/29/1899.

58 Quote from *Macomber v. Nichols;* Xenephon P. Huddy, *The Law of Automobiles,* 2nd ed. (Albany, NY: Matthew Bender, 1909), 22 n. 5; Claude Perrin Berry, *The Law of Automobiles,* 2nd ed. (Chicago: Callaghan, 1916), 18, 23, 25.

59 Charles Sumner Lobingier, "Bicycles," in Garland and McGehee, eds., *American and English Encyclopaedia of Law,* vol. 4, 18.

60 Berry, *Law of Automobiles,* 2nd ed., 30.

61 *House v. Cramer,* 134 Iowa 374 (1907); Berry, *Law of Automobiles,* 2nd ed., 14.

62 Claude Perrin Berry, *The Law of Automobiles,* 3rd ed. (Chicago: Callaghan, 1921), 11, 14, 30.

2. THE RIGHT SORT OF PEOPLE

1 "He Hated the Bicycles," *CDT,* 6/28/1891.

2 Anderson, *Imagined Communities;* "Bicycle Sidepaths," *GDN,* 4/18/1900.

3 While largely forgotten by the general public, sidepaths have occasionally been examined by local and academic historians: Dunham, "Bicycle Era," 480–83; Lehr and Selwood, "Two-Wheeled Workhorse," 3–13; McCally, "Bloomers and Bicycles," 14–17; Petty, "Bicycling in Minneapolis," 84–95; Longhurst, "Sidepath Not Taken."

4 Gant and Hoffman, *Wheel Fever,* 77.

5 Herlihy, *Bicycle,* 235–41, 251–62.

6 Herlihy has estimated 3 million bikes for 1895; Hounshell calculates 1.2 million annually for that period. By contrast, Epperson estimates that production exceeded 1 million only in 1899. David Herlihy, introduction to Dodge, *Bicycle;* Hounshell, *From the American System to Mass Production,* 191–215, esp. 201; Bruce Epperson, "How Many Bikes?"

7 Downey, *Telegraph Messenger Boys*, 74.

8 Stories in the *LAW Bulletin and Good Roads Magazine* (hereafter *LAW Bulletin*) 24 (1896): 7/3/1896, 9; 8/7/1896, 185; 7/3/1896, 3; 7/17/1896, 96.

9 "Have Bicycles an Earnest Purpose?" *Rochester Union and Advertiser*, 8/26/1889.

10 See Taylor, "Bicycle Boom," 213–40.

11 Frances Willard, *A Wheel Within a Wheel . . .* (Chicago: Women's Temperance Publishing Association, 1895), 11; Philip G. Hubert, Jr., "The Wheel of Today," in Sargent, *Athletic Sports*, 177. See also Gant and Hoffman, *Wheel Fever*, 100–102; Friss, "Cycling City," chapter 4.

12 Quote from Marguerite Merington, "Woman and the Bicycle," in Sargent, *Athletic Sports*, 209; see also Dunham, "Bicycle Era," 265–67.

13 Quote from *LAW Bulletin* 24, no. 2 (7/10/1896): 41. See also Marks, *Bicycles, Bangs and Bloomers;* Garvey, "Reframing the Bicycle"; Phillip Gordon Mackintosh and Glen Norcliffe, "Men, Women and the Bicycle: Gender and Social Geography of Cycling in the Late-Nineteenth Century," in Horton, Rosen, and Cox, *Cycling and Society*, 153–77; Macy, *Wheels of Change*.

14 Maurice Thompson, *Rosalynde's Lovers* (Philadelphia: Lippincott, 1901), 1.

15 "Some Odd Bike Suits," *CDT*, 5/1/1895.

16 Merington, "Woman and the Bicycle," 212.

17 "Negroes are Barred," *CDT*, 2/21/1894; see also Finison, *Boston's Cycling Craze*, 18–23; Ritchie, *Major Taylor*, 38–39.

18 Balf, *Major*, 77–78; see also Ritchie, *Major Taylor*, 10–11.

19 Mary Barnard Horne, *The Darktown Bicycle Club Scandal* (Boston: Walter H. Baker, 1897), 8, 16; see also Finison, *Boston's Cycling Craze*, 197–208.

20 Mason, "League of American Wheelmen," 105–7; Lisa, "Bicyclists and Bureaucrats," 392.

21 Quotes from Fein, *Paving the Way*, 24, 26; McShane, *Down the Asphalt Path*, 6–7, 19, 63–73; Mason, "League of American Wheelmen," 84–86; possibly apocryphal Twain story from "A Very Bad Road," *Good Roads* 1:3 (1892), 158.

22 Quote from Fein, *Paving the Way*, 29. See also Fuller, "Good Roads," 69; Mason, "League of American Wheelmen"; Hilles, "Good Roads Movement"; Campbell, "Good Roads Movement in Wisconsin," 273–93; Wells, "Changing Nature of Country Roads," 148–51.

23 Quote from Fein, *Paving the Way*, 35, 20–26; Fuller, "Good Roads," 69–70; Hugill, "Good Roads and the Automobile," 327–49.

24 Quote from "Roads for Cyclists," *CDT*, 5/24/1895; "Separate Roadway," *CDT*, 10/31/1894; "A Colorado Cycle-Path," *LAW Bulletin* 28, no. 12 (1898): 232; "Side Path Built," *Morning Oregonian* (Portland), 9/25/1896; "A Dollar Wheel Tax," *Morning Oregonian*, 5/5/1897; quote from "Sidepath League," *Daily Transcript* (North Adams, MA), September 9, 13, 14, 1897; Berger, *Roots of Tomorrow*, chapter 1.

25   *Annual Report of the City Engineer of Minneapolis* (Minneapolis, MN: Harrison and Smith, 1897), 36, 61, 151; "Cycle Paths of City," *St. Paul Globe*, 6/8/1902; "The Cycle-Paths of St. Paul," *LAW Bulletin* 28, no. 14 (1898): 262.

26   "Charles T. Raymond: A Brief Sketch . . . ," *Sidepaths* 4, no. 4 (February 1901): 72.

27   An 1895 bill failed on procedural grounds but was reintroduced in 1896. *Journal of the Senate of the State of New York*, 322; Act of March 4, 1896, ch. 68, 1896 N.Y. Laws 90.

28   "Charles T. Raymond," 73; "Roads and Side Paths," *LAW Bulletin* 23, no. 24 (6/12/1896): 864; "Roads versus Paths," ibid., 851.

29   "Charles T. Raymond," 72–73. See also Mason, "League of American Wheelmen," 121; William W. Armstrong, *The Higbie-Armstrong Good Roads Law . . .* (Buffalo, NY: LAW, 1898).

30   "A Cycling Center," *Rochester Union and Advertiser*, 10/19/1895.

31   "An Outrage on Cyclists," *Rochester Post-Express*, 4/18/1896; "Veto It, Governor," *Rochester Post-Express*, 4/20/1896; editorial, *Rochester Post-Express*, 5/6/1896.

32   Franklin Smith, "An Object Lesson in Social Reform," *Appleton's Popular Science Monthly* 50 (January 1897): 306–9.

33   "Wheelmen Pleased," *Rochester Democrat and Chronicle*, 4/25/1896; "Sidepath Bill is Dead," *Rochester Post-Express*, 5/7/1896.

34   "Sidepaths for Bicycles," *Rochester Post Express*, 5/13/1896; "Official Souvenir Program, LAW Good Roads Cycle Show," March 9–13, 1897, 1, in the RPL; Percy F. Megargle, "The Work of Side-Path Building," *LAW Magazine* 1, no. 8 (1901): 15–17; Smith, "Object Lesson," 311.

35   Act of March 11, 1897, ch. LIII §2, 1897 Wash. Sess. Laws 89; Act of March 18, 1896, ch. 62, 1896 N.J. Laws 100; "Cycling," *Trenton (NJ) Evening Times*, 3/22/1896. On Ontario, see Norcliffe, *Ride to Modernity*, chapter 5, n. 35.

36   For a more detailed account, see Longhurst, "Sidepath Not Taken," 566; "Charles T. Raymond," 73.

37   Act of March 27, 1899, ch. 152, 1899 N.Y. Laws 301.

38   Ibid.; Greene, *Highway Law*, 246; *Ryan v. Preston*, 10 N.Y. Ann. Cas. 5. (N.Y.S. 1901).

39   Quote from "Charles T. Raymond," 72–73; Act of March 27, 1899, ch. 152, 1899 N.Y. Laws 301; Act of April 24, 1900, ch. 640, 1900 N.Y. Laws 1393.

40   Greene, *Highway Law*, 335–38. An example of such a tag is misidentified in the Realia Collection, MSHS, as "Bicycle Path License Plate."

41   Radford, "From Municipal Socialism to Public Authorities," 867.

42   Quote from "A Special Tax," *LAW Bulletin* 23, no. 24 (6/12/1896): 851; "Special Tax on Bicycles," *LAW Bulletin* 25, no. 1 (1/1/1897): 12; "Get out of the Road," *Wichita Daily Eagle*, 5/7/1897. See also Gant and Hoffman, *Wheel Fever*, 84.

43   "Rights of Wheelmen," *CDT*, 5/24/1896.

44 "Get Good Roads," *CDT*, 2/28/1900; "Charles T. Raymond," 73.

45 "Charles T. Raymond," 73; Act of Feb. 18, 1899, S.B. 143, 1899 Or. Laws 152; *Ellis v. Frazier*, 38 Ore. 46 (Or. 1901); "Cycle Path Legislation," *LAW Magazine* 1, no. 10 (1901): 2; "Suit in Oregon," *Sidepaths* 3, no. 23 (1900): 442; "A New Law," *Sidepaths* 4, no. 3 (1901): 46.

46 Act of March 6, 1899, ch. 31, 1899 Wash. Laws 41; *People v. Bruce*, 23 Wash. 777 (1901); cf. "Washington Tax Law Illegal," *Chicago Legal News* 34, no. 56 (1901): 28.

47 *People v. Bruce*.

48 Act of April 11, 1899:35 § 2, 1899 Pa. Laws 36; *Westgate v. Spalding*, 8 Pa. D. 490 (Pa. Com. Pl. 1899)

49 Pa. Const. Art. III, § 20; *Keeler v. Westgate*, 10 Pa. D. 240 (Pa. Com. Pl. 1901); see also "Sidepath Law Inoperative," *Bucks County Gazette*, 5/10/1900.

50 *Porter v. Shields*, 200 Pa. 241 (1901); Act of Mar. 7, 1907:8 §1, 1907 Pa. Laws 10.

51 "Annual Report: Sidepath Commission by R. E. Archibald," 12/21/1901, Record Series: Highway Papers—Sidepath Commission, Warren County Archives, Lake George, NY; see also *Sidepaths* 3, no. 24 (1900): 456–57. Fulton and Seneca Falls counties likewise had budgets one-tenth the size of Monroe's. *Sidepaths* 4, no. 2 (1901): 30–33.

52 "Monroe County Sidepath Guide," 1900, Pamphlet Folder, RPL; also in NYS.

53 Act of April 10, 1900, ch. 658, 1900 Md. Laws 1047; Act of April 13, 1900, H.B. 605, 94 Ohio Laws 138; Act of May 4, 1900, ch. 757, 1900 R.I. Pub Laws 58; Act of June 17, 1901, ch. 180, 1901 Conn. Pub. Acts. 147; Act of May 27, 1901, ch. 4948, 1901 Fla. Laws 83; Act of April 2, 1901, ch. 126, 1901 Minn. Laws 153.

54 "No Let Up," *Sidepaths* 3, no. 23 (1900): 436; *LAW Magazine* 1, no. 11 (1901): 16.

55 "Sidepaths in Canada," *Sidepaths* 3, no. 23 (1900): 436–37; Act of March 29, 1901, ch. 53, 1901 S.M. 235; Norcliffe, *Ride to Modernity*, 149–57; Lehr and Selwood, "Two-Wheeled Workhorse," 6.

56 Salt Lake City, UT Code ch. LI § 727 (1903); "Cycle Path in the Granite State," *LAW Bulletin* 28, no. 22 (1898): 392; "Cycle-Paths in Ohio," *LAW Bulletin* 28, no. 16 (1898): 290; "Activity in the Far West," *LAW Magazine* 1, no. 6 (1900): 3.

57 "New Laws Needed," *St. Paul Globe*, 3/11/1900; "Wrong in Principle," *St. Paul Globe*, 4/7/1900.

58 *Bemidji Pioneer*, 5/3/1900; "Keeping up the Paths," *St. Paul Globe*, 2/30/1901.

59 "New Laws Needed," *St. Paul Globe*, 3/11/1900; "State Cycle License," *Minneapolis Journal*, 1/28/1901; "Plan for Next Season," *St. Paul Globe*, 3/28/1901.

60 *Journal of the Senate of the Thirty-Second Session of the Legislature of the State of Minnesota* (St. Paul, MN: McGill-Warner, 1901), 658; 1901 Minn. Laws 153.

61 Quote from "Want Commissioners Named," *St. Paul Globe*, 4/14/1901; "Cycle Paths of City," *St. Paul Globe*, 6/8/1902; "Cycle Path Plans," *Minneapolis Journal*, 4/15/1901; Isaac Houlgate, "Guide to Minneapolis Bicycle Paths," 1902,

pamphlet in MSHS; quote from Horace B. Hudson, *Dictionary of Minneapolis and Vicinity* (Minneapolis, MN: Hudson Publishing, 1906), 12.

62 *Ryan v. Preston;* see also *O'Donnell v. Preston*, 74 A.D. 86 (N.Y.S. 1902).

63 "Bicycle Sidepaths," *GDN*, 4/18/1900; McCally, "Bloomers and Bicycles," 14; "License System Commended," *LAW Magazine* 1, no. 6 (1900): 2.

64 "Cycle Paths," *LAW Bulletin* 28, no. 1 (1898): 42; "Cycle Path Legislation," *LAW Bulletin* 28, no. 27 (1898): 476; "Director Dodge Interested," *LAW Magazine* 1, no. 5 (1900): 2.

65 "First Tag Brought a V," *GDN*, 6/1/1899; "Bids for Bicycle Tags," *GDN*, 4/11/1900; "Three Cyclists Nabbed," *GDN*, 5/21/1900.

66 "Sidepath Funds Gone," *GDN*, 6/14/1900. In another cost-saving measure, the paths were to be covered with gravel instead of cinders. See "Preparations for Work," *GDN*, 5/30/1901; "Sale of Sidepath Tags Slow, " *GDN*, 5/2/1901.

67 "State Sidepath Commission," *Gloversville Daily Leader*, 9/13/1902.

68 "Lupton Bill Disappointing," *Brooklyn Daily Eagle*, 5/8/1907.

69 Compare "Side Paths of Monroe County," map dated 1897 and attributed to Frank J. Amsden, with "Good Roads Map" of Monroe County, dated 1902, RPL; quote from "Bicycle Sidepaths," *GDN*, 4/18/1900.

70 "The Basis of State Aid," *LAW Bulletin* 28, no. 17 (1898): 346; "Side Paths vs. Roads," *LAW Bulletin* 24, no. 3 (1896): 95; Novak, "The Myth of the 'Weak' American State," 758–59; Radford, "Municipal Socialism," 888.

71 Fein, *Paving the Way*, 35, 30. See also Lipin, "Cast Aside the Automobile Enthusiast."

3. THE RULES OF THE ROAD

1 *Automobile Parade* (Edison Manufacturing Company, 1900); *A Trip down Market Street before the Fire* (Miles Brothers, 1906), AFI/Post (George) Collection, LOC; *Speedy* (Paramount Pictures, 1928).

2 Wells, *Car Country*, 75.

3 Robert H. Merriam, "Bicycles and Tricycles," in Bureau of the Census, *Manufactures, Part IV of Special Reports on Selected Industries* (Washington, DC: U.S. Government Printing Office, 1905), 289.

4 "Bicycle Hit at Orpheum," *Variety* 37 (1915): 33; Ritchie, *Major Taylor*, 61; Herlihy, *Bicycle*, 377–82.

5 "Wheelmen Say Cycling is Dead," *CDT*, 11/19/1899.

6 Ibid.; see also Finison, *Boston's Cycling Craze*, 210; "The Bicycle and the Automobile," *Scientific American* 92 (9/23/1905): 234.

7 "Steinmetz Predicts," *Motor Age*, 6/11/1914, 22.

8 Quotes from Paxson, "The Rise of Sport," 159; "Sterling Elliott Signs Up," *American Motorist* 12 (May 1920): 44.

9 Report, March 1936, folder "0–871 League of American Wheelmen," RG 79 Records of the National Park Service, State Park Files, 1933–1947, NARA II.

10 UCTD, *Third Annual Report* (New York: UCTD, 1919), 16.

11 CTA, *Fourth Annual Report* (New York: CTA, 1920), 13–14, 17.

12 "Bicycle Output Was Reduced," *WSJ*, 7/16/1926; C. Arthur Fifer, *Do You Remember?* (Quincy, IL: n.p., 1951), 31–32.

13 McShane, *Down the Asphalt Path*, 125–48.

14 Oliver Wendell Holmes, *The Common Law* (Boston: Little, Brown, 1881), 113; R. Vashon Rogers, *The Law of the Road* (New York: Hurd and Houghton, 1876), 71; Norton, *Fighting Traffic*, 48.

15 James R. McConaghie, "The Use of Paint on Roads to Direct Traffic, II," *Good Roads* 63, no. 6 (1922): 47; "Road Signals," LAW *Bulletin*, 6/12/1896, 858.

16 Jakle and Sculle, *Signs in America's Auto Age*, 57; "Autoists, Horsemen and Cyclists," *Automobile Topics* 3, no. 14 (2/18/1902): 528; Norton, *Fighting Traffic*, 48.

17 Norton, *Fighting Traffic*, 63; the figures were 659 dead in auto crashes, 260 murdered. Wells, *Car Country*, 88.

18 McShane, "Origins," 380–81.

19 *Irwin v. Judge*, 81 Conn. 492, 71 Atl. 572 (1909), as reproduced in Berkeley Davids, *The Law of Motor Vehicles* (Northport, NY: Edward Thompson, 1911), 13, 163, 167.

20 McShane, "Origins," 392–93; Norton, *Fighting Traffic*, 50.

21 "New Automobile Laws," *Automobile Topics* 3, no. 14 (1/18/1902): 526; James H. Deering, *1905 Supplement to the Codes of California* . . . (San Francisco: Bancroft-Whitney, 1905), 857–66.

22 Quote from A. B. Barber, "Why Drivers' License Laws with Examination Are Needed," *Georgia Lawyer*, July 1931, 14; see also Roots, "Orphaned Right."

23 The home-rule revolution of the late nineteenth century greatly enlarged the powers of cities. Hall and Karsten, *Magic Mirror*, 213.

24 Norton, *Fighting Traffic*, 57, 61–62. Cf. Jakle and Sculle, *Signs in America's Auto Age*, 64.

25 Norton, *Fighting Traffic*, 52; McConaghie, "Use of Paint on Roads," 57, 62.

26 C. H. Shepherd, "Devices for Traffic Control," *American City* 26 (June, 1922): 583, emphasis added.

27 Quotes from *R. v. Cross* [1812] 3 Camp. 223; *Cohen v. Mayor* 113 N.Y. 532–535 (1889). See also Harold S. Buttenheim, "The Problem of the Standing Vehicle," *Annals of the American Academy of Political and Social Science* 133 (September 1927): 144–55; Segrave, *Parking Cars in America*, 5. Buttenheim and Segrave incorrectly paraphrase the *R. v. Cross* decision.

28 Fletcher Pratt, "No Parking," *American Mercury* 39 (October 1936): 155–56.

29 Report, March 1936.

30 "Traffic Control Lighting Equipment," *Good Roads* 63 (8/16/1922): 61. Chicago developed an alternative, timed system. Norton, *Fighting Traffic*, 134–38.

31 McShane, "Origins," 384.

32 "Space Grabbing Vehicle," *Electric Railway Journal* 52, no. 4 (7/27/1918): 149; Wis. Stat. § 85.69 (1929).

33 BSA, *Cycling* (New York: BSA, 1930), 23.

34 Norton, *Fighting Traffic*, 97.

35 Ibid., 71–79; McShane, *Down the Asphalt Path*, 187–89; Wells, *Car Country*, 93–95.

36 McShane, "Origins," 386; "Urges Pedestrians Must Be Regulated," *Automobile Topics* 44, no. 8 (1916): 819; "Fined for Getting Hurt," *Case and Comment* 29, no. 2 (March 1923): 44.

37 NCSHS, *Manual on Street Traffic Signs, Signals, and Markings* (Washington, DC: NCSHS, 1930); AASHO and NCSHS, *Manual on Uniform Traffic Control Devices for Streets and Highways* (Washington, DC: NCSHS, 1935).

38 Wells, *Car Country*, xxxii.

39 Sky, *National Road*, 155–60; Heitmann, *Automobile and American Life*, 76–79.

40 Thomas H. MacDonald, "Four Years of Road Building under the Federal-Aid Act," *Public Roads* 3 (June 1920): 11; Wells, *Car Country*, 129.

41 Heitmann, *Automobile and American Life*, 78. AASHO later became AASHTO.

42 McShane, *Down the Asphalt Path*, 58; Wells, *Car Country*, 76–7; Fein, *Paving the Way*, 88–90, 228–29; Heitmann, *Automobile and American Life*, 76–78, Holley, "Blacktop," 723–32.

43 Among many, see DiMento and Ellis, *Changing Lanes*, 15–21, 23–44.

44 Norton, *Fighting Traffic*, 175–81.

45 Ibid., 191, 186, 188–93.

46 NCSHS, *Tentative Draft of Model Municipal Traffic Ordinance . . .* (Washington, DC: National Capital, 1928), 9; NCSHS, *Final Text of Uniform Vehicle Code* (Geneva, NY: W. F. Humphrey, 1926), 66.

47 Bureau of Public Roads, *Uniform Vehicle Code . . .* , rev. ed. (Washington, DC: U.S. Government Printing Office, 1930), § 5.

48 Albert Sidney Bolles, *Business Man's Commercial Law Library*, vol. 2 (New York: Doubleday, 1922), 325; MTO section 12–14, quoted in *TLA*, 324. On the UVC's allowing bicycles on sidewalks, see Mionske, *Bicycling and the Law*, 67.

49 BSA, *Cycling*, 22.

50 *Luther v. State of Indiana*, 98 N.E. 640 (Ind. 1912); *Dice v. Johnson*, 175 N.W. 38 (Iowa 1919).

51 *Haynes v. Sprague et al.*, 137 Ore. 23 (1931).

52 *Kuczko v. Prudential*, 110 N.J.L. 111 (1933).

53 Bureau of Public Roads, *Uniform Vehicle Code . . . Act IV*, § 22.

54 See historical discussion of § 11–1205 in *TLA*, 320.

55 BSA, *Cycling*, 22; William Estabrook Chancellor, *Educational Sociology* (New York: Century, 1919), 204.

56 Quote from McShane, "Origins," 388; Andrews, *Managing the Environment*, 156; Herlihy, *Bicycle*, 360.

57 Berto, *Dancing Chain*, 97; Chancellor, *Educational Sociology*, 203–4.

58 *Parke Davis' Employees* (American Mutoscope and Biograph, © 1903, filmed 1899).

59 "Wheelmen Say Cycling Is Dead," 8; "Steinmetz Predicts," 22; Chancellor, *Educational Sociology*, 203; see also Herlihy, *Bicycle*, chapter 13.

60 "Figures on Wheels," *CDT*, 9/18/1898.

61 Andrew Rinker, *Annual Report of the City Engineer* (Minneapolis, MN: Syndicate Printing, 1911), 11e–14e.

62 Columbia Bicycles brochure (1911), 3–4, 32, series "Bicycles," Warshaw Collection, NMAH; *Motorcycling and Bicycling*, 12/6/1915, 41.

63 *Bridgeport Standard Telegram*, 2/15/1919; *Bill Henry* (Paramount Pictures, 1919); UCTD, *Third Annual Report*, 10, 13; United States Tariff Commission, *Tariff Information Surveys . . . C10*, rev. ed. (Washington, DC: U.S. Government Printing Office, 1921), 48.

64 Office of Brigade Signal Officer, Connecticut National Guard, to vice president, Pope Manufacturing Co., January 4, 1896, folder "Bicycle pps," RG 108, NARA I.

65 "August 10th, 1896 Report of 1st Lieut W. R. Abercrombie," RG 108, NARA I.

66 Quoted in Koelle, "Pedaling on the Periphery," 313. See also Sorensen, *Iron Riders;* Herlihy, *Bicycle*, 292.

67 Letters to the Adjutant General of the Army from C. S. Wilson, May 8, and Thomas C. Fry, May 11, 1898, and from "Chief Engnr," June 21, 1917, "Bicycles," Microfilm M698 reel 104, RG 94, "Records of Adjutant General," NARA I.

68 United States Tariff Commission, *Tariff Information Surveys*, 49; Berto, *Dancing Chain*, 107–8, 145–46.

69 Advertisement, *Boys' Life*, May 1934, 48.

70 "It Is Motorcycling and Bicycling Now," *Motorcycling and Bicycling*, 5/11/1915.

71 CTA, *Fourth Annual Report* 6–8, 12; Advertisement in *Boys' Life*, February 1917, 51.

72 Advertisements in *Boys' Life*, May 1925, 49; May 1932, 44; April 1932, 44.

73 CTA, "Cycle-Logical Ways to Happier Days" (1930), in the collection of the Brian Sutton-Smith Library and Archives of Play, Rochester, NY; advertisements in *Boys' Life*, June 1935, 28; August 1935, 49.

74 Downey, *Telegraph Messenger Boys*, 73; "Special Delivery Messenger, U.S. Post Office," (American Mutoscope & Biograph Company, 1903), Paper Print Collection, LOC; *Motorcycling and Bicycling*, 10/4/1915, 43; BSA, *Cycling*, 21; CTA, "Cycle-Logical."

75 Advertisement, *Boys' Life*, April 1927, 60; *Jahn's Administrator v. McKnight*, 25 Ky. L. Rptr. 1758, 78 S.W. 862 (1904).

76 *Clower v. Western Union*, 18 Ga. App. 775, 90 S.E. 730 (1916).

77 *Postal Telegraph-Cable Co. v. Minderhout*, 14 Ala. App. 392, 71 So. 89 (1916).

78 *Postal Telegraph-Cable Co. v. Murrell*, L.R.A. 1918D, 357, 201 S.W. 462 (1918).

79 *Western Union v. Ausbrooks*, 148 Tenn. 615, 257 S.W. 858 (1924).

80 Advertisement, *Boys' Life*, March 1926, 40; Downey, *Telegraph Messenger Boys*, 76–77.

81 Advertisements in *Boys' Life:* March 1916, 43; December 1917, 51; April 1917, 39.

82 Ernest Thompson Seton, *A Handbook of Woodcraft, Scouting, and Life-Craft* (New York: Doubleday Page, 1910), 15.

83 BSA, *The Official Handbook for Boys* (Garden City, New York: Doubleday, Page, 1912), 31.

84 UCTD, *Third Annual Report*, 31.

85 CTA, "Cycle-Logical Ways."

86 BSA, *Cycling*, 18–19.

87 "Boy Scouts' Bicycle Hike," *Boys' Life*, September 1912, 16; advertisement, *Boys' Life*, December 1915, 37; Charles Olive, "Selecting and Adjusting a Bicycle," *Boys' Life*, April 1923, 47; Irving Crump, "Twenty Years the Crowd's Hero," *Boys' Life*, April 1927, 8.

88 BSA, *Cycling*, 16.

89 Among many, see Seiler, *Republic of Drivers;* Urry, "'System' of Automobility"; Goodwin, "Reconstructing Automobility."

4. VICTORY BIKE BATTLES

1 Reproduced in the *Carmel Putnam County Republican* (New York), 1/18/1942; *Cuba Patriot* (New York), 1/22/1942. For background, see Bartels, "Office of Price Administration," 13.

2 "Leon Henderson, Price Boss," *Life*, 1/26/1942, 33; Robert McCall, "'And We'll Look Sweet,'" *Washington Post*, 1/29/1942; "Editorial," *New York Sun*, 1/16/1942; *News Parade: Washington in War Time* (Castle Films, 1942).

3 "Mr. Henderson Awheel," *NYT*, 1/17/1942.

4 "'Victory' Bicycles Are Planned," *Geneva Daily Times* (New York), 1/17/1942.

5 Bailey, *Home Front*, 9; Furness, *One Less Car*, 119–20; Fitzpatrick, *Bicycle in Wartime*, 171–74.

6 Most of the program was promulgated in *New Adult Bicycle Ration Regulations* (Washington, DC: U.S. Government Printing Office, July 1942), with amendments in quarterly reports.

7 Robert E. Sessions, director, Consumer Division, to Betty Sultini, May 29, 1942, folder "Bicycles Rationing R-7," RG 188, "Records of the Office of Price Administration, Rationing Department National Office, Automotive Supply Rationing Division, Bicycle Rationing Branch," NARA II. Unless otherwise noted, all file folders referenced in the rest of this chapter, labeled "Bicycle Transportation vs. Automotive," "Bicycle Production," "Rationing," "Progress Reports," "Press Releases," "Field Reports," and "Organizational Charts," are from this record group.

8 National Recovery Administration, *Code of Fair Competition for the Bicycle*

Manufacturing Industry (Washington, DC: U.S. Government Printing Office, 1934), 288.

9　"Amazing Return of the 'Bikes,'" *Popular Mechanics*, January, 1935, 62; see also "Sears,' Ward's Sales Helped," *WSJ*, 7/10/1934; "Bicycle Production," *WSJ*, 9/8/1936.

10　Quotes from "Our Hollywood Neighbors," *Movie Classic* 4 (March–July 1933): 71; ibid., 15; "My Beauty Hint," *Hagerstown Daily Mail*, 12/11/1933.

11　*Photoplay* 44–45 (July–December 1933): 87.

12　Garnett L. Eskew, "The Bike Completes a Cycle," *Rotarian*, August 1938, 34–36.

13　Ibid.; "Life Goes Bicycling," *Life*, 7/17/1939, 71.

14　"Shipments of Bicycles: Years 1935 to 1941 Inclusive," "Bicycle Production"; quote from Eskew, "The Bike Completes a Cycle."

15　Berto, *Dancing Chain*, 56, 108; "Life Goes Bicycling," 71.

16　Quote from Schwinn advertisement in *Life*, 8/11/1941, 15; Herlihy, *Bicycle*, 325–34; Berto, *Dancing Chain*, 145–47; Hadland and Lessing, *Bicycle Design*, 196.

17　BSA, *Cycling* (New Brunswick, NJ: BSA, 1949), 6.

18　Seattle branch of Mitsubishi Shoji Kaisha to manager, Osaka branch, July 26, 1934, box 5; memo, "Bicycle Business in California," July 30, 1935, box 6, "Seized Correspondence," RG 131 "Office of Alien Property," NARA II.

19　Eskew, "The Bike Completes a Cycle"; Paul W. Kearney, "Stopping Trouble on Two Wheels," *Rotarian*, August 1941, 19.

20　Using the GDP deflation method, the real value of bikes sold in 1900 would be around $701 million in 2009 dollars; in 1939, it was around $534 million. Robert H. Merriam, "Bicycles and Tricycles," *Census of Manufactures, Part IV* (Washington, DC: U.S. Government Printing Office, 1905), 289–92; *16th Census of the United States, 1940, Census of Business, 1939*, vol. 5 (Washington, DC: U.S. Government Printing Office, 1941), 188–89.

21　"Number of Automobiles and Bicycles Produced from 1937 through 1941," "Bicycle Transportation vs. Automotive."

22　"Bicycles: Do a Come-back," *WSJ*, 9/4/1941; "OPM Gives Radio, Bicycle Makers," *WSJ*, 12/17/1941.

23　Polenberg, *War and Society*, 32.

24　Fitzpatrick, *Bicycle in Wartime*, 172; "Sale of Bicycles to Adults Curbed," *NYT*, 4/3/1942; "New Bicycle Sales Banned," *WSJ*, 4/3/1942.

25　Robert E. Stone to Rolf Nugent, May 9, 1942, folder "Bicycles Rationing R-7"; Office of Price Administration, *Second Quarterly Report for the Period Ended July 31, 1942* (Washington, DC: U.S. Government Printing Office, 1942), 80.

26　These agencies and offices have a complex history. The OPA was created by the president's executive order of April 11, 1941. See Zimring, *Cash for Your Trash*, 90; Polenberg, *War and Society*, 7; Sparrow, *Warfare State*, 171–73; Graham, *Toward a Planned Society*, 70.

27　Zimring, *Cash for Your Trash*, 100.

28 "OPA Relaxes Bicycle Purchase," *WSJ*, 1/13/1943.

29 H. M. Meloney, BMA, "Preliminary Statement on Relationship of Bicycle to National Defense," April 29, 1942, "Bicycle Transportation vs. Automotive."

30 R. E. Stone to R. Nugent et al., "Comparison of Rubber Uses between Competitive Forms of Transportation," June 15, 1942, "Bicycle Transportation vs. Automotive."

31 Chart, "Travel per Pound of Crude Rubber: Thousands of Miles," "Bicycle Transportation vs. Automotive."

32 "Advance Release," June 4, 1942, "Bicycles Rationing R-7."

33 A. G. Richtmeyer, "A Study of the Relative Economy . . . ," June 22, 1942, "Bicycle Transportation vs. Automotive."

34 Ibid.

35 Memo from John F. Fennelly, End Products Committee, WPB, June 26, 1942, "Bicycle Transportation vs. Automotive."

36 Finlay, *Growing American Rubber*, 1, 107–39, 171–97; Frohardt-Lane, "Promoting a Culture of Driving," 337, 343; Heitmann, *Automobile and American Life*, 129–30.

37 Fennelly, memo; Zimring, *Cash For Your Trash*, 94.

38 Fennelly, memo.

39 Fennelly reported that "a different agency" was the Bureau of Public Roads, but it was probably the Bureau of Standards. Fennelly, memo; Robert E. Stone to John F. Fennelly, "Allotment of Rubber for New Adult Bicycles," June 27, 1942, "Bicycle Transportation vs. Automotive."

40 Dael Wolfle, "Psychologists in Government Service," *Psychological Bulletin* 39, no. 6 (June 1942): 392. By 1944, DeSilva was the Office of Program vice chairman of the WPB: Donald G. Marquis, "Social Psychologists in National War Agencies," *Psychological Bulletin* 41 (February 1944): 123. Harry Reginald De Silva, "An Experimental Investigation of the Determinants of Apparent Visual Movement" (PhD diss., Harvard University, 1927). For an example of DeSilva's extensive research, see Harry R. DeSilva, "Age and Highway Accidents," *Scientific Monthly* 47 (1938): 536–45; for samples of journalistic coverage, see Lewis Bergman, "Less Deadly than the Male," *NYT*, 7/14/1940.

41 Harry R. DeSilva, "Are Bicycles Needed to Supplement Existing Transportation?" n.d., "Bicycle Transportation vs. Automotive"; see also Frohardt-Lane, "Promoting a Culture of Driving," 348.

42 Fred Myers to Harry DeSilva, July 9, 1942, "Bicycle Transportation vs. Automotive."

43 Harry DeSilva to C. McFadden, "Facts about Bicycle Transportation," August 7, 1942, "Bicycle Transportation vs. Automotive."

44 "U.S. Trims List of Eligibles," *CDT*, 8/11/1942; "2 Plants Designated to Produce Bicycles," *NYT*, 9/3/1942; "88,000 Bicycles Set as October Quota," *NYT*, 9/27/1942; "OPA Relaxes Bicycle Purchase Rules," *WSJ*, 1/13/1943.

45 Untitled typescript, n.d. [October 1942], "Bicycle Transportation vs. Automotive."

46   Arthur Liebers, "More Bicycles to Keep," *NYT*, 3/22/1942; "War Increases Bicycle's Popularity," *NYT*, 1/13/1942; "Offers Bicycle Traffic Plan," *NYT*, 3/7/1942; "Bicycle Use Quadrupled," *NYT*, 3/7/1942; "He'll Be Riding Without," *CDT*, 3/8/1942.

47   William Strand, "Adult Bicycle Sales Banned," *CDT*, 4/3/1942; see also Charles E. Egan, "Sale of Bicycles to Adults Curbed," *NYT*, 4/3/1942.

48   "War Workers Use Bicycles," *American Bicyclist*, June, 1942, 32; "Cycling to Work," *American Bicyclist*, July, 1942, 28; "War Plant Employees Cycle," *American Bicyclist*, November, 1942, 30.

49   Advertisement, *Life*, 5/25/1943, 14.

50   AAA Research Report No. 20 (July 1943), and No. 23 (December 1943), in "Bicycle Transportation vs. Automotive."

51   Zimring, *Cash for Your Trash*, 89, 94.

52   Quote from Polenberg, *War and Society*, 32; Zimring, *Cash for Your Trash*, 94.

53   The large collection of correspondence in "Bicycle Rationing R-7" is organized alphabetically, by sender, in box 307 of RG 188.

54   Evan and Janet Gawne to Leon Henderson, June 13, 1942, "Bicycle Rationing R-7."

55   "Form Letter to Schoolchildren," January 19, 1943, box 305, "Rationing Department."

56   C. P. McFadden to Charles F. Phillips, December 17, 1942, "Bicycle Progress Reports 1942."

57   Ibid.

58   "Bicycle Production," A. H. Wyman to O. P. Hufstader, March 4, 1944, "Bicycle Production." A postwar publication supports these totals, estimating 144,000 bicycles manufactured yearly: Percy Bidwell, *What the Tariff Means to American Industries* (New York: Council on Foreign Relations, 1956), 74.

59   February and March 1943, "Press Releases."

60   Harry Gillogly to Elliott Taylor, February 5, 1944, "Bicycle Production"; "Comments from the Field on Bicycle Rationing," report, 1944; Russ Paul to Elliott Taylor, June 19, 1944, "Field Reports."

61   "Quarterly Report for the Months of July, August, and September 1944," "Bicycle Progress Reports 1942."

62   Arnold, Schwinn & Co., "A Survey Concerning Post-war Employment and Production in the Cycle Industry," n.d., "Bicycle Production."

63   Zimring, *Cash for Your Trash*, 97, 100–101; Frohardt-Lane, "Promoting a Culture of Driving," 355.

64   Norton, *Fighting Traffic*, 149–62, 204–5, 261–62; Frohardt-Lane, "Promoting a Culture of Driving," 338.

5. 1950s SYNDROME

1   *Leave It to Beaver:* "It's a Small World," pilot; "The Paper Route," season 1, episode 17; "Beaver's Prize," season 3, episode 4; "Beaver's Bike," season 3, episode 26 (1957–60; Universal, 2005), DVD.

2 Christian Pfister, "The '1950s Syndrome' and the Transition from a Slow-Going to a Rapid Loss of Global Sustainability," in Uekoetter, *Turning Points*, 92; Wells, *Car Country*, 287.

3 "Beaver Takes a Drive," *Leave It to Beaver*, season 5, episode 7.

4 "Wally's License," *Leave It to Beaver*, season 6, episode 3.

5 Vivanco, *Reconsidering the Bicycle*, 25–26.

6 "After Lean War Years," *WSJ*, 9/26/1945; "Bendix to Produce," *WSJ*, 8/14/1945; "Bicycle Output Expected to Top," *New York Herald Tribune*, 10/2/1947.

7 "Stiff Pedaling," *WSJ*, 5/18/1948; "Bicycle Makers Expect 2 Million," *WSJ*, 10/3/1947; "Bicycle Demand Put in Millions," *NYT*, 1/29/1947. Berto, *Dancing Chain*, 179, reports that 1.7 million bicycles were manufactured in 1946, 2.8 million in 1948, and 1.5 million in 1954.

8 Fiege, *Republic of Nature*, 392. It is unclear exactly when the LAW stopped functioning. There were only a few scattered chapters in the 1930s and 1940s. Hoffman puts its death at 1942, the year of the last national convention in Chicago. E. Peter Hoffman, "The League of American Wheelmen," in Leete, *Best of Bicycling!*, 397.

9 "New Executive Secretary of the Bicycle Institute," *NYT*, 11/4/1946. On the BIA, see Epperson, "The Great Schism," 78 n. 16.

10 Quote from Foster Hailey, "Bicycles Built for Millions," *New York Times Magazine*, 10/16/1949, 78–79; Herlihy, *Bicycle*, 336. On the increase in automobiles in Europe, see Ralph Buehler and John Pucher, "International Overview," in Pucher and Buehler, *City Cycling*, 16–17.

11 Oakley, *Winged Wheel*, quote from 127, 98–100, 134, 214.

12 *TLA*, 315–16.

13 UVC Act V, subsection 93(d) (rev. ed., 1944), emphasis added, reprinted in *TLA*, 1.

14 NCSHS, *Model Traffic Ordinance* (Washington, DC: U.S. Government Printing Office, 1946), 1.

15 North Carolina Law from § 20–38 (38), quoted in *TLA*, 26. For a specific example of state enactment, see Davis, "California Vehicle Code," 377.

16 "The Traffic Program," *Southeast Missourian*, 12/28/1948.

17 Theodore Malvin Matson, *Traffic Engineering* (New York: McGraw-Hill, 1955), 245.

18 Wells, *Car Country*, 274.

19 David R. Levin, *Legal Aspects of Controlling Highway Access* (Washington, DC: U.S. Government Printing Office, 1945), 31, 4; Netherton, *Control of Highway Access*, 5.

20 Rose, *Interstate*, 34, 46–47, 93; Wells, *Car Country*, 193; Wells, "Fueling the Boom," 72–81.

21 Wells, *Car Country*, 275; see also Rose and Mohl, *Interstate*; *Motormania* (Walt Disney, 1950); Walter Powers, "The Danger of Bike Riders," *Sarasota Herald-*

Tribune, 10/3/1965; McCann, *Completing Our Streets*, 10. For more on the mythology of road funding, see Blue, *Bikenomics*, 11–13.

22 Duany, Plater-Zyberk, and Speck, *Suburban Nation*, xiii; Hayden, *Building Suburbia;* Harris, *Second Suburb.*

23 Sellers, *Crabgrass Crucible;* Rome, *Bulldozer in the Countryside*, 16.

24 Rome, *Bulldozer in the Countryside*, 16; Wells, *Car Country*, 257, 261.

25 "After Lean War Years."

26 Percy Bidwell, *What the Tariff Means to American Industries* (New York: Council on Foreign Relations, 1956), 70; Furness, *One Less Car*, 115; Berto, *Dancing Chain*, 179, 199.

27 "Lucy's Bicycle Trip," *I Love Lucy*, season 5, episode 2 (1956); "Bicycle Trip for Two," *Father Knows Best*, season 6, episode 6 (1959); "Opie and the Spoiled Kid," *The Andy Griffith Show*, season 3, episode 21 (1960).

28 Ken Yarber, "Safety on Two Wheels," *Rotarian*, August 1953, 16.

29 Berto, *Dancing Chain*, 179, 199; Furness, *One Less Car*, 115; "Beaver's Bike," *Leave It to Beaver*, season 3, episode 26; advertisements from *Life*, 3/15/1948, 142, and 3/14/1949, 108.

30 See Orgeron, Orgeron, and Streible, *Learning with the Lights Off*, 9–11; Alexander, *Academic Films for the Classroom*, 5–10.

31 The President's Highway Safety Conference, *Preliminary Report of Committee on Education* (Washington, DC: U.S. Government Printing Office,1946), 11.

32 National Commission on Safety Education of the National Education Association, *Bicycle Safety in Action* (Washington, DC: National Education Association, 1950), 5.

33 *I'm No Fool with a Bicycle, with Jiminy Cricket* (Walt Disney Pictures, 1956). See also Furness, *One Less Car*, 115–17.

34 BSA, *Cycling* (New Brunswick, NJ: BSA, 1949), 5 (emphasis in original); *Bike Safety* (Centron, 1950); *Bicycle Clown* (Sid Davis, 1958).

35 *Drive Your Bike* (Sullivan, 1954).

36 *You and Your Bicycle* (Progressive Pictures, 1948, 1959).

37 *Bicycle Today, Automobile Tomorrow* (Sid Davis Productions, 1969).

38 Public Roads Administration, *Model Traffic Ordinance* (Washington, DC: U.S. Government Printing Office, 1946).

39 For current criminological concerns, see Shane D. Johnson, Aiden Sidebottom, and Adam Thorpe, *Bicycle Theft* (Washington, DC: U.S. Department of Justice, Office of Community Oriented Policing Services, 2008), 13–14, 42–44. Albert W. Whitney, *Man and the Motor Car* (Lansing: Michigan Inter-industry Highway Safety Committee, 1949), 249.

40 John Healey, "Big Increase in Bicycle Travel," *San Jose Evening News*, 8/22/1941; "Bicycle Smashing," *Life*, 7/14/1947, 77.

41 "Beaver's Bike."

42 *Bicycle Today, Automobile Tomorrow.*

43 Yasujiro Ozu, *Late Spring* (1949; Criterion, 2012), DVD.

44 Steele, "Making of a Bicycle Nation," 75. Rarely seen in the United States, this film's title is translated in various ways. Charles J. Fillmore and Miyo Kawai, *The Japanese Movie; Aoi Sanmyaku (The Green Mountain Ridge): Script with Notes and Translations* (Ann Arbor: University of Michigan Press, 1968), 96.

45 E. Peter Hoffman, "The Cycling Scene," in Leete, *Best of Bicycling!*, 73; Steele, "Making of a Bicycle Nation," 75.

46 "Japanese Bicycles," *LAW Bulletin* 24, no. 4 (7/24/1896): 25.

47 Chandler, *Inventing the Electronic Century*, 51.

48 Berto, *Dancing Chain*, 108–9; Steele, "Making of a Bicycle Nation," 72.

49 "Japan Factories Turn to Making," *WSJ*, 8/18/1922; Steele, "Making of a Bicycle Nation," 72; Berto, *Dancing Chain*, 108–9.

50 Mitsubishi Shoji Kaisha to Great Falls Paper Company, April 21, 1938, "Seized Correspondence of the Machinery Department of Mitsubishi Shoji Kaisha," RG 131 Records of the Office of Alien Property, NARA II.

51 "Trade and Industry," *Oriental Economist*, 4/20/1946, 254; Berto, *Dancing Chain*, 180–82.

52 Allinson, *Japan's Postwar History*, 52–82; Dower, *Embracing Defeat*, 75–76.

53 Dower, *Embracing Defeat*, 83–84, 533.

54 Steele, "Making of a Bicycle Nation," 75.

55 "Trade and Industry." The magazine's founder, Ishibashi Tanzan, had an incredibly complicated political history both before the war and after; "purged" by SCAP, he later served as prime minister in the mid-1950s.

56 "Blackmarket: Bicycle Production," May 20, 1947, folder "Bicycle General," Box 7728, RG 331, General Records of GHQ SCAP, NARA II.

57 Allinson, *Japan's Postwar History*, 74–75; Dower, *Embracing Defeat*, 533; Berto, *Dancing Chain*, 180–82.

58 Hoffman, "Cycling Scene," 73.

59 Takuya Yamazaki and Yuki Mabuchi, "Sports Betting and the Law in Japan," in Anderson, *Sports Betting*, 513–14.

60 Quotes from Yamazaki and Mabuchi's translation of the Bicycle Racing Act of 1948 in Anderson, *Sports Betting*, 517–19; Steele, "Making of a Bicycle Nation," 75.

61 "Bills and Resolutions Received from C.L.O.," National Diet Library, microfiche call number GS(A)-01806, reprinted in Bertrand M. Roehner, *Relations between Allied Forces and the Population of Japan . . .* (Paris: Institute for Theoretical and High Energy Physics, e-book, 2009), 32.

62 Hoffman, "Cycling Scene," 74; Anderson, *Sports Betting*, 517–19.

63 Dower, *Embracing Defeat*, 533–34; Chandler, *Inventing the Electronic Century*, 68.

64 Berto, *Dancing Chain*, 201.

65 MacArthur quoted in Shibusawa, *America's Geisha Ally*, 55, 56; Dower, *Embracing Defeat*, 550–51.

66 Bayly and Harper, *Forgotten Armies*, 116; cf. Fitzpatrick, *Bicycle in Wartime*, 144–56; Alan C. Headrick, "Bicycle Blitzkrieg: The Malayan Campaign and the Fall of Singapore," U.S. Naval War College report, 2/8/1994.

67 Pfister, "1950s Syndrome," in Uekoetter, *Turning Points*, 118.

68 Vivanco, *Reconsidering the Bicycle*, xx–xxi.

6. BIKES ARE BEAUTIFUL

1 *Bicycles Are Beautiful* (Lee Mendelson, 1974).

2 Department of Public Works, *California Bikeway Planning Criteria and Guidelines* (Washington, D.C.: US DOT, 1972), 1; Walter Rugaber, "U.S. Sets Safety Standards," *NYT*, 7/3/1974.

3 Berto, *Dancing Chain*, 201; "Bicycle Parts: Duty Suspension," *U.S. Congressional and Administrative News* 3 (1970): 6115–16.

4 Berto, *Dancing Chain*, 203, 201; Robert Frost, "On a Bicycle Built," *NYT*, 2/24/1965.

5 Department of Public Works, *California Bikeway Planning*, 1; Donald E. Mullen, "Bicycle Boom," *Beaver County Times* (Pennsylvania), 8/23/1972.

6 Gina Kolata, "How Safe is Cycling?" *NYT*, 10/22/2013; Mullen, "Bicycle Boom."

7 "Pedal-Pushing," *Life*, 5/10/1963, 17.

8 Johnny Lott, "Fred DeLong: Engineer's Passion," *Sumter Daily Item* (South Carolina), 8/9/1979; Richard Ballantine, *Richard's Bicycle Book* (New York: Ballantine, 1974), 251–56; Richard Ballantine, "Ten-Speed is Best," *Nashua Telegraph*, 5/17/1975, 14; Schwinn advertisement, *Life*, 5/30/1969, 52.

9 Berto, *Dancing Chain*, 203; Epperson, *Bicycles in American Highway Planning*, 74–75.

10 "A Bicycle Page for You," *WEC*, March, 1970, 41; Kirk, *Counterculture Green*, 30–31.

11 E. F. Schumacher, *Small is Beautiful: A Study of Economics As If People Mattered* (London: Blond & Briggs, 1973); Kirk, *Counterculture Green*, 30; *CoEvolution Quarterly* (Winter 1975): 97–98; Van der Ryn, *Design for Life*, 67.

12 Lillian Berson Frankel and Godfrey Frankel, *The Bicycle Book (Bike-Ways)* (New York: Cornerstone Library, 1972), 7; "Open a Bike Shop," *Mother Earth News*, *CDT*, 9/14/1975; Lott, "Fred DeLong," 10.

13 Bob Husky, "Bicycling for Fun, Health and Sport," *Palm Beach Post*, 5/17/1973; "Bicycling Growing," *Spartanburg Herald-Journal*, 5/1/1973.

14 Fiege, *Republic of Nature*, 392, 393–95; Leslie Maitland, "10,000 Cyclists," *NYT*, 4/23/1979.

15 "Millions of Americans Are Now," *New London Day*, 6/5/1973; "Minnesota State Bicycle Committee Report," January 15, 1977, in the collection of the Legislative Reference Library, St. Paul, Minnesota.

16   Ernest Del, Lawrence C. Moss, and Thomas Z. Reicher, *A Handbook for Bicycle Activists* (Stanford, CA: Stanford Environmental Law Society, 1976), 2.

17   "Safe Ways to School Days," *Lewiston Evening Journal* (Maine), 8/29/1940.

18   "Wants Bicyclists to Ride," *Pittsburgh Press*, 10/28/1939; Detroit Public Schools, *Traffic Safety in Detroit* (Detroit, MI: Board of Education, 1942), 88; "State Policeman Gives Advice," *New London Day*, 4/11/1951.

19   Walter Powers, "The Danger of Bike Riders," *Sarasota Herald-Tribune*, 10/3/1965; "Parents Say Ride Bike on Left," *Ocala Star-Banner*, 8/25/1966.

20   Claudette Durocher, "Bicycle Ordinance is Passed," *Nashua Telegraph*, 8/15/1973; "Not a Motor Vehicle," *Bangor Daily News*, 9/7/1973; Cattanach to Hasenorhl, October 18, 1977, folder "Correspondence, 1974–1977," Records of the Wisconsin Bicycle Coordinating Council, WHS.

21   "Bike Safety," *Palm Beach Post*, 4/7/1974; R. E. Ocker, "Cities Danger to Bicyclists," *Youngstown Vindicator*, 8/28/1975.

22   "Cycles Should Face Traffic," *Sarasota Herald-Tribune*, 9/24/1978.

23   "Bike Safety."

24   *Massey v. Scripter*, 64 Mich. App. 561 (1975); *Massey v. Scripter*, 401 Mich. 385 (1977).

25   *Drive Your Bike* (Glendale, CA: Sullivan, 1954).

26   Donald Pruden, *Around-Town Cycling* (Mountain View, CA: World Publications, 1975), 9; Bibs McIntyre, *The Bike Book: Everything You Need to Know about Owning and Riding a Bike* (New York: Harper & Row, 1972), 43–44; William C. Cramer Jr. and John D. Hadacek, "A Survey of Ohio Bicycle Law," 2 *Ohio N. U. L. Rev.* 524 (1974), 525 n. 9; see also "Correspondence, 1974–1977."

27   "Cyclists Creating a Problem," *Ludington Daily News*, 5/30/1990; "Bicycle Safety," *Lakeland Ledger* (Florida), 4/9/2005; "Change Law for Bike," *Ocala Star-Banner*, 7/18/1986.

28   Sophie Kerr, *Wife's Eye View* (New York: Rinehart, 1947), 92; Judy Blume, *Tiger Eyes* (New York: Bradbury, 1981), 41; see also 72. The 2013 Delacorte edition reversed these instructions, which now read: "'Remember . . . ride with the traffic,' Walter tells me. . . . 'With the traffic,' I repeat."

29   "Minnesota State Bicycle Committee"; "Hitchin' Rack," *Boys' Life*, September 1977, 4; "Cyclist Fights 'Dumb Law,'" *New London Day*, 8/4/1979; "More on Bike Safety," *St. Petersburg Times*, 6/8/1982.

30   "Bike Paths Are the Answer," *Boca Raton News*, 11/28/1973.

31   E. Peter Hoffman, "200,000 Miles of Bikeways," in Leete, *Best of Bicycling!*, 290; McIntyre, *Bike Book*, 159.

32   Department of Public Works, *California Bikeway Planning*, 1.

33   Ibid., 11; Charlie Hudson, "Hollywood Legend West Dedicates," *South Dade News Leader*, 9/16/2012; Hoffman, "200,000 Miles of Bikeways," 287–90; BIA, *Boom in Bikeways* (New York: BIA, 1968); Walter Lewis Cook, *Bike Trails and*

Facilities: A Guide to Their Design, Construction and Operation (Wheeling, WV: American Institute of Park Executives, 1965).

34   Berto, *Dancing Chain*, 201; "Udall Urges More Bicycle Paths," *NYT*, 5/2/1964; DOI, *Trails for America* (Washington, DC: US Government Printing Office, 1966), 126.

35   Nationwide Trails System Hearings, 90th Congress, first session, on H.R. 4865 and related bills. (Washington DC: US Government Printing Office, 1967), 1, 42.

36   Ibid., 144. Aspinall also pressured the United Auto Workers representative on the subject (160).

37   DOI, *Establishing Trails on Rights of Way* (Washington, DC: US Government Printing Office, 1971); "Rails to Trails Funding," and Rich Landers, "Railbed Offers 'Bargain' Bikeway," *Spokane Spokesman-Review*, 7/29/1979.

38   Pucher and Buehler, *City Cycling*, 113; Department of Public Works, *California Bikeway Planning*, 11.

39   Robert Cantwell, "Where All Roads Lead to Roam," *Sports Illustrated*, 5/26/1975, 36–44.

40   117 Cong. Rec. 10830 (1971); resolution quoted in Department of Public Works, *California Bikeway Planning*, xii.

41   Department of Public Works, *California Bikeway Planning*, xii, 48.

42   Mary Perot Nichols, "Start Pedaling, John," *Village Voice*, 6/7/1971; "Bikes Shifting," *Reading Eagle*, 12/25/1974; Del, Moss, and Reicher, *Handbook*, 23.

43   "Bikeway Planning and Design," *CoEvolution Quarterly*, Spring 1975, 120; quote from Epperson, "Great Schism," 85.

44   Cantwell, "Where All Roads," 36; Johnson, "Transformation of Civic Institutions," chapter 10; Curt Johnson, "Solon Relates Fight," *Eugene Register-Guard*, 12/3/1971; Jerry Uhrhammer, "Cyclists Battle Proposal," *Eugene Register-Guard*, 4/3/1973.

45   "Count 'Em," *Bend Bulletin*, 7/31/1972; Ed Kenyon, "'Plot' to Unseat Bike," *Eugene Register-Guard*, 2/1/1973; Daniel Panshin, letter to the editor, *Sports Illustrated*, 6/30/1975.

46   Edward Neilan, "Bicycle Boom Here to Stay," *Wilmington Star-News* (North Carolina), 5/16/1972; Opinion of the Justices to the Senate, 370 Mass. 895 (1976).

47   Quote from Epperson, "Great Schism," 81; Feige, *Republic of Nature*, 394; Federal-Aid Highway Act of 1973, Public Law 93–87, 87 Stat. 262.

48   Godfrey Frankel, *Bike-Ways* (New York: Sterling, 1950); "Bike Route Hearings Set," *Washington Afro-American* 3/5/1974; Colin Stewart, "Pedal (and Coast?)," *Salt Lake City Deseret News*, 6/1/1973.

49   "Millions of Americans," *New London Day*, 6/5/1973; "Bike Trail Opens May 14," *Milwaukee Sentinel*, 5/5/1966.

50   DOI press release, February 5, 1967, Bureau of Outdoor Recreation, Press

Releases 1963–1974, RG 48, Records of the Office of the Secretary of the Interior, NARA II.

51 "Phase I of Bike Route," *Salt Lake City Deseret News*, 5/31/1973; Mark Albright, "Officials 'Rethink' Bike Path Plans," *St. Petersburg Evening Independent*, 8/20/1974; Roger Miller, "Bike Path Established," *Bowling Green Daily News*, 7/6/1975.

52 Ann Baker, "Springfield Bike Group," *Eugene Register-Guard*, 2/21/1974; Richard Ballantine, *Richard's Bicycle Book* (New York: Ballantine, 1974), 243–44; Del, Moss, and Reicher, *Handbook*, 2.

53 "Ed Mollring on Bicycle Paths," *Prescott Courier*, 8/18/1974; "Bicycle Path Plan," *Prescott Courier*, 2/2/1976.

54 "City's Bike Route Redrawn," *Wilmington Morning Star* (North Carolina), 5/10/1979.

55 Tom O'Hara, "Optimism, Hard Work Not Enough," *Daytona Beach Morning Journal*, 7/15/1977.

56 *Kirksey v. Jackson*, 461 F. Supp. 1282 (S.D. Miss. 1978).

57 City of St. Paul Planning Department, "Bicycle Feasibility Study," February 1974, Minnesota Department of Transportation Library; James Longhurst, "'Awheel from Chicago to the Twin Cities,'" in Vrtis and Wells, *Two Cities, One Hinterland*.

58 National Highway Traffic Safety Administration (NHTSA), *Pedestrian and Bicycle Safety Study, Highway Safety Act of 1973 (Section 214)*, 3. The Highway Safety Act of 1973 was arguably part of the wave of public-interest law that began with the 1966 Auto Safety Act. See Hall and Karsten, *Magic Mirror*, 336.

59 NHTSA, *Pedestrian and Bicycle Safety Study*, 67; *TLA*, 324.

60 Quoted in Wachtel, "Bicycles and the Law."

61 *TLA*, 320; Del, Moss, and Reicher, *Handbook*, 59; Mionske, *Bicycling and the Law*, 57–59.

62 *Albrecht v. Broughton*, 6 Cal. App. 3d 173 (Cal. App. 1st Dist. 1970).

63 Puerto Rico and the District of Columbia had their own implementations. *TLA*, 320–21; Maryland Citizens' Bicycle Study Committee, *A Report on the Status of Bicycling in Maryland* (January 1979), I-9–I-10, in the collection of the Maryland State Archives.

64 *Townsend v. State*, 309 So. 2d 887 (La. App. 3rd Cir. 1975); *Vaughn v. Cortland* 1980 WL 352137 (Ohio App. 11 Dist. 1980).

65 *Owen v. Burcham* 100 Idaho 441 (1979).

66 *I Like Bikes* (Centron, 1978).

67 *Only One Road* (AVS, 1975).

68 "Minnesota State Bicycle Committee"; "Testimony for the Governor's Advisory Bicycle Coordinating Council," September 18, 1978, Records of the League of American Wheelmen- La Crosse Chapter, Area Research Center, La Crosse, Wisconsin.

69 *TLA*, 1, 316–17; Wachtel, "Bicycles and the Law."

70 Epperson, "Great Schism," 84; Hurst, *Cyclist's Manifesto*, 97.

71 *Bendix v. U.S.*, 79 Cust. Ct. 108 (1977).

72 Forester, *Effective Cycling*, 3.1, 3.1.3.

73 Ibid., 4.6.3.

74 "Minnesota State Bicycle Committee Report," 13.

75 *Taylor v. Goodwin* [1879] 4 QBD 228; Forester, *Effective Cycling*, 3.0.2.

76 Adolphe V. Bernotas, "Cycling Clubs Stress Competence," *Nashua Telegraph*, 7/15/1980.

77 Epperson, "Great Schism," 92; c.f. Forester, "Letter to the Editor," 31–51; quotes from Forester, *Effective Cycling*, 4.6.5.

78 David Nilsson, "Bikeway Plan Called Bum Steer," *Pittsburgh Press*, 5/24/1981; Albright, "Officials 'Rethink' Bike Path Plans."

79 *TLA*, 322. The 1946 MTO repeated the 1944 UVC language: see MTO (1946), section 113 (c). See also Mionske, *Bicycling and the Law*, 66.

80 Del, Moss, and Reicher, *Handbook*, 2; *Best v. Avon Lake*, 1979 WL 207596 (Ohio App. 9th Dist. 1979).

81 Frederick Wolfe, *The Bicycle: A Commuting Alternative* (Edmonds, WA: Signpost, 1979), 67; Forester, *Effective Cycling*, 4.1.1.

82 Keith Kingbay, *Inside Bicycling* (Chicago: Regnery, 1976), 52; Forester, *Bicycle Transportation*, 120.

83 Petty, "Impact of the Sport"; CPSC, *Sprocket Man* (Washington, DC: U.S. Government Printing Office, 1975), 1; *Forester v. CPSC*, 559 F.2d 774 (D.C. Cir. 1977).

84 See Forester, "Bikeway Controversy," 7–17.

85 Nilsson, "Bikeway Plan Called Bum Steer"; Sue Vaughan, "Bike Lanes Remain Unrealized Dream," *Spokane Spokesman-Review*, 5/24/1983.

86 Department of Transportation and DOI, *Bicycling for Recreation and Commuting* (Washington DC: US Government Printing Office, 1972), 16.

87 H.R. 955, 95th Congress (1977–78); Pub. L. 95–599, the Surface Transportation Assistance Act of 1978.

CONCLUSION

1 Hardin, "Tragedy of the Commons," 1243–48; Ostrom, *Governing the Commons*, 1, 30–33. Although Ostrom does not include the road in her very broad definition of common-pool resources, I contend that the public road fits within it.

2 Pierson, "The Study of Policy Development," 42, 37.

3 Quote from Urry, "System of Automobility," 25; see also Goodwin, "Reconstructing Automobility," 60–78.

4 National Bicycle Dealers Association, "Industry Overview 2013," http://nbda.com/articles/industry-overview-2012-pg34.htm, accessed 3/1/2014; Pucher, Buehler, and Seinen, "Bicycling Renaissance in North America?"

5   See the Intermodal Surface Transportation Efficiency Act (ISTEA) Public Law 240, 102nd Cong., 1st sess. (December 18, 1991), and the Transportation Equity Act for the 21st Century (TEA-21) Public Law 178, 105th Cong., 2nd sess. (June 9, 1998).

6   "Uses of the Bicycle," *Wheelman* 1 (October 1882): 22; "Manufacturers Booming the Bike," *Spokane Press*, 6/29/1904; "Bicycles: Do a Come-back," *WSJ*, 9/4/1941; "The Amazing Return of the 'Bikes,'" *Popular Mechanics*, January 1935, 62; Frankel, *Bike-Ways*, 9; Martin J. Shannon, "Bicycle Makers Rolling," *WSJ*, 10/7/1965; "Open a Bike Shop," *Mother Earth News*, *CDT*, 9/14/1975; Michael Cabanatuan, "San Francisco Bicycle Boom," *San Francisco Chronicle*, 12/12/2013.

7   "Bicycle Sidepaths," *GDN*, 4/18/1900; Paul W. Kearney, "Stopping Trouble on Two Wheels," *Rotarian*, August 1941, 20; Walter Powers, "The Danger of Bike Riders," *Sarasota Herald-Tribune*, 10/3/1965; McIntyre, *Bike Book*, 159–61.

8   People for Bikes, "Green Lane Project," http://www.peopleforbikes.org/green-lane-project/pages/about-the-project, accessed July 20, 2014.

9   Lewis Mumford, *The Highway and the City: Essays* (New York: Harcourt, 1963), 248.

10 See Ostrom, *Governing the Commons*, 58.

11 Ibid., 1, ch. 3.

SELECT BIBLIOGRAPHY

Alexander, Geoff. *Academic Films for the Classroom: A History*. Jefferson, NC: McFarland, 2010.

Allinson, Gary D. *Japan's Postwar History*. Ithaca, NY: Cornell University Press, 1997.

Anderson, Benedict R. *Imagined Communities: Reflections on the Origin and Spread of Nationalism*. Rev. ed. New York: Verso, 2006.

Anderson, Paul M., ed. *Sports Betting: Law and Policy*. The Hague, The Netherlands: T. M. C. Asser, 2012.

Andrews, Richard N. L. *Managing the Environment, Managing Ourselves: A History of American Environmental Policy*. New Haven, CT: Yale University Press, 2006.

Bailey, Ronald H. *The Home Front: USA*. Alexandria, VA: Time-Life Books, 1978.

Balf, Todd. *Major: A Black Athlete, a White Era, and the Fight to Be the World's Fastest Human Being*. New York: Three Rivers, 2008.

Balogh, Brian. *A Government Out of Sight: The Mystery of National Authority in Nineteenth-Century America*. New York: Cambridge University Press, 2009.

Bartels, Andrew H. "The Office of Price Administration and the Legacy of the New Deal, 1939–1946." *Public Historian* 5 (Summer 1983): 5–29.

Bayly, Christopher Alan, and Timothy Norman Harper. *Forgotten Armies: The Fall of British Asia, 1941–1945*. New York: Penguin, 2004.

Berger, Knute. *Roots of Tomorrow: Tales of Early Seattle Urbanism*. Crosscut Public Media, e-book, 2014.

Berto, Frank. *The Dancing Chain: History and Development of the Derailleur Bicycle*. San Francisco: Cycle Publishing/Van Der Plas Publications, 2013.

Bijker, Wiebe. *Of Bicycles, Bakelites, and Bulbs: Toward a Theory of Sociotechnical Change*. Cambridge, MA: MIT Press, 1995.

Bijker, Wiebe, Thomas Hughes, and Trevor Pinch, eds. *The Social Construction of Technological Systems: New Directions in the Sociology and History of Technology*. Cambridge, MA: MIT Press, 2012.

Blomley, Nicholas. *Rights of Passage: Sidewalks and the Regulation of Public Flow*. New York: Routledge, 2011.

Blue, Elly. *Bikenomics: How Bicycling Can Save the Economy.* Portland, OR: Microcosm, 2013.

Campbell, Ballard. "The Good Roads Movement in Wisconsin, 1980–1911." *Wisconsin Magazine of History* 49 (Summer 1966): 273–93.

Chandler, Alfred Dupont. *Inventing the Electronic Century: The Epic Story of the Consumer Electronics and Computer Industries.* Cambridge, MA: Harvard University Press, 2005.

Clayton, Nick. "SCOT: Does it Answer?" *Technology and Culture* 43 (April 2002): 351–60.

Clementson, George Burr. *The Road Rights and Liabilities of Wheelmen.* Chicago: Callaghan, 1895.

Davis, J. Allen. "The California Vehicle Code and the Uniform Vehicle Code." *Hastings Law Journal* 14 (1962): 377–98.

DiMento, Joseph F. C., and Cliff Ellis. *Changing Lanes: Visions and Histories of Urban Freeways.* Cambridge, MA: MIT Press, 2013.

Disco, Nil, and Eda Kranakis, eds. *Cosmopolitan Commons: Sharing Resources and Risks across Borders.* Cambridge, MA: MIT Press, 2013.

Dodge, Pryor. *The Bicycle.* New York: Flammarion, 1996.

Dower, John. *Embracing Defeat: Japan in the Wake of World War II.* New York: Norton, 1999.

Downey, Gregory J. *Telegraph Messenger Boys: Labor, Technology, and Geography, 1850–1950.* New York: Routledge, 2002.

Duany, Andres, Elizabeth Plater-Zyberk, and Jeff Speck. *Suburban Nation.* New York: North Point, 2010.

Dubber, M. D., and M. Valverde, eds. *Police and the Liberal State.* Stanford, CA: Stanford University Press, 2008.

Dunham, Norman L. "The Bicycle Era in American History." PhD diss., Harvard University, 1956.

Epperson, Bruce D. "How Many Bikes?" *Proceedings of the 11th International Cycle History Conference.* San Francisco: Van Der Plas Publications, 2001.

———. "The Great Schism: Federal Bicycle Safety Regulation and the Unraveling of American Bicycle Planning." *Transportation Law Journal* 37 (2010): 73–118.

———. *Peddling Bicycles to America: The Rise of an Industry.* Jefferson, NC: McFarland, 2010.

———. *Bicycles in American Highway Planning: The Critical Years of Decision-Making, 1969–1991.* Jefferson, NC: McFarland, 2014.

Fein, Michael R. *Paving the Way: New York Road Building and the American State, 1880–1956.* Lawrence: University Press of Kansas, 2008.

Fiege, Mark. *The Republic of Nature: An Environmental History of the United States.* Seattle: University of Washington Press, 2013.

Finison, Lorenz. *Boston's Cycling Craze, 1880–1900: A Story of Race, Sport, and Society.* Amherst: University of Massachusetts Press, 2014.

Finlay, Mark R. *Growing American Rubber: Strategic Plants and the Politics of National Security.* New Brunswick, NJ: Rutgers University Press, 2009.

Fitzpatrick, Jim. *The Bicycle in Wartime: An Illustrated History.* Kilcoy, Australia: Star Hill Studio, 2011.

Forester, John. *Bicycle Transportation: A Handbook for Cycling Transportation Engineers.* Cambridge, MA: MIT Press, 1994.

———. "The Bikeway Controversy." *Transportation Quarterly* 55 (Spring 2001): 7–17.

———. "Letter to the Editor." *Transportation Law Journal* 39, no. 1 (2011): 31–51.

Friss, Evan. "The Cycling City: Bicycles and the Transformation of Urban America." PhD diss., City University of New York, 2011.

———. "Writing Bicycles: The Historiography of Cycling in the United States." *Mobility in History* 6 (2015): 127–33.

Frohardt-Lane, Sarah. "Promoting a Culture of Driving: Rationing, Car Sharing, and Propaganda in World War II." *Journal of American Studies* 46, no. 2 (May 2012): 337–55.

Fuller, Wayne E. "Good Roads and Rural Free Delivery of Mail," *Mississippi Valley Historical Review* 42, no. 1 (1955): 67–83.

Furness, Zack. *One Less Car: Bicycling and the Politics of Automobility.* Philadelphia: Temple University Press, 2010.

Gant, Jesse, and Nicholas Hoffman. *Wheel Fever: How Wisconsin Became a Great Bicycling State.* Madison: Wisconsin Historical Society, 2013.

Garvey, Ellen Gruber. "Reframing the Bicycle: Advertising-Supported Magazines and Scorching Women." *American Quarterly* 47, no. 1 (1995): 66–101.

Goodwin, Katherine J. "Reconstructing Automobility: The Making and Breaking of Modern Transportation." *Global Environmental Politics* 10, no. 4 (November 2010): 60–78.

Graham, Otis L. *Toward a Planned Society: From Roosevelt to Nixon.* New York: Oxford University Press, 1976.

Hadland, Tony, and Hans-Erhard Lessing. *Bicycle Design: An Illustrated History.* Cambridge, MA: MIT Press, 2014.

Hall, Kermit L., and Peter Karsten. *The Magic Mirror: Law in American History.* New York: Oxford University Press, 2008.

Hardin, Garrett. "The Tragedy of the Commons." *Science* 162 (1968): 1243–48.

Harris, Dianne. *Second Suburb: Levittown, Pennsylvania.* Pittsburgh: University of Pittsburgh Press, 2010.

Hayden, Dolores. *Building Suburbia: Green Fields and Urban Growth, 1820–2000.* New York: Vintage, 2004.

Heitmann, John. *The Automobile and American Life.* Jefferson, NC: McFarland, 2009.

Henderson, Jason. *Street Fight: The Politics of Mobility in San Francisco.* Amherst: University of Massachusetts Press, 2013.

Herlihy, David. *Bicycle: The History.* New Haven, CT: Yale University Press, 2004.

Hilles, William C. "The Good Roads Movement in the United States: 1880–1916." Master's thesis, Duke University, 1958.

Holley, J. I. B., Jr. "Blacktop: How Asphalt Paving Came to the Urban United States." *Technology and Culture* 44 (October 2003): 723–32.

Horton, Dave, Paul Rosen, and Peter Cox. *Cycling and Society.* Burlington, VT: Ashgate, 2007.

Hounshell, David A. *From the American System to Mass Production, 1800–1932: The Development of Manufacturing Technology in the United States.* Baltimore: Johns Hopkins University Press, 1985.

Hugill, Peter J. "Good Roads and the Automobile in the United States, 1880–1929." *Geographical Review* 72, no. 3 (1982): 327–49.

Hurst, Robert. *The Cyclist's Manifesto: The Case for Riding on Two Wheels Instead of Four.* Guilford, CT: Falcon, 2009.

Jakle, John A., and Keith A. Sculle. *Signs in America's Auto Age: Signatures of Landscape and Place.* Iowa City: University of Iowa Press, 2004.

Johnson, Steven Reed. "The Transformation of Civic Institutions and Practices in Portland, Oregon, 1960–1999." PhD diss., Portland State University, 2002.

Kirk, Andrew G. *Counterculture Green: The Whole Earth Catalog and American Environmentalism.* Lawrence: University Press of Kansas, 2007.

Koelle, Alexandra V. "Pedaling on the Periphery: The African American Twenty-Fifth Infantry Bicycle Corps and the Roads of American Expansion." *Western Historical Quarterly* 41 (Autumn 2010): 305–26.

Leete, Henry M., ed. *The Best of Bicycling!* New York: Trident, 1970.

Lehr, John C., and H. John Selwood. "The Two-Wheeled Workhorse: The Bicycle as Personal and Commercial Transport in Winnipeg." *Urban History Review* 28, no. 1 (1999): 3–13.

Lipin, Lawrence M. "'Cast Aside the Automobile Enthusiast': Class Conflict, Tax Policy, and the Preservation of Nature in Progressive-Era Oregon." *Oregon Historical Quarterly* 107, no. 2 (2006): 166–95.

Lisa, Gregory C. "Bicyclists and Bureaucrats: The League of American Wheelmen and Public Choice Theory Applied." *Georgetown Law Journal* 84 (1995): 373–98.

Longhurst, James. "The Sidepath Not Taken: Bicycles, Taxes, and the Rhetoric of the Public Good in the 1890s." *Journal of Policy History* 25, no. 4 (2013): 557–86.

Macy, Sue. *Wheels of Change: How Women Rode the Bicycle to Freedom (with a Few Flat Tires along the Way).* Washington, DC: National Geographic, 2011.

Mapes, Jeff. *Pedaling Revolution: How Cyclists Are Changing American Cities.* Eugene: Oregon State University Press, 2007.

Marks, Patricia. *Bicycles, Bangs and Bloomers: The New Woman in the Popular Press.* Lexington: University of Kentucky Press, 1990.

Mason, Philip Parker. "The League of American Wheelmen and the Good-Roads Movement, 1880–1905." PhD diss., University of Michigan, 1957.

McCally, Karen. "Bloomers and Bicycles: Health and Fitness in Victorian Rochester." *Rochester History* 69, no. 2 (2008): 1–27.

McCann, Barbara. *Completing Our Streets: The Transition to Safe and Inclusive Transportation Networks*. Washington, DC: Island Press, 2013.

McShane, Clay. *Down the Asphalt Path: The Automobile and the American City*. New York: Columbia University Press, 1994.

———. "The Origins and Globalization of Traffic Control Signals." *Journal of Urban History* 25 (March, 1999): 379–404.

McShane, Clay, and Joel A. Tarr. *The Horse in the City: Living Machines in the Nineteenth Century*. Baltimore: Johns Hopkins University Press, 2007.

Mionske, Bob. *Bicycling and the Law: Your Rights as a Cyclist*. Boulder, CO: Velo Press, 2007.

National Committee on Uniform Traffic Laws and Ordinances. *Traffic Laws Annotated*. Washington, DC: US Government Printing Office, 1979.

Netherton, Ross De Witt. *Control of Highway Access*. Madison: University of Wisconsin Press, 1963.

Nolte, Sharon H. *Liberalism in Modern Japan: Ishibashi Tanzan and His Teachers, 1905–1960*. Berkeley: University of California Press, 1987.

Norcliffe, Glen. *Ride to Modernity: The Bicycle in Canada, 1869–1900*. Toronto: University of Toronto Press, 2001.

Norton, Peter. *Fighting Traffic: The Dawn of the Motor Age in the American City*. Cambridge, MA: MIT Press, 2008.

Novak, William J. *The People's Welfare: Law and Regulation in Nineteenth-Century America*. Chapel Hill: University of North Carolina Press, 1996.

———. "The Myth of the 'Weak' American State." *American Historical Review* 113, no. 3 (2008): 752–72.

Oakley, William. *Winged Wheel: The History of the First Hundred Years of the Cyclists' Touring Club*. Godalming, UK: Cyclists' Touring Club, 1977.

Orgeron, Devin, Marsha Orgeron, and Dan Streible, eds. *Learning with the Lights Off: Educational Film in the United States*. New York: Oxford, 2012.

Ostrom, Elinor. *Governing the Commons: The Evolution of Institutions for Collective Action*. Cambridge: Cambridge University Press, 1990.

Penn, Robert. *It's All about the Bike: The Pursuit of Happiness on Two Wheels*. New York: Bloomsbury, 2010.

Petty, Ross D. "The Impact of the Sport of Bicycle Riding on Safety Law." *American Business Law Journal* 35, no. 2 (1998): 185–224.

———. "Bicycling in Minneapolis in the Early Twentieth Century." *Minnesota History* 62 (Fall 2010): 84–95.

Pierson, Paul. "The Study of Policy Development." *Journal of Policy History* 17, no. 1 (2005): 34–51.

Platt, Harold L. *The Electric City: Energy and the Growth of the Chicago Area, 1880–1930*. Chicago: University of Chicago Press, 1991.

Polenberg, Richard. *War and Society: The United States, 1941–1945*. Philadelphia: Lippincott, 1972.

Pucher, John, and Ralph Buehler, eds. *City Cycling*. Cambridge, MA: MIT Press, 2012.

Pucher, John, Ralph Buehler, and Mark Seinen. "Bicycling Renaissance In North America? An Update and Re-appraisal of Cycling Trends and Policies." *Transportation Research Part A* 45 (2011): 451–75.

Radford, Gail. "From Municipal Socialism to Public Authorities: Institutional Factors in the Shaping of American Public Enterprise." *Journal of American History* 90 (December 2003): 863–90.

Ritchie, Andrew. *Major Taylor: The Extraordinary Career of a Champion Bicycle Racer*. Baltimore: Johns Hopkins University Press, 1988.

Rome, Adam. *The Bulldozer in the Countryside: Suburban Sprawl and the Rise of American Environmentalism*. New York: Cambridge University Press, 2001.

Roots, Roger I. "The Orphaned Right: The Right to Travel by Automobile, 1890–1950." *Oklahoma City University Law Review* 30 (Summer 2005): 245–68.

Rose, Mark H. *Interstate: Express Highway Politics, 1939–1989*. Knoxville: University of Tennessee Press, 1990.

Rose, Mark H., and Raymond A. Mohl. *Interstate: Highway Politics and Policy Since 1939*. Knoxville: University of Tennessee Press, 2012.

Segrave, Kerry. *Parking Cars in America, 1910–1945: A History*. Jefferson, NC: McFarland, 2012.

Seiler, Cotton. *Republic of Drivers: A Cultural History of Automobility in America*. Chicago: University of Chicago Press, 2008.

Sellers, Christopher. *Crabgrass Crucible: Suburban Nature and the Rise of Environmentalism in Twentieth-Century America*. Chapel Hill: University of North Carolina Press, 2012.

Shibusawa, Naoko. *America's Geisha Ally: Reimagining the Japanese Enemy*. Cambridge, MA: Harvard University Press, 2006.

Sky, Theodore. *The National Road and the Difficult Path to Sustainable National Investment*. Newark: University of Delaware Press, 2011.

Sorensen, George Niels. *Iron Riders: The Story of the 1890s Fort Missoula Buffalo Soldiers Bicycle Corps*. Missoula, MT: Pictorial Histories, 2000.

Sparrow, James T. *Warfare State: World War II Americans and the Age of Big Government*. New York: Oxford University Press, 2011.

Steele, M. William. "The Making of a Bicycle Nation: Japan." *Transfers* 2, no. 2 (2012): 70–94.

Street, Roger. *The Pedestrian Hobby-Horse: At the Dawn of Cycling*. Christchurch, UK: Artesius, 1998.

Taylor, Michael. "The Bicycle Boom and the Bicycle Bloc: Cycling and Politics in the 1890s." *Indiana Magazine of History* 104 (September 2008): 213–40.

Troesken, Werner. "Water and Urban Development." *Journal of Urban History* 32 (May 2006): 619–30.

Troesken, Werner, and Rick Geddes. "Municipalizing American Waterworks, 1897–1915." *Journal of Law, Economics, and Organization* 19 (October 2003): 246–67.

Uekoetter, Frank, ed. *The Turning Points of Environmental History.* Pittsburgh: University of Pittsburgh Press, 2010.

Urry, John. "The 'System' of Automobility." *Theory, Culture and Society* 21, no. 4–5 (2004): 25–39.

Van der Ryn, Sim. *Design for Life: The Architecture of Sim Van der Ryn.* Layton, UT: Gibbs Smith, 2005.

Vivanco, Luis A. *Reconsidering the Bicycle: An Anthropological Perspective on a New (Old) Thing.* New York: Routledge, 2013.

Vrtis, George, and Christopher W. Wells, eds. *Two Cities, One Hinterland: An Environmental History of the Twin Cities and Greater Minnesota.* Forthcoming.

Wachtel, Alan. "Bicycles and the Law: The Case of California." *Environs* 18 (1994): 105–24.

Wall, Derek. *The Commons in History: Culture, Conflict, and Ecology.* Cambridge, MA: MIT Press, 2014.

Wells, Christopher W. "The Changing Nature of Country Roads: Farmers, Reformers, and the Shifting Uses of Rural Space, 1880–1905." *Agricultural History* 80 (Spring 2006): 143–66.

———. *Car Country: An Environmental History.* Seattle: University of Washington Press, 2012.

———. "Fueling the Boom: Gasoline Taxes, Invisibility, and the Growth of the American Highway Infrastructure, 1919–1956." *Journal of American History* 99 (2012): 72–81.

Wilhelm, Kathryn E. "Freedom of Movement at a Standstill? Toward the Establishment of a Fundamental Right to Intrastate Travel." *Boston University Law Review* 90 (2010): 2461–97.

Wray, J. Harry. *Pedal Power: The Quiet Rise of the Bicycle in American Public Life.* Boulder, CO: Paradigm, 2008.

Zimring, Carl A. *Cash for Your Trash: Scrap Recycling in America.* New Brunswick, NJ: Rutgers University Press, 2009.

INDEX